# THE EUROPEAN UNION AND GENDER EQUALITY

Agnès Hubert

# THE EUROPEAN UNION AND GENDER EQUALITY

Free, Thrive, Lead: striving for a better future

 **FEPS**
Primer Series

This book has been produced with the financial support
of the European Parliament.

Bibliographical information of the German National Library
The German Library catalogues this publication in the
German National Bibliography; detailed bibliographic information
can be found on the internet at: *http://dnb.dnb.de*.

ISBN 978-3-8012-3102-3

Copyright © 2022 by Foundation for European Progressive Studies
FEPS Editors: Dr L. Andor, Dr A. Skrzypek, L.Thissen
FEPS Project Coordinator: E. Gil

Published by
Verlag J.H.W. Dietz Nachf. GmbH
Dreizehnmorgenweg 24, D-53175 Bonn

Published in association with the
Foundation for European Progressive Studies
*www.feps-europe.eu*
European Political Foundation – N° 4 BE 896.230.213

**FEPS**
Primer Series

– Vol. 2

Cover design und typesetting: Rohtext, Bonn
Cover picture: © Priscilla Beccari, https://priscillabeccari.com/
Printing and processing: Bookpress, Olsztyn

Find us on the internet: *www.dietz-verlag.de*

# Contents

# Foreword

*"If you see inequality as a 'them' problem or 'unfortunate other'*
*problem, that is a problem."*

– Kimberlé Crenshaw
  Lawyer, civil rights activist and intersectional feminist

The feminist movement and its claims remain, more than ever, a cornerstone of ongoing struggles for social justice. Here lies precisely the central contribution of this FEPS primer *"Gender Equality and the European Union. Free, Thrive, Lead: striving for a better future"* by Agnès Hubert. By building on her first-hand experience within the European institutions and as a recognised European gender policy expert, she maps out the expanding field of gender and EU politics. She sets out with the task of depicting the gendered nature of European integration and gender relations in the EU as a political system under the impulse of feminist and progressive actors. This primer brilliantly illustrates how gender equality and the European project are two sides of the same coin.

By delving into the developments of gender equality policy of the EU from its historic pathways (Part II) up until today (Part III), Agnès Hubert's primer is an invitation to navigate through the various milestones, obstacles and achievements along the road to equality giving an overview of the fundamentals and new directions. With every page, she embarks us on the incremental yet sustained developments that anchored the equality principle as one of the strongholds of the European project. The historic legal and policy tools are explored from the very first inscription of the equality principle in the 1957 Treaty of Rome to the influence of the Fourth World Conference on Women in Beijing in 1995 until the present-day EU Gender Equality policy and most notably the much-awaited Gender Equality Strategy 2020-2025.

Beyond a mere chronological account, the reader will meet with some of the leading figures who each made the difference in their determined endeavour to bring the European project in line with active citizenship and inclusive democracy ideals. On this journey, Agnès Hubert namely (re-)introduces us to key feminist and progressive actors such as Eliane-Vogel Polsky, Vasso Papandreou, Yvette Roudy up until Helena Dalli giving these stories in the construction of Europe the visibility they deserve. More precisely, she illustrates how they have all, in their own singular ways, directly contributed to shaping advances for women's rights and gender equality in the EU. This story tells us how every success within this "velvet triangle" was bolstered by a unique community of feminist actors gathering academics, policymakers, activists, NGOs including the European Women's Lobby, and women's organisations such as PES Women to cite just a few, all driven by a deep commitment towards the crafting of a feminist Europe.

Despite significant advances in the area, it becomes however very quickly evident from this primer that women in Europe still face significant social, economic and political barriers in their everyday life. Amongst the rich amount of useful reference points and tools the reader will encounter throughout the different chapters, the European Gender Equality Index published annually by EIGE (European Institute for Gender Equality) is always a sobering reminder that the road to gender equality is still a long one. According to its last edition at the time of writing, the index still stood at 68 points out of 100 with barely noticeable improvements of just +4.9 points since 2010[1]. Persisting gender gaps continue to prevent women to stand on an equal footing in the distribution of employment, decision-making,

---

[1]     EIGE, 'Gender Equality Index 2021 - Health' (Vilnius, 2021), https://eige.europa.eu/publications/gender-equality-index-2021-health."language":"en","page":"196","publisher-place":"Vilnius","source":"Zotero","title":"Gender Equality Index 2021 - Health","URL":"https://eige.europa.eu/publications/gender-equality-index-2021-health","author":[{"family":"EIGE","given":""}],"issued":{"date-parts":[["2021"]]}}}],"schema":"https://github.com/citation-style-language/schema/raw/master/csl-citation.json"}

economic resources, time, and access to health (including sexual and reproductive health)[2]. Admittedly, these imbalances are not without consequences on the many forms of violence women and girls are confronted with in various situations. Ranging from the everyday sexism to their most severe instances epitomised by the prevalence of femicides across Europe and beyond[3], all these instances form part of a *continuum of violence*[4] eventually building up a heavy climate of intimidation, fear, discrimination, exclusion and insecurity curtailing women's and girls' opportunities and freedoms. Trends of de-democratisation across Europe and its gendered aspects also raise serious concerns due to the backlash in women's rights and gender equality in the face of growing ultra-conservative and antifeminist mobilisations. That is not to mention how the COVID-19 crisis has unearthed deep cracks in the social order. Additionally, this pandemic has posed new short-term and long-term challenges for gender equality as widely evidenced in this primer. On the one hand, women have namely been at the forefront of the battle against the pandemic making up the majority of the health and care economy workforce whilst also representing the most severely undervalued sectors. On the other hand, there are serious concerns about the impact of the adverse effects of the pandemic on women's jobs and economic security as women tend to be overrepresented in many of the sectors most affected by the crisis. At the same time, the changing work patterns resulting from the widespread use of telework also deserve a close gender-impact assessment analysis, not least when it comes to the interplays with these newly emerging work dynamics and the impacts of women's (still) disproportionate care responsibilities in a long-run perspective.

---

2    Ibid.

3    EIGE, 'Gender-Based Violence - Measuring Femicide in the EU and Internationally: An Assessment' (Publications Ofce of the European Union, 2021), https://eige.europa.eu/publications/measuring-femicide-eu-and-internationally-assessment.

4    Liz Kelly, *Surviving Sexual Violence* (University of Minnesota Press, 1988).

As slow and fragile as progress towards gender equality may seem in light of the primer's introductory considerations, the importance of tireless feminist mobilisation and support has remained more timely than ever. In echo with the thinking of the eminent feminist theorist and social activist bell hooks[5] (1952-2021), it is not so much about knowing when contemporary feminist movements started to emerge but rather how, almost everywhere across the globe, individual women progressively started speaking up against sexism and patriarchy[6]. In this light, the feminist movement does not aim to benefit just a group of women or to privilege women over men. It arises anytime and anywhere women and men oppose gender inequalities, and it truly comes to life when groups of people mobilise around a determined strategy to transform in a meaningful way all our lives by putting an end to sexist behaviours and structures. In light of this perspective, it can be argued that seizing the European Union to tackle gender inequalities has been one such promising strategy for women to see their own cause advance in a Europe that needed (and still needs) to be made *by* and *for* women.

All in all, it might still be open for discussion what a truly feminist society should look like in practice as there are as many definitions of feminism as there are people. However, what is clear is that building a fair, equal and sustainable society will require an inclusive approach capable of overcoming the one-size-fits-all formula to ensure everyone, regardless of their gender, finds their place. That is for instance why "*Part I: When inequalities meet gender*" seeks to equip the reader with the adequate lenses to better understand not only inequalities from a feminist standpoint but also the socially constructed nature of gender (roles) behind its corresponding inequalities. In the same way, inclusive feminism must go hand in hand with an inter-

---

5    Born Gloria Watkins, bell hooks always decapitalised her pen name as a way of keeping the public's focus on her work, not "who she is". See 'Why Bell Hooks Didn't Capitalize Her Name', *Washington Post*, accessed 1 March 2022, https://www.washingtonpost.com/lifestyle/2021/12/15/bell-hooks-real-name/.

6    bell hooks, *Feminist Theory from Margin to Center* (Boston, MA: South End Press, 1984).

sectional approach rooted in the understanding that various forms of inequality often operate together and exacerbate each other. By drawing on a selection of key feminist literature, Part I, therefore, encourages not only to think *about* but also *beyond* gender as a category for analysis. Raising important questions about post-covid outlooks, Agnès Hubert's account demonstrates that the EU of tomorrow cannot content itself with a "return to normal". In order to shape the future of Europe in gender-just terms, her conclusion encourages us to consider a comprehensive epistemological review of the place of gender equality in the European economy and society.

Providing the reader with the essential ins and outs of the field at EU level, the great value of this primer is to offer every progressive actor the right tools to be able to envision all spheres of European politics and beyond through the prism of gender equality. This primer is a must-read for students, practitioners, activists, and policymakers at a time when the European Union stands at a defining crossroads between remaining a mere bystander of the tangible risks of seeing the rollback of gender equality or, instead, profiling itself at the vanguard of the defence of women's and human rights. Beyond merely recognising it as one of the EU's core values, this timely contribution is a fantastic intervention setting gender equality an essential precondition for the achievement of any aspiration of a social Europe that wants itself a fair, inclusive place full of opportunity for everyone.

Laeticia Thissen
FEPS Policy Analyst for Gender Equality

# Preamble

When everything goes wrong, we turn to women. This joke made in the aftermath of the bursting of the financial bubble in 2008 is again valid in times of covid-19 when the leadership of women in fighting the virus was celebrated and nurses and caregivers applauded. This expression of acknowledgment is however fraught with ambivalent meanings, given how slow our European societies are in challenging the standards of a patriarchy that is still felt as comfortable by some, and reassuring by others. Meanwhile, women's breakthrough in education still fails to be mirrored by their situation on the labour market, and women's rights are being questioned by anti-gender movements, demonstrating that the emancipation movements' victory is an unfinished and fragile one indeed.

"A decision made in Brussels", these few words are still enough to stigmatise institutions unloved by citizens, often disqualified as 'undemocratic'. The "nons" and "nees" to the 2005 French and Dutch referendums rejecting the proposed Constitution for the EU, and the fallout from the financial crisis of 2008 have revived a sense of rampant right-wing radicalism, whetting the appetite of political scavengers that feed on ego-minded nationalism and fear. Both right-wing radicalism and nationalism oppose European integration and love patriarchy.

Just over half a century earlier, there was no such confusion: By the end of the Second World War, women had distinguished themselves among nurses but also as pilots, in the Resistance movement and by taking on the jobs of men who had gone to the front, thus playing the pivotal role of keeping society afloat. In the aftermath of the war, the new French, German and Italian constitutions gave women equal rights in the wake of a general fight against totalitarianism. This was the period when new international human rights instruments were created and those states which had not yet done so granted women voting rights. In 1949, Simone de Beauvoir wrote

*Le Deuxième Sexe* (The Second Sex), denouncing the 'otherness' of women as a cultural construct imposed on them by society to justify their confinement to the family sphere. This foundational book, widely known for one of its central statements "One is not born, but rather becomes, woman", has constituted a springboard for the 'second wave' feminist movements in the 1960s and 70s. In parallel, Churchill, Monnet, Schuman, and Adenauer passionately defended a peace-loving Europe which would unite in solidarity and prosperity in the aftermath of the war. The attempt to create a defence community having been rejected in August 1954 in bellicose debates in the French parliament, the strategic coal and steel industries went on to form the heart of the first pooling of interests between former enemies. Before long, supra-national mechanisms emerged with the birth of the European Economic Community in 1957. The rest would follow naturally.

The parallels between women's liberation movements and the European unification process can easily be drawn. These two movements were both in full effervescence following the devastating consequences of the war. Women's right to equality and the patient building of a European power seemed to go naturally hand in hand.

More than half a century later, these two trends have solidly established themselves as alive and sustainable, although with a chronic disease of "stop and go". They are however beyond their "lite" versions and the simplifying logics of essentialism for the women's lib movement, or federalism for European unification. Over time, their scope has expanded to new members for the EU and new understandings of gender for feminist movements, but also to new issues (through the deepening and widening of EU policies and through intersectional approaches of feminist policy). They have become more complex, dense, and entangled. Even now, despite the challenges posed by right-wing radicalism, Brexit[1] and the hardship created

---

1  See, for instance, Mary Honeyball and Hannah Manzur, "Women & Brexit: Assessing the impact of Brexit on Women and Gender Equality in the UK" (2019), http://womenandbrexit.com/wp-content/uploads/2019/10/Women-Brexit-Report.pdf

by the pandemic, European integration and gender equality remain projects which hold promises for the future, supported by progressive ideals, social and political movements, and an institutional architecture.

On the one hand, the past seventy years have amply proved that a United Europe is a better deal than competing nation states despite the multiple challenges and crises posed to the EU from right-wing radicalism to nationalism and Brexit. The unfortunate departure of the United Kingdom has even served as a glue for other Member States and the waiting list of countries aspiring to membership remains long.

This success goes hand in hand with sustained economic development since the end of the Second World War; living standards are higher than in most regions of the world; social protection systems remain strong despite the pressures of globalisation and the constraints of integration, which have reduced the fiscal choices of governments. Today, the prospects of seeing European nations clash or seeing small states threatened by the power of the big ones are hardly on the agenda. Even the great divide between east and west that was enshrined in Yalta was diluted by the fifth and sixth EU enlargements between 2004 and 2013 with the last addition of Croatia. European integration has evolved into European 'reconfiguration'. [2]

On the other hand, feminism, in the sense of a belief that men and women should have equal rights and opportunities for the benefit of society as a whole, continues to exist and has a future[3] despite the numerous counter movements it has continuously faced. In fact, the inequalities in wages, income, respect, power, time and even happiness persist. Despite 'cancel culture' doomsayers forecasting the disappearance of feminism or its absorption into neoliberalism,[4] and seeing that some cohorts of women have succeeded 'like men in a world made for men', it is tempting to believe that gender equality

---

2      Desmond Dinan, "Europe Recast, a History of European Union" (Basingstoke: Palgrave Macmillan, 2004).

3      Sylvia Walby, *The Future of Feminism* (Cambridge: Polity Press, 2011).

4      Nancy Fraser, "Feminism, Capitalism and the Cunning of History" New Left Review 56 (Mar/Apr 2009): 97–117.

is no longer an issue since 'it already exists'. Indeed, there are more women than ever before in governments and parliaments. Projects and programmes are implemented at different levels to correct inequalities. It has become less and less acceptable to display male chauvinist behaviours. In the wake of the #Metoo movement, sexual harassment and violence against women are now being denounced publicly. Girls perform better than boys in the school system and more of them graduate from higher education. As a result of its achievements, feminism is taking on new forms. Mobilisation for parity democracy, against gender-based violence and the specific poverty of women, but also gender mainstreaming and intersectionality (see part III) and an increased presence of women in public decision-making have brought new concerns to the heart of public policies. In the field of political philosophy, feminism is a prime mover in the search for new forms of social justice[5] but also the search for peace.[6] Feminism also develops its own "potential for synthesis"[7] with ecological projects,[8] forms of growth, human rights and social democracy.[9] Far from painting a rosy image of reality, many authors also highlight new threats to the advances of feminism constituted by xenophobia, cultural protectionism, environmental catastrophism, and neoliberalism. These threats also hamper European integration.

5    Nancy Fraser "From Redistribution to Recognition? Dilemmas of Justice in a 'Post-Socialist' Age," *New Left Review* I, no. 212 (July/August 1995): 68-93; Axel Honneth, *The Struggle for Recognition* (Cambridge: Polity, 1995).

6    "to counter catastrophism, men identify with God and women identify with the earth", says Richard Rorty, *Contingence, Irony and Solidarity* (Cambridge University Press, 1989); Jean-Claude Ameisen, *La sculpture du vivant* [The Sculpture of Life], (Paris: Édition du Seuil, 2007) connects knowledge and trust.

7    Walby, *The Future of Feminism* (2011)

8    See, for instance, the ecofeminist idea of an 'indifferent Gaia' by Isabelle Stengers, *Au temps des catastrophes: Résister à la barbarie qui vient* (Paris: Editions La Découverte, 2009); the confidence in the infinite force of the Earth; or the concept of 'Gyn-ecology' coined by Mary Daly, *The Metaethics of Radical Feminism* (Boston: Beacon Press, 1978).

9    Walby, *The Future of Feminism* (2011)

Enough said to try convincing the reader that the construction of Europe and the emancipation of women are two historical projects that go hand in hand. They thrive together and suffer together, one drags the other to Olympus or oblivion. We need to explore how this invisible relationship has worked in practice in the last seventy years and what is in it for the future.

This interconnection is, in many respects, paradoxical. Indeed, the beginnings of a united Europe were initiated by men – the 'founding *fathers* of Europe' – at a time when few or no women could yet make their voices heard in the public sphere.[10] Even though there has been much progress, the European institutions continue to be led at the highest levels mainly by men. European Council meetings, the ultimate decision-making instance of the EU, count very few women heads of state or government (4 out of 27 in 2021). The European Commission, for the first time in its history headed by a woman with Ursula von der Leyen, counts an almost gender balanced college of commissioners (13 of 27). The European Parliament counted 40.6 percent women following the 2019 European elections, a figure which has fallen back to 39.6 after Brexit.[11] Similarly, women and many feminists have shown indifference if not reluctance towards a new political construction such as the EU which they perceive likely to threaten the achievements of their national struggles.[12] Even

10    For more on the Founding *Mothers* of Europe, see Anne-Laure Briatte, Éliane Gubin and Françoise Thébaud, ed., *L'Europe, une chance pour les femmes?* (Paris: Édition de la Sorbonne, 2019),  http://www.editions-delasorbonne.fr/en/livre/?GCOI=28405100154540; see also Maria Pia di Nonno, "The Founding Mothers of Europe: The Role of Simone Veil and Sofia Corradi in Defence of the European Values" in *Peace and European values as a potential model for integration and progress in a global world*, ed. Jesús Baigorri, Jürgen Elvert (Brussels: Peter Lang Group, 2019), 239-258,  https://iris.uniroma1.it/handle/11573/1342982#.YT9elJ4zak0

11    Giulio Sabatti (Members Research Service), "EP infographic 'Members of the European Parliament from February 2020'". September 23, 2020, https://www.europarl.europa.eu/RegData/etudes/ATAG/2020/646202/ EPRS_ATA(2020)646202_EN.pdf

12    Eg Drude Dalherup, a renowned Danish feminist academic, was one of the leading figures in the no-campaigns in the Danish referenda on new EU Treaties (in 1992, 1993, 1998).

more women were only distantly interested in European processes and resisted the advances in integration when they were submitted to a referendum (1992 in France and Denmark, 2005 in France and the Netherlands).

The fact remains that this paradox, which holds for political agents and institutions, is invalidated by the ideas mobilised to bring these projects to life. Indeed, the peace objective which initially supported the European project is also, historically, at the origin of a large part of European women's and feminist movements. Likewise, European integration was woven by the methodical and patient construction of "de facto solidarities", to use Robert Schuman's words,[13] not by force but by negotiation and a logic of complementarity. Finally, the European project, reacting to the horrors of the Second World War, was born with democracy and respect for human rights in its DNA. The deepening of democracy, taken up as an objective in the preamble to the treaties, cannot be conceived today without recognising the rights of women. Finally, the tension that exists between the European Union and member states in many ways overlaps with the obstacles that the patriarchal state has erected in the path of female emancipation.

The common ideological progressive roots of these two movements create the basis for exploring how *interests*, *ideas* and *institutions* have combined to integrate a gender perspective in the pursuit of European integration.

In order to improve the participation and economic, political and social representation of women in decision-making, the gender perspective implies a critical analysis of policies in light of the power relations on which they are based. In the same way, the relationship between Member States and the European Union has to be based on a fertile complementarity, which excludes domination and subordination.

---

13     Robert Schuman, "Declaration of 9 May 1950," *European Issue*, 204 (2011): 1, https://www.robert-schuman.eu/en/doc/questions-d-europe/ qe-204-en.pdf

From a theorical perspective, the construction of Europe and gender equality have scarcely been framed together. The classic literature explaining European integration[14] falls into specific schools of thought: functionalism, neo-functionalism[15] and intergovernmentalism,[16] later supplemented by theories of multi-level governance, cognitive theory, Europeanisation[17]and constructivism. In these works, gender is not among  the parameters of analysis, except for the essays of a few young authors self-defining as constructivist.[18]

As for the literature on gender in political science, it has mainly focused on the opportunities and limits of women's activism to develop or transform public policies. In the context of European policies, it is notable and symptomatic how, after a period of general disinterest, the novelty of the concept of *gender mainstreaming* in the 1990s coincides with the emergence of a relatively abundant literature both on the institutional innovation the concept entails[19] and on the European policy on equality between women and men (or certain aspects of it).[20]

---

14    Mark Pollack, "Theorising EU Policy-Making," in *Policy-Making in the European Union*, ed. Helen Wallace and Mark Pollack, (Oxford: Oxford University Press, 2005); Ben Rosamond, *Theories of European Integration* (Houndsmills: MacMillan, 2000).

15    Ernst Haas, ed., *The uniting of Europe: political, social, and economic forces, 1950–1957* (Notre Dame, USA: University of Notre Dame Press, 2004 [1958]).

16    Andrew Moravcsik, "Preferences and power in the European Community: A liberal intergovernmentalist approach," *Journal of Common Market Studies* 31, no. 4 (1993): 473-524.

17    Kevin Featherstone and Claudio Radaelli, ed., *The politics of Europeanization* (Oxford: Oxford University Press, 2003).

18    Gender, Power and European Integration Theory Kronsel Annica (2005) In Journal of European Public Policy 12 (6): p.1022-1040.

19    Kathrin Zippel, *The Politics of Sexual Harassmen* (Cambridge University Press, 2006);  Eleonor Lepinard *L'égalité introuvable: La parité, les féministes et la République* (Paris: Presses de la Fondation Nationale des Sciences Politiques, 2007).

20    Catherine Hoskyns, Integrating Gender: Women, Law and Politics in the European Union (Verso 1996); Sylvia Walby, "The European Union and Gender Equality: Emergent Variety of Gender Regimes," *Social*

The very first attempt to engage a dialogue between European integration theories and gender studies was eventually published in 2016 by Gabriele Abels and Heather MacRae (ed.)[21]. The authors conclude that

*in an era of crises, both analysts and practitioners of European integration would do well to [... gender] their perspectives. The gender gap in support for integration cannot be closed by superficial public relations strategies that do not address the underlying power structures of integration.*[22]

We will join the authors in seeking to demonstrate that the significance of the theoretical attempt to gender European integration goes far beyond the analysis of a policy. It is a 'plea to rethink the ways that integration policies have addressed gender issues'.

Going backwards is often the best way to look far forward. Can we rely on the historical, philosophical and political correspondences between the aspirations for the unification of Europe and those which denounced the oppression of women and advocated their emancipation? From the federalism of Victor Hugo or Immanuel Kant, from the feminist visions of Olympe de Gouge and Mary Wollstonecraft, from the concrete political translations of their ideas from the post-WWII period to the twenty-first century, what should we remember? The ideas that have served these two movements (solidarity to guarantee peace, respect for human rights, the deepening of democracy) have shifted over time. For a variety of reasons which will become clearer in this *Primer*, the space for a gendered expression of interests has been more open in the European sphere than in most national public spaces. It will be apparent when reviewing the story of some seventy years of development of the 'European policy on equality between women and men' that women have played a significant role in setting the agenda and putting in place the instru-

---

*Politics* 11, no. 1, (2004); Sophie Jacquot, *Transformations in EU Gender Equality: From Emergence to Dismantling* (London: Palgrave, 2015).

21  Gabriele Abels and Heather MacRae, ed., *Gendering European Integration Theory: Engaging new Dialogues*. (Opladen/Berlin/Toronto: Barbara Budrich Publishers, 2016).

22  Abels and MacRae, *Gendering Integration Theory*, 291.

ments that have made it possible. In fact, this policy represents an eloquent example of progress pushed by its main stakeholders which would nevertheless not have seen the light of day without the mobilisation of the ideals enshrined in the treaties and their construction by the institutions.

### Timeline of women's suffrage in EU countries and the United Kingdom

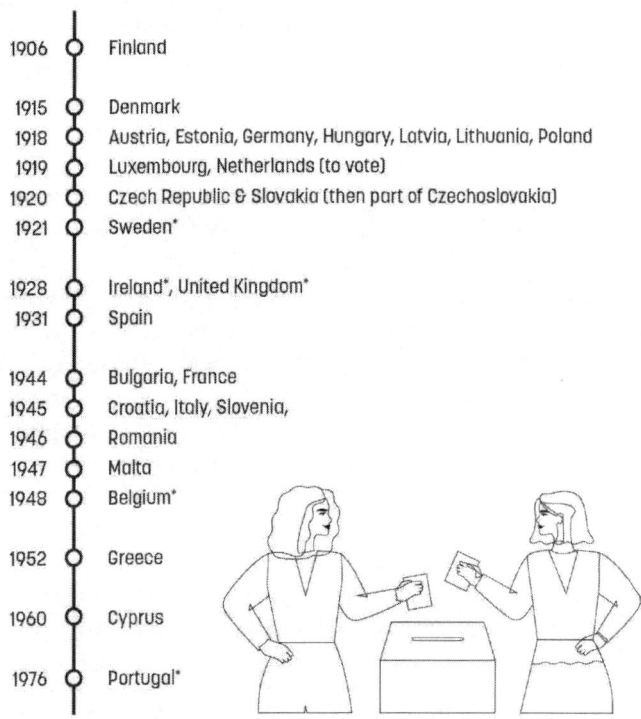

| | |
|---|---|
| 1906 | Finland |
| 1915 | Denmark |
| 1918 | Austria, Estonia, Germany, Hungary, Latvia, Lithuania, Poland |
| 1919 | Luxembourg, Netherlands (to vote) |
| 1920 | Czech Republic & Slovakia (then part of Czechoslovakia) |
| 1921 | Sweden* |
| 1928 | Ireland*, United Kingdom* |
| 1931 | Spain |
| 1944 | Bulgaria, France |
| 1945 | Croatia, Italy, Slovenia, |
| 1946 | Romania |
| 1947 | Malta |
| 1948 | Belgium* |
| 1952 | Greece |
| 1960 | Cyprus |
| 1976 | Portugal* |

*The date signifies the year women were granted the full right both to vote and to stand for election. In some cases, rights were initially subject to conditions or restrictions, after being lifted later on (relevant countries marked by an asterisk).*

Source :
Inter-Parliamentary Union "A World Chronology Of The Recognition Of Women's Rights To Vote And To Stand For Election, retrieved from : http://archive.ipu.org/wmn-e/suffrage.htm

# Introduction

It is now widely recognised that the European Union has played a leading role in the promotion of gender equality, not only within the European Union but worldwide. Over the years its institutions, pressed by civil society activists and served by proactive public servants and favourable circumstances, have developed legislation, programmes, strategies, instruments and tools to promote equality, measure and monitor progress, giving rise to a policy in its own right. Since 2019, a dedicated EU commissioner has even been established to promote equality with the appointment of the Maltese labour politician Helena Dalli.

Paradoxically, the EU's specific contribution to gender equality has not yet convinced European women to support European integration: fewer women than men have voted in European elections,[23] very few of them took part in the consultations launched in March 2021 on the future of Europe,[24] and their attitude towards the EU is generally less positive than men's as it appears in the Eurobaro-

---

23    Although sociodemographic analysis shows there has been an increase in turnout for all population groups, men (52%, +7pp) remain slightly more likely to vote than women (49%, +8pp) – see European Parliament, "The 2019 Post-electoral Survey: Have European Elections Entered a New Dimension? Complete Survey Results," (Brussels: European Union, 2019), https://op.europa.eu/en/publication-detail/-/publicatio n/42b98847-db51-11e9-9c4e-01aa75ed71a1/language-en

24    Of the people contributing to this platform, 57% self-identified as men, and 15% as women, according to its third interim report – see Kantar Public, *Contributions per Member State on the Multilingual Digital Platform of the Conference on the Future of Europe* (Brussels: Conference on the Future of Europe, November 2021), 10, https://futureu.europa. eu/rails/active_storage/blobs/eyJfcmFpbHMiOnsibWVzc2FnZSI6IkJ- BaHBBam1MIiwiZXhwIjpudWxsLCJwdXIiOiJibG9iX2lkIn19--0fe069d- c36072188453cf63db1f14b9530316ddd/Report%20Kantar%20COFE%20 MEMBER%20STATE_contributions%20November_final.pdf

meter surveys.[25] Even in the most recent period when trust in the EU has reached its highest levels in more than a decade[26] in reaction to Brexit and illiberal governments, women's level of trust remains more reticent.

Still, the construction of a united Europe and the liberation of women have developed in parallel in western Europe since World War II as a reaction to the barbarity of the war and for the building of peace and solidarity. Both movements have changed the way we live, travel, interact, and see our future. It is then puzzling to note that these two movements, which seem to have much in common, are not perceived to be in a complementary relationship. The way European integration is materialising, in substance and in process, does not convince women. Gender equality is still a marginal policy in the EU (the proverbial cherry on the cake) and mainstream policies too often destroy the benefits of gender advances. This results in contradictory measures like proclaiming childcare is a priority of the EU (Barcelona targets, the 2019 work-life balance directive) while promoting austerity policies which impose budgetary cuts in public social services like childcare; like prioritising economic objectives in the most liberal sense (favouring competition over cooperation) to the detriment of social inclusion; like praising the role of women in the economy while the majority of women are still in insecure, underpaid and precarious jobs. In addition, the 'solidarity component' of the EU which women would care for, is not dominant in its public image.

25     According to a Eurobarometer conducted in February-March 2021, interest in EU politics is significantly correlated with gender (as well as age, education and socioeconomic situation). As the survey unveils, EU matters is mostly an issue of interest for men and the most socially and economically advantaged. Kantar Belgium, "Standard Eurobarometer 94 (Winter 2020-2021): Public opinion in the European Union" (Brussels: European Commission, Directorate-General for Communication, 2021), https://doi.org/10.2775/841401

26     With a turnout of 50.6%, according to the "2019 European Parliament Election Results" (Brussels: EU Parliament, 22 October 2019), ://www.europarl.europa.eu/election-results-2019/en/turnout/

The EU gender equality policy has drawn an increasing interest from researchers and analysts over the years and is singularised as an original policy field which has relied on the dynamic interaction of three key elements, or explanatory variables since its early days: *institutions* (processes, context), *interests* (actors, power) and *ideas* (content, evidence, values), known as the '3 Is'.[27] The rich and well-documented body of knowledge produced about inequality and discrimination in general, as they persist all over Europe, but also the creation of a supranational stakeholder community and a supportive set of institutions continue to attract the attention of scholars worldwide. It is a policy worth looking into from a political science and Europeanist perspective, but also from a feminist and progressive perspective.

No other policy since the beginning of the European Economic Community has pushed the boundaries of European competences to such an extent. No other policy has gained so much support from an original community of stakeholders (the "velvet triangle"[28] of feminist activists, researchers and policy makers), no other policy has benefitted so much from its progressive institutionalisation and still, no other policy has known so many ups and downs, in synchrony with the ups and downs of European integration itself.

We will take the reader through an overview of seventy years of the European gender equality policy decade after decade, describing its successes and disappointments as it developed under the pressure of women's rights players, the various institutions and a variety of other factors.

Today's strength of the EU's gender equality policy lies in the original constellation of institutions, instruments and tools which have

---

27   Bruno Palier, and Yves Surel, *Les "trois I" et l'analyse de l'Etat en action* (Paris: Presses de Science Po, 2005), https://spire.sciencespo.fr/hdl:/2441/d7a7evb2ctdg4i89gglrnilo2/resources/2005-les-trois-i.pdf

28   A term coined by Alison Woodward, see "Building Velvet Triangles: Gender and Informal Governance," in *Informal Governance in the European Union*, ed. Thomas Christiansen and Simona Piattoni (Cheltenham: Edward Elgar, 2003), 76-93.

emerged over the years. While some of them are robust, others are more fragile and subject to critical reviews, often not sufficiently binding for a proper and even policy implementation, and conceived from too limited a perspective to properly address the systemic sources of inequality.

These insufficiencies have been revealed in recent years in two defining moments:

First, its 2004-2013 enlargement by 13 new Member States[29] has been a historical revolution for an EU led by ageing governance structures. In the accession agenda, gender equality has been treated as a formal process, disconnected from the people it is supposed to address. Eastern and Central European Member States formally translated the *acquis* as they had to comply with it. However, there was a lack of involvement of civil society, and later the economic and financial (and migration) prevailed. What should have been felt as a positive impact on the situation of women (the consolidation of equal rights) was blighted by the difficult, precarious and low-paid labour market opportunities for women, the closure of former childcare facilities, and the damage to the social sphere by liberal economic choices which came in reaction to a communist past. On this unfortunate bedrock, rising illiberal regimes have legitimised a backlash against culturally progressive policies and generated anti-gender movements which affect not only women but also the LGBTIQ community, closing the emerging public debates on new freedoms regarding one's sexual orientation and sexual identity.

The second defining moment is still 'work in progress': the corona crisis has raised major questions about our governance structures and the role of inequalities in the spread of the pandemic. The priority given to the economic or financial sectors when 'all we need is care'; the shrinking of public services in the name of budget austerity; the persistent pay discrepancies in sectors like health, education and care (occupied in majority by women); the performance of women leaders in managing the crisis - all are calling for a more

---

29    10 (in 2004), 2 (in 2007) and 1 (in 2013)

systemic handling of gender inequalities and a reconfiguration of our governance structures and priorities.

Looking to the future, shouldn't we ask why the practical and mental load for family care is still mainly borne by women? How can we care for people and the environment if competition and profit-making remain the rules of the game? How can the redistribution of resources be more efficient?

By easing the financial constraints on public budgets to face the pandemic, the EU has made a huge step forward. The European Council, in a pressing context with leaders sharing very different views, reached the remarkable consensual decision of temporarily giving up on financial austerity in the name of saving lives – but how long will the well-being of its citizens remain a priority over economic growth for the EU?

The pandemic has generated a plethora of research and studies[30] advocating for investment in caring activities[31] and fighting inequalities, with gender inequalities turning out to be at the heart of all these injustices suddenly under the spotlight. How do researchers recommend to shape responses to the crisis? Under scrutiny are the allocation of funds of the Next Generation EU recovery facility, with findings far from satisfactory regarding its gender dimension (or the lack thereof).[32]

---

30 See for instance European Institute for Gender Equality (EIGE), *Gender equality and the socio-economic impact of the COVID-19 pandemic* (Luxembourg: Publications Office of the European Union, 2021); Gender Five Plus, *Towards a gendered recovery in the EU: women and equality in their aftermath of the COVID 19 pandemic* (Brussels: 2021), https://www.genderfiveplus.com/covid19-gender-equality-eu; or World Bank Group, *Gender Dimensions of the COVID-19 Pandemic: Policy note* (Washington, D.C.: World Bank Group, 2020).

31 Barbara Helfferich, *Towards a fairer, care-focused Europe* (FEPS/FES, 2021), https://www.feps-europe.eu/attachments/events/policy%20study_care4care.pdf

32 Elisabeth Klatzer and Azzurra Rinaldi, *#nextGenerationEU Leaves Women Behind: Gender Impact Assessment of the European Commission, Proposals for the EU Recovery Plan. Preliminary Study* (Brussels: The Greens/EFA Group in the European Parliament, 2020), https://alexan-

*Quo vadis Europe*? As a number of progressive thinkers today, we at FEPS believe that the European Union needs new driving forces. It was the case before the health crisis, it is even more so today. One of these driving forces must be redistributing power and resources by re-setting priorities, caring for people, and putting solidarity first–all issues widely known and theorised in feminist thinking for decades already.

Gender equality and European integration must recognise what they have in common. The common thread in the journey we undertake here endeavours to bring closer together these two dynamics which have, in parallel, already shaped huge political and societal transformations since World War II. The underlying question will be how more explicit synergies between gender equality and European integration can renew progressive thinking.

drageese.eu/ wp-content/uploads/2020/07/Gender-Impact-Assessment-NextGenerationEU_Klatzer_Rinaldi_2020.pdf

# Part I:
# When inequalities meet gender

Gender equality remains one of the most misunderstood concepts in contemporary discourse, although it has been widely studied since the emergence of feminist scholarship in the 1960s. Some see it as a corporatist claim of (mostly privileged) women to fit in a man's world through equal rights. Others have embraced the term of gender to express a much wider and more fluid notion than its traditional binary understanding, based on the understanding that the categories of women and men are socially constructed. Finally, some see it as a transformative notion where gender equality is the cornerstone for a better, fairer and more caring society.

While feminism and the fight for gender equality have over time become subject to many interpretations, the most crucial understanding of feminism for progressives is to be inclusive, intersectional and genuinely empowering, in a way that serves social justice for all.

In order to understand the underpinning concepts of gender equality in all its meanings and uses, we will briefly explore the definitions of the terms *inequality* and *gender,* and the controversies they may generate in public policy-making in the EU.

The term *gender* appeared on the EU agenda (although never in the treaties) in the nineties to refer to the social construction of relations between sexes. In this precise context, it mostly appeared in association with the term *mainstreaming* as a practical translation of the new article of the Treaty of Amsterdam (TFEU) stating that the EU should "combat discrimination based on sex" (Art 19), and "eliminate inequalities, and [...] promote equality, between men and women" – "in all its activities" (Art 8). Since then, while keeping the premise of social construction, gender has increasingly been used with the addition of *identity.* This perspective encourages a re-thinking of the boundaries created by assigning rigid and stereotyped sets of social norms and behaviours to individuals that uphold many forms of discrimination. Obviously, the term is not politically neutral. For instance, at the other end of the spectrum, the use of the term gender in the Istanbul Convention was invoked by some governments as a justification for refusing to ratify this comprehensive text to prevent and combat violence against women. Anti-gender movements made up of conservative and most often religious adepts, contest the rights of LGBTIQ persons and praise anti-gender equality family values.

As to the term (*in-*) *equality*, it has deep roots amongst progressive thinkers, often framed as underpinning universalist values. While there is a consensus that inequalities should be corrected by public policy, social democrats are struggling as to the extent and meaning of compensatory policies and at which level of policy-making it should be done. The concept has often failed to be linked with the uneven social roles occupied by women and men. Therefore, we will seek to demonstrate that a European and feminist perspective is now necessary to effectively address inequalities in the current transitions.

## Inequalities, principles and realities from a feminist perspective

Inequality is traditionally not perceived as problematic for liberal thinkers. On the contrary, it is supposed to constitute an incentive for economic growth whilst the market is supposed to correct the most blatant inequalities.[33] However, this has proved tragically wrong. We are living, in Europe, in very affluent societies which are increasingly unequal.[34] Even liberal thinkers have come to realise re-

---

33    This liberal view was theorised by Milton Friedman and the Chicago school, as well as Friedrich Hayek.

34    Oxfam, "5 shocking facts about inequality" (2020), https://www.weforum.org/agenda/2020/01/5-shocking-facts-about-inequality-according-to-oxfam-s-latest-report

cently that the so-called 'trickle-down effect' whereby wealth would automatically benefit the most deprived in the end, does not work.

The current public health crisis, adding to the impact of the 2008 financial crisis, has exacerbated social inequalities. The situation of some social groups (single parents, migrant women, older women, and also increasingly lower middle-class families) is becoming unbearable while the richest ten percent of the population own the majority of the world's wealth. This trend started in the eighties and translated into a steady decline of the electorate of Social Democratic parties in Europe and beyond. The time is then ripe to revisit the roots of progressive ideas to address inequalities and the theories behind a just society - but from a strongly European and feminist perspective.

For progressive thinkers, the fair distribution of resources aims at ensuring a harmonious and well-educated society, free of the ills of injustice, violence and poverty. This mainly is the role of any welfare state: to reduce inequalities with social spending, progressive taxation and labour rights. However, since the early 1980s, the hegemonic neoliberal doctrine has favoured a shrinking state depleted of resources due to unjust systems of tax revenue, and generated a severe lack of social cohesion between countries, regions and people, to stimulate competition. This model, which has driven the governance of the European Union in the last 20 years, has created not only inequality, but also a grave democratic deficit fuelling the rejection of the EU in referenda, low participation in European elections, and the success of fake news which have fed into Brexit[35] and other anti-European movements. This neoliberal governance of the economy has impacted less educated women the hardest as competition lowered the cost of labour, creating new forms of low-paid, often part-time jobs without social safety nets in the service sector. In the first decade of the century, highly educated women have massively entered into traditionally male-dominated employment. Meanwhile, most of the new jobs in the care sector were created with the underlying

---

35    The fake news item 'financing of the NHS vs the EU' was what stuck
      with the electorate.

assumption that women have 'naturally endowed' skills to care for others by equating this type of work with the stereotypical image of the housewife confined to the private sphere. Women have also been paying the price for the shrinking of public services with lower stable employment and reduced social services and assistance.

The corona crisis has amplified existing inequalities including gender inequalities, revealing their systemic nature. According to Thomas Piketty, author of the bestselling book *Capital in the Twentieth Century* (2013),[36] inequalities are built into the current economic system as wealth grows faster than economic output (returns on capital exceed the rate of growth). This has been the case since the end of the 19th century and the rise of capitalism. A relative balance has been maintained by the redistribution created by two World Wars and the growth period of the sixties, but in the last 40 years, nothing has disrupted the steady concentration of wealth, making the gap between the return on capital over labour ever larger. This context is unlikely to see a reduction of gender inequalities, given that the largest proportion of capital (and access thereto) is owned by men. As a 2021 Oxfam report denounced ahead of the World Economic Forum, the world's ten richest men have seen their combined wealth increase by half a trillion US dollars since the start of the pandemic whilst women were the hardest hit being over-represented in the low-paid precarious professions and thus paying the largest toll to the same pandemic.[37] Commenting on the report, Oxfam international executive director Gabriela Bucher goes on arguing: "Women and marginalised racial and ethnic groups are bearing the brunt of

---

36    Thomas Piketty, *Capital in the Twentieth Century* (Cambridge, MA: Harvard University Press, 2013).

37    Esmée Berghout et al, *The Inequality Virus: Bringing together a world torn apart by coronavirus through a fair, just and sustainable economy* (Oxford: Oxfam International, 25 January 2021), https://oxfamilibrary. openrepository.com/bitstream/handle/10546/621149/bp-the-inequality-virus-250121-en.pdf

this crisis. They are more likely to be pushed into poverty, more likely to go hungry, and more likely to be excluded from healthcare." [38]

As a wild guess, is it useful to wonder if this wealth gap would have come about in a more gender-equal world? Would more gender equality in leadership positions today foster a more equal distribution of wealth? Would it generate more investments in education, health, care services or sustainable development? Fresh thinking to overcome the current crisis needs to take a serious look at the gender perspective. But where shall we start?

Many great thinkers who have theorised some of the most fundamental human principles such as democracy, freedom and equality have been either blatantly misogynistic or have adopted a universalist approach turning a blind eye on gender imbalances. From Aristotle to Rousseau, political philosophers considered women as a submissive appendix to men. In *Politics*, we can read: "The male is by nature superior, and the female inferior, one rules and the other is ruled; this principle of necessity extends to all mankind".[39] Later, Philosophers like John Stuart Mill, Condorcet or Poulain de la Barre theorised how women suffered a lower status than men in classical thought.[40] More recently, the family as a production unit[41] or the

---

38  *Mega-rich recoup COVID-losses in record-time yet billions will live in poverty for at least a decade* (Oxford: Oxfam International, 25 January 2021), https://www.oxfam.org/en/press-releases/mega-rich-recoup-covid-losses-record-time-yet-billions-will-live-poverty-least

39  For a more detailed analysis of Aristotle's *Politics* within which he makes claims about women and their place in his conception of politics, see María Luisa Femenías, "Women and Natural Hierarchy in Aristotle," *Hypatia* 9, no. 1 (1994): 164–72.

40  See for instance Robert Dimand and Chris Nyland, ed., *The Status of Women in Classical Economic Thought* (Cheltenham, UK: Edward Elgar, 2003).

41  See for instance the seminal work of the materialist feminist scholar Christine Delphy who draws on the case of rural women whose work is made invisible: Delphy Christine, *L'Ennemi principal* (Paris: Syllepse, 2013); or more recent research on family firms conducted by Paula Rodríguez-Modroño et al., *The hidden role of women in family firms* (Sevilla: Universidad Pablo de Olavide, 2015), https://ideas.repec.org/p/pab/wphaei/15.01.html.

specific inequalities created by the socially constructed distribution of roles have still not featured on the radar of modern thinkers of welfare. In *A Theory of Justice* (1971), John Rawls defines social justice in terms of equality of rights and of priority given to individuals who receive the smallest quantity of basic resources (primary goods). Although revolutionary at the time, his social justice concept considers neither the position of women nor the organisation inside the family within his visions of a just society.[42]

In this regard, Nobel prize winner and social justice theorist Amartya Sen (who had to bring up his children as a single parent) is one of the rare exceptions in his category, aware of the different life experiences and aspirations of women and men. His theory of democracy based on people's capabilities,[43] measured by the *functionings*[44] of individuals is a very good start. Martha Nussbaum advanced Sen's theoretical approach by 'qualifying' capabilities and exerting a feminist critique which takes us into much of today's debates on paid and unpaid work.[45] Nussbaum highlights some of the problematic assumptions and conclusions of output-based measures of development like GDP (or GNP) which do not consider social requirements limiting the access to resources for some social groups, such as women.[46] Specifically, Nussbaum mentions that output-based approa-

---

42    Martha Nussbaum, "Rawls and Feminism," in *The Cambridge Companion to Rawls*, ed. Samuel Freeman (Cambridge University Press, 2003), 489-520.

43    Amartya Sen, *Equality of What?* The Tanner Lecture on Human Values (Stanford, CA: Stanford University, 22 May 1979).

44    Functionings are actions (doings) but also states of the body and the mind (beings) which individuals can transform into achievements. For instance, an individual's level of happiness is a functioning, as well as his marital status, his income, the kind of job he has, and how much he works. Sen argues that what is important, out of concern for freedom and responsibility, is that people have access to good levels of functionings. The set of functioning levels that an individual is able to achieve is called a capability and he favours a definition of social justice in terms of equality of capabilities.

45    Martha Nussbaum, "Rawls and Feminism," 2003

46    Martha Nussbaum, "Promoting women's capabilities," in *Global tensions: challenges and opportunities in the world economy*, ed. Lourdes Ben-

ches ignore the distribution of needs for the varying circumstances of people, for example a pregnant woman needs more resources than a non-pregnant woman or a single man. Also, output-based measures ignore unpaid work, which includes child rearing and the societal advantages that result from a mother's work. Marilyn Waring, a political economist and activist for women's rights, elaborates on the example of a mother engaged in childcare, domestic care and producing goods for the informal market, all of which are usually done simultaneously.[47] These activities provide economic benefits, but are not valued in national accounting systems, suggesting that the definition of employment used in output-based measures is inappropriate.[48]

Contemporary feminist economists such as the International Association for Feminist Economics (IAFFE)[49] join Sen and Nussbaum's view that economics should be less focused on mechanisms (like income) or theories (such as utilitarianism) and more on well-being, a multidimensional concept which includes income, health, education, empowerment and social status. They argue that economic success cannot be measured only by goods or domestic products but must include human well-being. Aggregate income is not sufficient to evaluate general well-being, because individual entitlements and needs (health, longevity, access to property, education, time) must also be considered.

Similar conclusions were reached in 2008 by Stiglitz, Sen and Fitoussi in their report on the "measurement of economic performance and social progress". The OECD continued to work on the issue, producing a new *Beyond GDP* report in 2018 on measuring what

ería and Savitri Bisnath (New York: Routledge, 2004), 200–214.

47  Waring, Marilyn "Counting for something! Recognising women's contribution to the global economy through alternative accounting systems" in *Gender and Development* 11, no. 1 (2003).

48  This is a very topical issue in our post covid-19, digital, platform economies as shown by the French sociologist Marie Anne Dujarie, *Troubles dans le travail: sociologie d'une catégorie de pensée* (Paris: Presses Universitaires de France, 2021).

49  For publications, events, and introductory videos on feminist economics by IAFFE, see http://www.iaffe.org/

counts for economic and social performance. Stating that GDP has been caught to have misled policy makers who adopted wrong policies concentrating on the wrong indicators, this report called for a dashboard of indicators. Together, these indicators should reveal who is benefitting from growth, whether that growth is environmentally sustainable but also how people feel about their lives and what factors contribute to an individual or a country's success. In the same vein, the European Commission, within its own Beyond GDP initiative has recently produced a comprehensive report on *resilience*[50] presenting four prototype dashboards to monitor four interrelated dimensions: social and economic, geopolitical, green, and digital. In the Commission's report, gender is one of the categories mentioned for increased inequalities, and it utilises the European Gender Equality Institute's (EIGE) work on post-covid public health. The questions of the reproductive sphere and the valuation of unpaid work are however still far from being considered as part of the measurement of the wellbeing of Europeans.

## The meaning of gender

Rational vs. emotional, strong vs. weak, active vs. passive, calculated vs. sensitive, culture vs. nature, public vs. private, politics vs. family: the dichotomies of traditional gender norms or stereotypes present in everyday life have placed men in the public world of politics and women in the private, domestic and (supposedly) non-political world of the home, without any analysis of the power relations they entail. The belief that women's and men's behaviour, life and work choices, their skills and social roles are predetermined by their anatomy was not thoroughly questioned or analysed by the social sciences until the emergence of gender studies, some fifty years ago. Gender studies as a field of academic research developed in the wake of the *women's liberation movements* beginning in the late 1960s.

---

50    European Commission, *First Strategic Foresight Report* (Brussels: 2020), https://ec.europa.eu/info/strategy/strategic-planning/strategic-foresight/2020-strategic-foresight-report_en

Gender studies (initially called women's studies) has a distinctive engagement with interdisciplinarity, using a scientific approach which relies on theoretical input from social science, biology, philosophy, psychoanalysis, history, sociology and economy to explain the social, economic, political and cultural construction of gender. The objective is to understand how purely anatomical sexual differences and socially constructed gender roles are used in power strategies to control bodies and normalise inequality, discrimination and domination. Gender studies go beyond the mere notion of biological sex traits, which are considered as one of the differences amongst all those which make each of us unique. The concept of gender as a *category of analysis* was coined in the 1980s by the seminal work of US historian Joan Scott[51] to highlight the unequal processes which create various forms of differentiation between the sexes.

It is crucial for progressives to fully understand the scientific context and its correct academic uses, particularly in times when conservative activists tend to caricature the notion of gender, precisely because it is poorly understood, in public debates.

On the EU's agenda the term *gender* did not become salient until the 1990s, when it mainly referred to the social construction of relations between women and men, highlighting the deep-seated power relations at stake in their interaction. It appeared in association with the term *mainstreaming* at the time of the UN's Fourth World Conference on Women in Beijing (1995). Although the Treaties themselves do not use the word 'gender', it has been widely used in official texts, secondary legislation, and even in the name of institutions (e.g. EIGE, the European institute for Gender Equality).

During the 1990s, a large progressive consensus embraced the term gender to add a layer of clarification to policies: *male dominance*[52] was not biological but socially constructed, hence *deconstruction* was a political choice. Claiming that "[g]ender neutrality is thus

---

51    Joan Scott, "Gender a useful category of historical analysis," *The American Historical Review* 91, no. 5 (December 1986), 1053-1075.

52    Pierre Bourdieu coined the term in French *La Domination Masculine* (Paris: Seuil, 1998). He exposes a male form of dominance which is so anchored in our social practices and our unconscious that we hardly

simply the male standard", Catharine MacKinnon had demonstrated how the law and jurisprudence often ignored the particular disadvantages faced by women, resulting in persisting social injustice.[53] Therefore, the paradigmatic change operated by the EU attracted the interest of many feminist researchers to look closer into EU gender equality policy.

The effervescence that surrounded movements to put women's rights, but also more broadly LGBTIQ people's rights (including related advanced such as the legalisation of same sex marriage in many countries) onto the international political agenda was soon met with a ferocious counter-attack initiated by the Vatican in the 1990s. An unlikely[54] alliance of fundamentalist and conservative circles followed suit, contesting what they label a 'gender theory' and 'gender ideology'.[55] On the one hand, the latter expressions are used to vilify the concept of gender, which they claim enfeebles the traditional family, ie the supposedly fragile 'last pillar' of their societal vision. On the other hand, the introduction of the 'gender theory' contributed to creating confusion around the real concerns raised using the concept of gender – which was crafted by social science as a lens to see the ways in which gendered power relations permeate structures and institutions. As we will see later, the term gender has thus been instrumentalised by some governments and political actors who have

---

perceive it; something so deeply engrained into our collective expectations that we find it difficult to call into question.

53    Catharine McKinnon, *Toward a Feminist Theory of the State*, (Cambridge, MA: Harvard University Press, 1989).

54    To find out more about how anti-gender actors have used gender as an umbrella to build right-wing, conservative alliances against gender equality and progress towards social equality at large, see for instance Eszter Kováts and Maari Põim, ed. *Gender as a symbolic glue: The position and role of conservative and far right parties in the anti-gender mobilization in Europe.* (Brussels: FEPS-FES, 2015), https://www.feps-europe.eu/Assets/Publications/PostFiles/314_1.pdf

55    Florence Rochefort, "Genre, religions et sécularisation" in *Qu'est ce que le genre?* ed. Laurie Laufer and Florence Rochefort (Paris: Payot, 2014), 213- 23, analyses the discourse of representatives of the Catholic, Protestant and Orthodox Christian, Jewish, Muslim and Buddist faiths in their hearings for the French law on same-sex marriage passed in 2013.

used it to prevent further advances for gender equality, the most emblematic recent example being the current blockages of the Council of Europe's ratification process of the Convention on preventing and combatting violence against women and domestic violence (known as the Istanbul convention).[56]

Fig. 1    The first massive demonstrations against what was named by opponents the theory of gender or gender ideology took place in Paris before the vote of the law on same sex marriage in 2013

The Council of Europe Convention on preventing and combating violence against women (**'Istanbul Convention'**), which came into force in 2014, is the first legally binding international instrument on preventing and combating violence against women and girls at international level. It establishes a comprehensive framework of legal and policy measures for preventing such violence, supporting victims and punishing perpetrators. As of November 2021, it has

---

56    Council of Europe, "Istanbul Convention Action against violence against women and domestic violence" (Strasbourg, 2022), https://www.coe.int/en/web/istanbul-convention

been signed by all EU Member States, and ratified by 21 (Austria, Belgium, Croatia, Cyprus, Denmark, Estonia, Finland, France, Germany, Greece, Ireland, Italy, Luxembourg, Malta, Netherlands, Poland, Portugal, Romania, Slovenia, Spain and Sweden). However, in July 2020, the Polish government announced its intention to withdraw from the Convention. The Convention also provides for EU accession, to the extent of its competences.

The reluctance of the remaining EU Member States to ratify is, as pointed out by Vice President Timmermans in a parliamentary debate, based on misinterpretations on the use of the term gender in the Convention, as the Convention is about protecting women against violence, not about challenging traditional families or imposing an ideology.[57]

Particularly, the misconceptions some Member State governments are using not to ratify the Convention are as follows.[58] Firstly, they alledge that the Convention would support a 'destructive gender ideology'. That is simply untrue: "Gender refers to how social structures can lead to a lack of respect for women's rights, resulting in increased violence, thus serving as an interpretation tool. Regardless, it does not force the countries to adopt that position nor does it replace any biological definition."[59]

Secondly, they are apprehensive that the Istanbul Convention would legally force countries to introduce a third gender. In fact, the convention does not oblige states to recognise a third sex under domestic law. The term 'third sex'

57    Rosamund Shreeves, Ülla Jurviste (Members' Research Service), Legislative Train Schedule: women's rights and gender equality - FEMM – EU accession to the [...] ('Istanbul Convention') 2016-03 (European Parliament, 20 February 2022), https://www.europarl.europa.eu/legislative-train/theme-a-new-push-for-european-democracy/file-eu-accession-to-the-istanbul-convention

58    EU Observer, "Five Istanbul Convemtion Myths" (2020) https://euobserver.com/opinion/149358

59    Ibid.

does not even appear in the text. Thirdly, the Istanbul Convention is said to threaten the nuclear family and traditional family values. This is also not true. The Convention does not lead to forcing men or women into a certain lifestyle. It merely stipulates that women who are subjected to domestic violence have the right to receive the protection and support they need to leave a violent relationship.

The theoretical discourse around the term gender has been rich in academic and progressive circles, not without giving rise to debate, especially regarding the recognition of sexual orientations which deviate from the dominant heteronormative model, but also more recently about sexual identities and the need for policy intervention to prevent discrimination against LGBTIQ persons. It never claimed, however, to result from a theory, much less an ideology. There is no such thing as 'a gender theory' but instead, gender is a tool to offer a new lens on reality.

Inspired by Michel Foucault's analysis[60] of the body and sexuality as power constructs, Judith Butler committed to break down the distinction between biological bodies and socially constructed gender differences, arguing that the distinction between male and female bodies is itself arbitrary and an artefact of a social order organised by normative heterosexuality.[61] For her, as for British social anthropologist Henrietta Moore, "bodies are not simply bodies but they express a revised understanding of gender identity as not simply imposed through patriarchal structures but as a set of norms that are lived and transformed in the embodied practices of women and men".[62]

These academic debates contributed to giving a voice to people who had long remained invisible in the discussions about gender

---

60    For Foucault, the body is not sexed prior to its determination within a discourse through which it becomes invested with an idea of natural or essential sex. – Michel Foucault, *History of Sexuality Volume 1: introduction* (New York: Vintage Books, 1980).

61    Judith Butler, *Gender Trouble* (New York: Routledge, 1990).

62    Henrietta Moore, "'Divided We Stand': Sex, Gender and Sexual Difference," *Feminist Review 47, no.* 1 (1994), 78-95.

equality, in particular trans[63] women and intersex[64] people. Scholars helped raise awareness of the discrimination they were facing and created a greater understanding of the specific social, legal and economic challenges involved.

The EU was prompt to react, asking its European Network of legal experts in gender equality and non-discrimination to produce a first report in 2012 on the situation in 30 countries. This research was followed by surveys conducted by the Fundamental Rights Agen-

---

63    "*Trans* is an inclusive umbrella term referring to people whose gender identity and/or a gender expression differs from the sex they were assigned at birth. Gender identity is how we see ourselves: an internal and personalised perception of our own gender. This may differ from the sex we were assigned at birth or how society might label us. The term trans includes, but is not limited to: men and women with transsexual pasts, and people who identify as transsexual, transgender, transvestite/cross-dressing, androgynous, polygender, genderqueer, agender, gender variant, or with any other gender identity and/or expression which is not standard male or female, and express their gender through their choice of clothes, presentation or body modifications, including undergoing multiple surgical procedures." – See ILGA Europe, *The definition: what is trans?* (Ixelles: International Lesbian, Gay, Bisexual, Trans and Intersex Association, 2019), https://ilga-europe.org/what-we-do/our-advocacy-work/trans-and-intersex/trans

64    "Intersex people are born with physical, hormonal or genetic features that are neither wholly female nor wholly male, or a combination of female and male, or neither female nor male. Many forms of intersex exist; it is a spectrum or umbrella term, rather than a single category. An intersex individual is born intersex. Some common intersex variations are diagnosed prenatally via genetic screening. Intersex differences may be visibly apparent at birth. Some intersex traits become apparent in puberty, or when trying to conceive, or through random chance. Other instances may only be discovered during an autopsy. The lowest popular statistic is around 1 in 2,000 people (.05% of births) but a more likely figure is closer to 1.7%. This makes intersex differences about as common as red hair." – See ILGA Europe, *Definitions: what is intersex?* (Ixelles: International Lesbian, Gay, Bisexual, Trans and Intersex Association, 2019), https://ilga-europe.org/what-we-do/our-advocacy-work/trans-and-intersex/intersex

cy (FRA) in 2014[65] and more recently in 2020.[66] Similar publications include the European network of legal experts' 2018 comparative analysis on "Trans and intersex equality rights in Europe"[67] and a European Commission 2020 report drafted by the research consultancy ICF "Legal gender recognition in the EU – The journeys of trans people towards full equality".[68] FEPS, together with Fondation Jean Jaurès, published an article by Flora Bolter highlighting the intersection between gender and sexual identity/orientation showing how violence impacts LBTIQ women in a much more acute manner.[69] On the basis of this accumulated knowledge of existing discrimination and difficulties inflicted on the grounds of sexual orientation, identity and expression, the European Commission presented its *LGBTIQ Equality Strategy 2020-2025 in the EU* in December 2020.[70] The strategy proposed to present an initiative in 2021[71] to extend the

65    Fundamental Rights Agency (FRA), "Being Trans in the EU: Comparative analysis of the EU LGBT survey data" (Luxembourg: Publications Office of the European Union, 09 December 2014), https://fra.europa.eu/en/publication/2014/being-trans-eu-comparative-analysis-eu-lgbt-survey-data

66    FRA, "A long way to go for LGBTI equality," https://fra.europa.eu/en/publication/2020/eu-lgbti-survey-results

67    European network of legal experts in gender equality and non-discrimination, "Trans and intersex equality in Europe: a comparative analysis" (Brussels: Directorate-General for Justice and Consumers, https://ec.europa.eu/info/sites/default/files/trans_and_intersex_equality_rights.pdf

68    European Commission, "Legal gender recognition in the EU: The journey of trans people towards full equality" (Directorate-General for Justice and Consumers, June 2020), https://ec.europa.eu/info/sites/default/files/legal_gender_recognition_in_the_eu_the_journeys_of_trans_people_towards_full_equality_sept_en.pdf

69    Find out more about the publication series "Stop Gender-based violence" by FEPS and Fondation Jean Jaurès at https://www.feps-europe.eu/articles/36-project/78-feps-fjj-gender-based-violence-publication-series.html

70    European Commission, "LGBTIQ Equality Strategy 2020-2025," https://ec.europa.eu/info/sites/default/files/lgbtiq_strategy_2020-2025_en.pdf

71    And indeed, a communication was issued in December 2021: https://ec.europa.eu/info/sites/default/files/1_1_178542_comm_eu_crimes_

list of EU crimes under Article 83(1) TFEU to cover hate crime and hate speech, including when targeted at LGBTIQ people. Moreover, it endeavours, among others, to bring forward the legislation on the mutual recognition of parenthood in cross-border situations (planned for end of 2022) and commits to ensure that LGBTIQ concerns are considered across EU policy-making, striving for an EU where people "in *all* their diversity, are safe and have equal opportunities to prosper and fully participate in society".[72]

## EU Legal foundations of gender equality and anti-discrimination

The multiple meanings and debates around gender have highlighted the need for gender equality to be simultaneously *transformative* and *inclusive.* In order to deliver a gender justice transformation, fundamental change need to take place (overcoming the public-private divide, challenging the patriarchal structures of society, recognising the connections between women's socio-economic disadvantage and their political status); At the same time, no such transformative change can take place without adopting an intersectional approach, taking into account all the specific challenges faced by the most underrepresented and underprivileged social groups, in order to achieve a genuine "Union of Equality".[73]

---

en.pdf)

72    European Commission, "Legal gender recognition in the EU: the journeys of trans people towards full equality" (June 2020), https://ec.europa.eu/info/policies/justice-and-fundamental-rights/combatting-discrimination/lesbian-gay-bi-trans-and-intersex-equality/studies-and-research-lgbti-equality_en

73    In her inaugural address, the president of the EU Commission declared her determination to strive for a "Union of equality" in the context of LGBTQI rights. Ursula von der Leyen, "Building the world we want to live in: A Union of vitality in a world of fragility," (SPEECH/20/1655, Brussels, 16 September 2020), European Commission, 15, https://ec.europa.eu/commission/presscorner/api/files/document/print/ov/speech_20_1655/SPEECH_20_1655_OV.pdf

Therefore, in order not to let ourselves be misled by the confusion brought by recent anti-gender trends, we need to build on the founding principles enshrined in the agreed texts of the European Treaties which offer solid support for a sound understanding of the concepts of gender equality and discrimination.

## Equality between women and men and non-discrimination in the EU Treaties: *Objectives*

### In the Treaty on European Union (TEU)

Article 2 (TEU) states: "The Union is founded on the values of respect for human dignity, freedom, democracy, equality, the rule of law and respect for human rights, including the rights of persons belonging to minorities. These values are common to the Member States in a society in which pluralism, **non-discrimination**, tolerance, justice, solidarity and **equality between women and men** prevail."

Article 3 (TEU) adds: "It shall combat **social exclusion and discrimination**, and shall promote social justice and protection, **equality between women and men**, solidarity between generations and protection of the rights of the child."

### In the Treaty on the Functioning of the European Union (TFEU)

Article 8 TFEU specifies that "In all its activities, the Union shall aim to eliminate inequalities, and to promote equality, between men and women."

Article 10 TFEU contains a similar obligation for **all the discrimination grounds** mentioned in Article 19 TFEU, including sex: "In defining and implementing its policies and activities, the Union shall aim to **combat discrimination based on sex, racial or ethnic origin, religion or belief, disability, age or sexual orientation**."

Additionally, in the declaration on Art 8 TFEU "[the] Conference agrees that, in its general efforts to **eliminate in-**

**equalities between women and men**, the Union will aim in its different policies to combat all kinds of **domestic violence**. The Member States should take all necessary measures to prevent and punish these criminal acts and to support and protect the victims."

### In the EU Charter of Fundamental Rights

In addition, the Charter of Fundamental Rights of the EU prohibits discrimination on any ground, including sex (**Article 21**).

It recognises the right to **gender equality in all areas**, and is thus not limited only to employment, and it also recognises the possibility of **positive action** (see glossary) for its promotion (**Article 23**).

Furthermore, it also defines **rights related to family protection and gender equality**. The reconciliation of family/private life with work is an important aspect of the Charter; the Charter guarantees, inter alia, the **"right to paid maternity leave and to parental leave"** (**Article 33**).

Since the entry into force of the Lisbon Treaty, the Charter has become a binding catalogue of EU fundamental rights (see **Article 6(1)** TEU). The Charter applies to the EU institutions, bodies, offices and agencies, and to the Member States when they are implementing Union law (**Article 51(1)** of the Charter), i.e. when they are acting 'within the scope' of Union law.

## Equality between women and men and non-discrimination: *the legal basis*

The principle that men and women should receive **equal pay for work of equal value** is now enshrined **Article 157** of the Treaty on the Functioning of the European Union (TFEU). **Article 153** TFEU allows the EU to act in the wider area of **equal opportunities and equal treatment in employment**

**matters,** and within this framework Article 157 TFEU authorises **positive action** to empower women.

In addition, Article 19 TFEU provides for the adoption of legislation to combat all forms of discrimination, including on the basis of sex.

Legislation against **trafficking in human beings,** in particular women and children, has been adopted on the basis of **Articles 79 and 83** TFEU.

The Rights, Equality and Citizenship programme finances, among others, measures contributing to the **eradication of violence against women,** based on **Article 168** TFEU.

We should also mention the *European Pillar of Social Rights* (2017), which has no legally binding value, but is an important instrument as it creates a **common framework for the social rights of European citizens** yet to be defined. The European Pillar of Social Rights includes twenty principles on social matters, eg on equal opportunities, access to the labour market, working conditions, social protection and social inclusion. Gender equality is one of these 20 key principles (addressed in the first chapter, "Equal opportunities and access to the labour market"). Another one demands equal opportunities regardless of gender, racial origin, religion or belief, disability, age or sexual orientation.

An action plan on the European Pillar of Social Rights was presented by the European Commission in March 2021 and approved at the Porto Summit in May 2021.

# Part II:
# From equal pay to parity democracy, the EU gender equality policy

Equality between women and men was not explicitly part of the political design imagined by the Fathers of Europe or their successors. It imposed itself on the European agenda for economic reasons. The interaction between feminist actors in the field, experts, activists and European institutions contributed to its fortuitous development, strengthening the political dimension of the Union. It was, for instance, in 1966, female factory workers in Herstal (Belgium) who upheld Article 119 of the Treaty of Rome when striking for equal salaries. As the European Economic Community (EEC) was widening and deepening, the claims of the Women's Liberation Movement for sexual and reproductive rights and equal civil rights were rising (even if the latter often tended to remain more strongly rooted in the national context). As the demands of the labour market became more pressing due to the expanding service economy in the early eighties, drawing a mainly female labour force, the scope of the EU's equality policy surpassed the focus on equal pay to acknowledge the importance of the private sphere (eg conciliation between work and family, gender-based violence). Thereby, EU equality policy *de facto* progressed through concrete actions, expanding the field of competences of the European Union and the response capacity of institutions to major social advances.

Equality (of pay, first, then of treatment at work, then of opportunities) gradually became a European policy that developed alternately in harmony and tension with the needs of the market, the critical contributions of feminists, and political opportunities. The impact of this policy area on the progress of European integration is greater than its perceived status, as is typical for an area of shared competence between the Union and its Member State. From the outset, equality policy prompted a mobilisation of those who saw the potential of Article 119 to give legitimacy to their demands, as will be highlighted below. European integration served as a strong lever for advancing equality in the Member States, and equality between women and men contributed to the Europeanisation of aspects of social and employment policies.[74]

As we go through the practical developments of the last seventy years, decade after decade, we will combine a chronological and thematic presentation to highlight the decisive role of the feminist actors in the emergence and implementation of the European policy to promote equality. We will focus on key moments, including circumstances where the achievements of equality were threatened; We will explore the structural transformations induced by this policy in the nineties, the 'golden age of European integration', and move on to the turbulent first two decades of the twenty-first century.

## The 1960s: Equal pay enshrined in the Treaty of Rome

Article 119 of the 1957 Treaty of Rome (which commits each Member State to ensure the application of the principle of equal pay for male and female workers for the same job) was introduced at the request of the French government. This request may seem paradoxical on the part of a state which was among the last in Europe to grant the right to vote to women in 1945. To plunge back into the climate of the time, let us recall this anecdote, reported by the French historian Michèle Perrot, of a member of the French parliament who insisted on awarding women the right to vote, "only after the return of all the prisoners of war, because in the absence of their natural tutelage, women voters could find themselves distraught." [75]

---

74      Gabriele Abels and Joyce Mushaben, *Gendering the European Union* (London: Palgrave, 2011).

75      Michelle Perrot, "Preface" in *Femmes et République*, ed. Scarlett Beauvalet et al. (Paris: La Documentation Française, 2020).

Even if the theorists of a United Europe subscribed to a tradition of emancipation, the origin of this request from France was motivated by considerations linked to the conditions of economic competition between Member States and not to women's rights. In the interwar period, the French industry (employers and unions) had benefitted from a situation of reinforced protection, subject to the demands of a more generous social model than in other Member States (paid holidays, payment of overtime). Consequently, it was hardly able to face competition within the common market. Industrialists were therefore very reluctant to accept the opening of borders unless the French government promised to make their agreement subject to equalisation or harmonisation of social provisions across Member States. Equal pay for women was one of these conditions, as the textile sector of northern France, which employed predominantly female workers, had to pay real salaries. Indeed, what was a legal obligation in France under the new constitution of 1945 was not so for the powerful textile industry in the Netherlands, where it was customary for women workers to receive only 'pin money' for their work.

A constellation of circumstances helped make this request from France acceptable to its partners.

After the Indochina War, the Suez crisis and in the midst of the Algerian war, the French political climate in 1957 was unstable, which pushed the negotiators of the European project to conclude swiftly. Paul-Henri Spaak, the Belgian Minister of Foreign Affairs, responsible for coordinating the first intergovernmental conference of the European Community, reported these concerns in his memoirs. The defeat of the EDC (European Defence Community) three years earlier had rekindled fear of the old demons of Franco-German warmongering. It was in the own interest of the Community's national governments, but also in that of the Americans who were banking on Spaak's enterprise to ensure the success of the Marshall Plan, that an agreement be negotiated as quickly as possible. Finally, German Chancellor Conrad Adenauer and French Prime Minister Guy Mollet agreed in November 1956 to integrate into the social chapter of the Treaty a provision promising equal pay for male and female workers, which allowed France to be flexible in its demands for the equalisation or harmonisation of social provisions and accept the dismantling of customs barriers.

This Franco-German agreement was based on the conclusions of the *Ohlin Report*, named after the Swedish Trade Minister who was entrusted with the chairmanship of a group of experts on the social aspects of integration by the International Labour Office (ILO). In general, this report was confident in the ability of market forces to cope with the differences in social obligations existing from one Member State to another. But the differences in legislation regarding women's wages – and to a lesser extent the provisions governing paid leave – were presented as needing harmonisation. Indeed, the additional wage costs weighing on industrialists in countries such as France (whose legislation provided for equal remuneration for men and women) over those payable by the Dutch industry for example (which could continue to pay women 'pin money') were too much of a distortion of competition to be absorbed by the market.

This singling out of equal pay in the Ohlin report is explained by the precedent of the ILO Convention (No. 100) on "equal pay for men and women workers for work of equal value", adopted in 1951. This had generated, studies, research, and the development of a unique expertise within the Geneva-based organisation, from which the group of experts chaired by Ohlin was able to draw inspiration.

The origin of this convention dates back to the very first inclusion of the principle of "equal pay for equal work" in the preamble to the ILO Constitution in 1919. Women, who were then very poorly represented in decision-making spheres, were not at the origin of this inscription. According to the testimony of Marguerite Thibert, a senior official at the International Labour Office, the request for this registration came from a group of male trade unionists who, after the First World War, "feared a degradation of the wages of men who had returned to civilian life" to whom their bosses could say that the work was also well done by the women."[76]

---

76    Agnès Hubert, *L'Europe et les femmes, identités en mouvement* (Rennes: Apogée, 1998).

Subsequently, "equal pay, for equal work, for all human beings, without discrimination" would be required in the Universal Declaration of Human Rights of the United Nations of 1948[77] and the principle of equal opportunities again features in the Declaration of Philadelphia adopted in 1944 by the ILO.[78]

## The implementation of Article 119

An article of the Treaty of Rome thus opened a breach allowing the European Economic Community (precursor to the European Union) to be involved in a major societal transformation. The history of the first years of its implementation nevertheless tends to prove that the impact of this article would not have been so considerable without the pugnacity of a few women determined to transform promises into reality. They met with the claims of a movement for rights for equal pay which emerged in female industrial worker's strikes in the sixties, relayed by women activists.

Under Article 119, "Each Member State shall during the first stage ensure and subsequently maintain the application of the principle that men and women should receive equal pay for equal work."[79] But when in May 1960 the Council of Ministers agreed to step up the pace of dismantling customs barriers between the six Member States (with a view to completing the first phase provided for by the Treaty in December 1961), nothing had been done to achieve equal pay for women and men. France, anxious to remind its partners of their commitments on the social chapter, then recalled that the commitment of the Six on women's wages was an integral part of the

---

[77]     United Nations, Universal Declaration of Human Rights (New York, 1948), https://www.un.org/en/about-us/universal-declaration-of-human-rights

[78]     International Labor Organization, *Declaration concerning the aims and purposes of the ILO* (Philadelphia, USA: 09 December 1944), https://www.ilo.org/dyn/normlex/en/f?p=1000:62:0::NO:62:P62_LIST_EN-TRIE_ID:2453907:NO#declaration

[79]     See full Art 119 in the Treaty of Rome (1957), https://www.equalrightstrust.org/sites/default/files/ertdocs//rometreaty.pdf

implementation of the first phase and remained a condition for its acceptance of tariff dismantling.

French president Charles de Gaulle and his government were then suspected of seeking a pretext to delay the establishment of the common market. The Council of Ministers, pressed by the French insistence and wishing to unblock the situation, agreed to ask the European Commission to establish a programme for the implementation of Article 119. At the end of 1960 time was pressing as the second stage loomed by the end of 1961. The European Commission therefore requested Member States to report before June 1961 the measures they had taken at national level for the article's implementation. Since not a single notification reached the Commission by this date, on the pretext of a lack of factual information on women's pay, it was decided to create an 'Article 119 expert group'.

With the fateful date of 31 December 1961 set for the transition to the second phase approaching, this group concluded its first rushed meeting with a list of measures to be taken to achieve equal pay. Its conclusions helped calm French demands and satisfy the members of the Council, content to have found some technical obstacles to justify political delay.

Thus, on 31 December 1961 a resolution was adopted which the feminist jurist Eliane Vogel Polsky later called a "coup de force", ie a power grab.[80] This text provided for the equalisation of salary scales and the elimination of discriminatory clauses in collective agreements within three years. Governments were also to adopt "all appropriate measures" to guarantee access to the control of the European Court of Justice in the event of an infringement of the provisions of Article 119. Besides, the European Commission was requested to deliver a report on the measures taken by the Member States at the end of each stage.

---

80    Eliane Gubin, "Eliane Vogel Polsky, une femme de conviction" (Brussels: Institut pour l'égalité des femmes et des hommes Belgique, 2007), https://igvm-iefh.belgium.be/fr/publications/eliane_vogel-polsky_een_vrouw_met_overtuiging

The first report of the Article 119 expert group notably put Belgium and the Netherlands in the dock for not having adopted any measures allowing possible recourse to the court of law, but it fell on deaf ears.

As economic conditions were changing, immigrant workers started to replace women workers in the textile industry, lowering the pressure on the industry to pay equal rates. Equal pay dropped on the political agenda. The Article 119 group continued to produce reports which were received with decreasing interest in the Council of Ministers as it faced the worst political crisis in the history of the EEC in 1965.

After the setback of 1961, it took almost a decade for women and equal pay to re-emerge on the European agenda. Two impulses were decisive in galvanising a select number of gender-sensitive actors who found opportunities to revive the cause of women: the *Herstal equal pay strike* and the *Sullerot study*.

It was not until fifteen years later that the European Court of Justice effectively put an end to this indifference. In the *Defrenne II* judgment, the Court would recognise that there has been a violation of the Treaty with the complicity of the institutions: "The obligation imposed by the Treaty has not been fulfilled and the common institutions have insufficiently reacted to this state of deficiency" (paragraph 33), adding that "to admit the contrary would risk making the violation of the law a rule of interpretation". Even if the data were lacking to assess the extent of the wage disparities, this 'arrangement' on the provisions of the Treaty remains nonetheless serious and unique in the history of a community created in the respect of the rule of law. In fact, for fifteen years (1961-1976), that is up until the Defrenne II judgment, millions of women workers were effectively deprived of the possibility to claim the equal pay they were entitled to. The Defrenne case was eventually brought to the Court by **Eliane Vogel Polsky**, a Belgian lawyer appalled by the condition of women factory workers in Herstal who believed in the potential of the new European supranational law. She would be a major agent for the promotion of gender equality in the EU for over 50 years.

## The Herstal equal pay strike

On 2 June 1966, a large-scale march was launched by 3000 female workers from the National Belgian Arms Factory (known as Fabrique Nationale or FN) in Herstal, a small city near Liège, Belgium. While the manufacture was experiencing an economic boom and generating major profit, anger arose as women denounced the injustice around their significantly lower pay compared to men which not at all compensated for the execrable conditions in which they had to work (hence the appellation 'machine women'). Their requests for a more decent salary having been repeatedly ignored, they took to the streets, carrying banners calling for the application of Article 119. As Charlotte Hauglustaine, one of the strike leaders, reports, "women who were skilled operators working on three machines earned less than a young man sweeper from the same factory".[81] After three months of strike, they obtained a salary increase of 2 francs out of the 5 they demanded at the start of the conflict. However, the reference to the Treaty of Rome had empowered women, "giving this strike a scale quite different from that of a simple local struggle for wage improvements".[82] This was when European law was mentioned for the first time, giving the movement international impact: women in trade unions all over Europe expressed their solidarity with the FN workers. Their fight became emblematic as a strike for equality. It would also have repercussions at the level of the European Parliament with the convening of an extraordinary meeting of the Social Committee "to assess the application of Article 119".[83]

Europe taking to the streets contrasts with the negotiations between elites in the hushed corridors that usually characterised European decision-making processes; This experience introduced very concretely the role of stakeholders in the heart of Europe. This in-

---

[81]     Charlotte Hauglustaine features in the Gender Five Plus 30-minute documentary film *Eliane Vogel Polsky, champion of the cause of women in Europe*, directed by Haleh Chinikar and Agnès Huber (Gender 5+, 2018), https://vimeo.com/manage/videos/297136091

[82]     *Eliane Vogel Polsky* documentary by Haleh Chinikar and Agnès Huber (Gender 5+, 2018)

[83]     *Eliane Vogel Polsky* documentary

terest was not going to falter. Indeed, the Herstal strike was instrumental in the development of a process that would culminate in the Defrenne II judgment in 1976.

## The Sullerot study

But before we get to the seventies and the Defrenne judgments, let us recall another hallmark of this period. Concerned with the lack of existing comparative studies on women's labour force on the one hand and met with the obligation to produce regular reports for the expert group on Article 119 on the other hand, the European Commission tasked Evelyne Sullerot (a French sociologist and founding member of the French planned parenthood programme) with the drafting of a comparative study. The *Sullerot report* (1979) entitled "The employment of women and the problems it raises in the Member States of the European Community"[84] prompted a renewal in institutional attention to gender equality policy. It revealed that the gender pay gap was significant in all Member States but that fundamental changes were underway all across Europe. The increase in life expectancy and the reduction of the number of pregnancies (as children survived) was transforming the use of time by women. Their roles and aspirations could no more be confined by their maternal function. Time devoted to maternity in the 1970s represented on average one seventh of the average lifespan of a European woman. Hence came a new wave of energy to be directed to other activities. This analysis, according to the Director General for Social Affairs of the time, was opening a vision of the future relevant to develop Community initiatives.

---

84    Evelyne Sullerot, "The Employment of Women and the Problems it raises in the Member States of the European Community," [abridged and translated edition (Brussels: Commission of the EC, 1979)], https://op.europa.eu/en/publication-detail/-/publication/26ae80db-e1ba-440f-9459-28a85e50c895

# The 1970s: The European Court of Justice rules on equal pay

In the early seventies, before the oil shocks, the European economies were still flourishing in their *Glorious Thirties*[85] following the Second World War. The EEC was depicted as a success story, attractive to new Member States. Its first enlargement to include the United Kingdom, Ireland and Denmark took place in 1973 with the UK insisting on a social program.

## Women's liberation movements

At the same time, the second wave of feminism was spreading in the literature and on the ground through the action of feminist writers and activists all over Europe[86] as attested in particular by the sudden best seller status of numerous feminist classics. In *The Second Sex* (*Le Deuxième Sexe*, 1949) Simone de Beauvoir had coined the famous expression "One is not born, but rather becomes, woman" rejecting gender roles and the idea of women as the "insignificant other" as social inventions to be deconstructed. De Beauvoir's revolutionary ideas laid the foundation for the second wavers movements in the 1960s and 1970s. *Our Bodies Ourselves*, written by a collective of Boston academics in 1970, was initially circulated by hand in the form

---

85    The term *Glorious Thirties* describes nearly thirty years of economic growth and prosperity after the end of WWII (between 1945 and the oil crisis of 1973). This growth was in large part due to reflationary policies by Western states and principally inspired by the Keynesian school of thought.

86    Sibilla Aleramo, *Una donna* (Turin: STEN Società Tipografica Editrice Nazionale, 1906); Elena Gianini Belotti, *Dalla parte delle bambine: l'influenza dei condizionamenti sociali nella formazione del ruolo femminile nei primi anni di vita* (Milano: Giangiacomo Feltrinelli Editore, 1973) – an analysis of the social conditioning of little girls to submission;  Alice Schwartzer, *Der kleine Unterschied und seine großen Folgen: Frauen über sich – Beginn einer Befreiung* (Frankfurt am Main: S. Fischer Verlag, 1975). The French publishing house *Les editions des femmes*, created in 1973, continues to print feminists literatur to this day, https://www.desfemmes.fr/

of stapled pages, soon became an underground success mainly by word-of-mouth and was published in 1973. Informing about women's health and sexuality, it had a tremendous impact on the lives, health and human rights of women across the globe.[87] Readers in Europe found great sources of inspiration in North-American authors like Kate Millett (*Sexual Politics*)[88] and Shulamit Firestone (*The Dialectic of Sex: The Case for a Feminist Revolution*, 1970).[89] The same year, a series of symbolic but powerful feminist demonstrations were happening across Europe. In Paris, France's women's liberation movement paid tribute to the wife of the Unknown Soldier by laying a wreath at the foot of the Arc the Triomphe with the famous inscription "There

87  The story of *Our Bodies, Ourselves* (the book) and Our Bodies Ourselves (the organisation, aka the Boston Women's Health Book Collective) – is long and fruitful – see https://www.ourbodiesourselves.org/our-story/

88  A classic of feminism and one of radical feminism's key texts, *Sexual Politics* analyses the subjugation of women in prominent art and literature in the 20th century, specifically looking at the ubiquity of male domination in culture. Millett argues that "sex has a frequently neglected political aspect" and goes on to discuss the role that patriarchy plays in sexual relations, looking especially at the works of D.H. Lawrence, Henry Miller, and Norman Mailer. Millett argues that these authors view and discuss sex in a patriarchal and sexist way. In contrast, she applauds the more nuanced gender politics of homosexual writer Jean Genet. Other writers discussed at length include Sigmund Freud, George Meredith, John Ruskin, and John Stuart Mill. Kate Millett, *Sexual Politics* (Garden City, NY: Doubleday, 1970).

89  This book, written over a few months when Firestone was 25, has been described as a classic of feminist thought. Firestone argues that the "sexual class system" predates and runs deeper than any other form of oppression, and that the eradication of sexism will require a radical reordering of society: "The first women are fleeing the massacre, and, shaking and tottering, are beginning to find each other. [...] This is painful: no matter how many levels of consciousness one reaches, the problem always goes deeper. It is everywhere. [...] feminists have to question, not just all of *Western* culture, but the organisation of culture itself, and further, even the very organisation of nature." The goal of the feminist revolution, she wrote, must be "not just the elimination of male privilege but of the sex distinction itself" so that genital differences no longer have cultural significance.

is one person more unknown than the unknown soldier, his wife". In London, the election of Miss World was spoilt by feminist activists. In 1971, 343 women in France had the courage to sign a petition (the 'Manifesto of the 343') written by Simone de Beauvoir reading out in public space that they had had an illegal abortion. In Amsterdam – in the whole of the Netherlands and neighbouring countries such as Belgium – the group *Dolle Mina* (translated the 'Mad Mina') campaigned for equal rights for women. Centres for battered women and women's groups for peace, civil rights and abortion were burgeoning underground, in Western and Eastern Europe.[90]

In the second half of the 1970s, the dynamism of the women's movements was brought to the attention of governments as they prepared for the first World Conference on Women organised by the United Nations in Mexico (1975).

## Women's rights in European institutions

While the mobilisation for women's rights focused first and foremost on reproductive rights, civil rights and violence against women, all issues outside the European Treaty competences, it nevertheless formed the ground on which the European institutions would take new initiatives and upgrade the status of women's rights in their structures and in legislation.

A 'Women's Bureau' was created in the European Commission services, assisted by an advisory committee[91] made up of Member States representatives. In June 1979, the first directly elected European Parliament created an *ad hoc* committee for women's rights chaired by socialist MEP Yvette Roudy. She lead the adoption of a

---

90    For more development and bibliographic references, see chapter 2 (European feminism in the seventies) of Catherine Hoskyns' "Integrating *gender, women law and politics in the European Union*"; Joyce Mushaben, "From Losers to Winners: East German Women," in *What remains? The Dialectical Identities of Eastern Germans* (forthcoming 2022); and Donna Harsch, *Revenge of the Domestic: Women, the Family, and Communism in the German Democratic Republic* (Princeton: Princeton University Press, 2018).

91    An advisory committee which still exists these days – see description in Part III (velvet triangle and other bodies).

For the vast majority of men and women in Europe, parliamentary democracy remains the best possible system.

**Fig. 2** "Women have your say" poster during the 1979 european elections.

resolution on the position of women in the European Community in 1981, presenting an exhaustive list of gender-specific problems and discrimination experienced by women, exacerbated by the economic crisis at the time,[92] which later was to become permanent in 1984 (see part III). At that time, the European assembly was chaired by a woman, Simone Veil, one of 68 women (out of 410 members) sitting in that new parliament. Prior to the first direct elections, MEPs were delegates of national assemblies. As the table below illustrates, female representation was marginal but the first direct elections marked a dramatic increase in comparison to the previous legislature.

Lastly, three new EEC directives for equality were presented to the Council and adopted, which marked the beginning of a set of secondary legislation instruments with a structuring effect for women to emerge as agents in the public sphere:

- The 1975 Council Directive on equal pay,[93]

---

92    European Parliament Resolution on the Position of Women in the European Community of 11 February 1981 (OJ C 50, 9.3.1981), 35.

93    No longer in force today, Council Directive 75/117/EE of February 19, 1975, on the Approximation of the Laws of the Member States Relating to the Application of the Principle of Equal Pay for Men and Women (OJ L 45, 19.2.1975), 19-20, https://eur-lex.europa.eu/legal-content/en/ALL/?uri=CELEX%3A31975L0117
was replaced by Directive 2006/54/EC of the European Parliament and

- The 1976 Council Directive on equal treatment as regards access to employment, vocational training and promotion, and working conditions,[94]
- And the 1978 Council Directive on equal treatment in matters of social security.[95]

In all Member States, these directives have empowered actors and legitimated the claims for women's rights.

Representation of female MEPs. Source: European Parliamentary Research Service
Source: https://epthinktank.eu/2014/03/05/europes-first-women/

|  | 1952 | 1958 | 1972 | 1979 | Post-1979 direct EP elections |
|---|---|---|---|---|---|
| **Female MEPs** | 1 | 4 | 5 | 11 | 68 |
| **Total seats** | 78 | 142 | 142 | 198 | 410 |
| **%** | 1 | 3 | 3 | 6 | 16 |

Fig. 3

## The Defrenne trials

Action of the European Court was decisive to implement the principle of equal pay and to grant women's rights issues the political attention they deserve.

of the Council of 5 July 2006 on the Implementation of the Principle of Equal Opportunities and Equal Treatment of Men and Women in Matters of Employment and Occupation (recast, OJ L 204, 26.7.2006), 23-36, https://eur-lex.europa.eu/legal-content/en/TXT/?uri=CELEX-%3A32006L0054

94   Council Directive 76/207/EEC of 9 February 1976 on the Implementation of the Principle of Equal Treatment for Men and Women as Regards Access to Employment, Vocational Training and Promotion, and Working Conditions (OJ L 039, 14/02/1976), 40-42, https://eur-lex.europa.eu/LexUriServ/LexUriServ.do?uri=CELEX:31976L0207:en:HTML

95   Council Directive 79/7/EEC of 19 December 1978 on the Progressive Implementation of the Principle of Equal Treatment for Men and Women in Matters of Social Security (OJ L 6, 10.1.1979), 24-25, https://eur-lex.europa.eu/legal-content/EN/ALL/?uri=celex%3A31979L0007

Following the Herstal female factory workers' strike, the Belgian government, within the framework of a general revision of the legislative provisions regarding the female workforce, had introduced a provision establishing the right for any worker to claim before the national courts the application of the principle of equal pay, in application of Article 119. With a view to test these new provisions, Eliane Vogel Polsky and Marie Therese Cuvelliez, two committed feminist lawyers and activists for the European cause and the rights of women, introduced the first recourse claiming the application of Article 119 before the Brussels Labour Court in February 1968 in the name of the plaintiff, their client Gabrielle Defrenne. This flight attendant, an employee of Sabena (then the national airline company in Belgium), contested the obligation imposed on female staff to have to quit their job at age 40, unlike their male counterparts. She demanded compensation for loss of income relying on the Belgian government's obligation under Article 119 of the Treaty of Rome.

Three successive 'Defrenne' trials followed, ending with a historic judgment of the European Court of Justice in 1976. In its Judgment of April 8, 1976 (Case 43-75),[96] the Court recognised the *direct effect* of Article 119, including the duty of national courts to ensure the protection of the right to equal pay, thereby holding Member States responsible for not having kept to their commitments under the Treaty and recognising the full competence of the Community to oversee the implementation of the principle of equal pay. It also established that the principle laid down in Article 119 is "one of the foundations of the community,"[97] paving the way for all the actions necessary to be taken to actually fulfil this principle.

96    ECJ Judgment of the Court of 8 April 1976, Gabrielle Defrenne v Société anonyme belge de navigation aérienne Sabena, Reference for a preliminary ruling: Cour du travail de Bruxelles, Belgium. *The principle that men and women should receive equal pay for equal work*, case 43-75. (ECLI:EU:C:1976:56), https://eur-lex.europa.eu/legal-content/EN/TXT/?uri=CELEX%3A61975CJ0043

97    ECJ Judgment of the Court of 8 April 1976, Defrenne v Sabena

# The 1980s: Inequalities on the labour market

From the very beginning of the 1980s, European Integration was at a standstill. From 1979, the oil shock and the election of Margaret Thatcher and Ronald Reagan set the tone for the dominance of liberal ideology which would poison progress in European integration and gender equality: As expressed by President Reagan in his inaugural speech, "political action is at the service of economic and financial private interests which bear the dynamism of the economy". The 'Iron Lady' championed this philosophy on the European scene. The first woman in power in the highest spheres of the EU, she also set the example of a nationalist and antisocialist leader, going to war in the Falklands, bashing trade unions and systematically quashing initiatives for a more social Europe, not to mention gender equality. Having risen from her father's greengrocer shop to become prime minister, Thatcher believed only in the credo that those who want equality will have to earn it through their own merit.

In this rather inhospitable context for a more feminist Europe, socialist Jacques Delors, who was president of the European Commission for ten years (1985-1995), would focus on the only 'acceptable' issue for all Member States: the completion of the internal market. This trade and technical integration was not likely to catch the interest of the women's movement or of those European women who were struggling to take advantage of new openings in the labour market while still bearing the main (yet mostly invisible) responsibility for care and domestic work.

Nonetheless, pressure for releasing women from their domestic burdens came from employers since the early eighties. As the service sector and its demands for a flexible, non-unionised and docile labour force was increasing, the Union of Industrials and Employers' Confederation of Europe[98] called on public authorities to reconcile

---

98    Known by the acronym of UNICE after the French name *Union des Industries de la Communauté Européenne* which was renamed 'Business Europe'.

family and work life. This led the European Commission to promote a 'childcare network of experts' in the early 1980s.

## New anchorage in the institutions

Since the UN first World Conference on Women in Mexico in 1975 and a mid-term review in Copenhagen in 1980 aimed to review progress in implementing its goals, women's rights had started to be institutionalised. In Member States, structures were set up to deal with the issue: the Equal Opportunities Commission in the UK, a Minister for equality in France (in 1981), in Germany the Federal Ministry for Youth, Family and Health was renamed to the Federal Ministry for Youth, Family, *Women*, and Health in 1986, in Italy parity and the Department for Equal Opportunity (*il Dipartimento per le Pari Opportunità*[99]) were placed under the responsibility of the Ministry of Employment, then of the Prime Minister (and back). Meanwhile in European institutions, the newly elected European Parliament in 1984 decided to have a fully recognised Committee for women's rights established permanently with 25 committee members (30 after Spain and Portugal joined) with the objective of monitoring the application of the directives in force on the areas of equal opportunity whilst considering issues such as education, employment, vocational training, new technologies and migrant women. In the future it would then be endowed with the task of drawing up reports, meeting monthly and organising regular hearings on all sorts of issues relevant for women. The European Commission transformed its Women's Bureau into a 'unit for equal opportunities for women and men' which would work in close cooperation with women's experts and representatives of the Member States, meeting at regular intervals with the 'Advisory Committee for Equality'. It also created a women's information service. Trade Unions had appointed officers in charge of women's rights in the 1970s. This set of institutions would have to wait until the end of the decade to be completed by civil so-

---

99    Il *Dipartimento per le Pari Opportunità,* http://www.pariopportunita.gov. it/ [website in Italian]

ciety organisations assembled under the umbrella organisation the European Women's Lobby (EWL), created on 22 September 1990.

As of the beginning of the 1980s, the first initiatives of this new set of institutions were to develop multi-annual action programmes clearly defining a budget, objectives, and a strategy comprising actions to translate legal equality into factual equality. The first three-years programmes concentrated on the implementation of Article 119. The second enlarged the scope to vocational training and *positive action*, including looking into questions of childcare, a concern expressed by the business sector.

## European Networks of Experts

The European Network of Childcare Experts was created in 1986 and renewed for ten years. With one expert per Member State and a European coordinator, it created new insights over the needs of parents and children and how they were met in Member States. It also looked at carers' working conditions, and at the integration of children with special needs, formulating recommendations to improve the situation of families. Building on this solid set of accumulated knowledge, the network's experts drafted the text of a fairly progressive Council recommendation on childcare adopted in March 1992.[100] For the very first time, a European legislative text addressed the role of men in parenthood and how fathers should be encouraged by public policy to participate equally in their parental responsibility.[101] The network also worked on elderly care and started to prepare the first binding community text (a directive) on the issue of reconciling work and family life. Yet this text, adopted in 1997 on the basis of an

---

[100]  Council Recommendation 92/241/EEC of 31 March 1992 on Child Care (OJ L 123 , 08/05/1992), 16-18, https://eur-lex.europa.eu/LexUriServ/Lex-UriServ.do?uri=CELEX:31992H0241:EN:HTML

[101]  Council Recommendation 92/241/EEC Art 6: "Sharing of responsibilities As regards responsibilities arising from the care and upbringing of children, it is recommended that Member States should promote and encourage, with due respect for freedom of the individual, increased participation by men, in order to a achieve a more equal sharing of parental responsibilities between men and women and to enable women to have a more effective role in the labour market."

agreement of the social partners, did not contain provisions likely to induce actual change in the sharing of tasks within families.[102]

Unfortunately, the European Network of Childcare Experts was dismantled in 1996, together with nine other networks created after the same model in the 1980s and 1990s to document and assist policy makers with expertise.

These networks created grounded knowledge which was essential to decision-makers in fields which had a deficit of data and few specialised analysts. Legal experts were monitoring the implementation of directives and confronting the interpretation of the new rights granted by the European legal order. Employment specialist produced original reports on the world of work and its trends, including the reality lived by women (working time, flexicurity, etc). The IRIS community network for vocational training for women researched and experimented conditions of training, including the provision of childcare, to effectively help women progress in the world of work. ILE (Local Employment initiatives) raised the concerns of women entrepreneurs, *positive action* experts advised companies' human resources departments on the smooth development of measures to promote equality, education specialists addressed the unequal treatment of girls and boys in  education, a network of journalists and media operators created initiatives to bring awareness of inequality issues into the media sector and finally a mixed group of academics, journalists, legal experts and innovative thinkers documented the deficit of women in decision-making positions and designed initiatives to improve the situation.

---

102    Council Directive 97/81/EC of 15 December 1997 concerning the Framework Agreement on part-time work concluded by UNICE, CEEP and the ETUC - Annex: Framework agreement on part-time work, https://eur-lex.europa.eu/legal-content/EN/TXT/?uri=celex-%3A31997L0081. This directive has now been overtaken by the EU Directive 2019/1158 of the EP and the Council on work-life balance for parents and carers and repealing Council Directive 2010/18/EU adopted on 20 June 2019, https://eur-lex.europa.eu/legal-content/EN/TXT/PD-F/?uri=CELEX:32019L1158&from=EN

These networks, together with the new institutional structures (women's rights specialised structures in the European Parliament, the European Commission, governments and NGOs were integral parts of what academics[103] dubbed the *velvet triangle* (see Part III). The triangle members include bureaucrats, elected officials, academics and NGO representatives, who are all adhering to particular discourses of gender equality with the agenda to achieve change. This gave a very special quality to policy-making at European level at a time when European women had massively accessed the labour market (from 32 percent in 1980 to 43 percent in 1983), big changes were happening in education (longer studies, more women in tertiary education), in families (the contraceptive revolution and the promulgation of divorce by mutual consent in the 1960s and 1970s).

## Sexual harassment in the workplace

The increasing participation of women in the labour market also brought new and controversial issues which, thanks to the collaboration and activism of an expert community, was brought on the political agenda. This was the case for sexual harassment at a time when it was common to deny the guilt of the perpetrator by shaming and blaming the victim because of the way she dressed, spoke or behaved. A coalition of progressive lawyers, equality activists and politicians convinced the European Commission to take a leading role in Europe by producing a recommendation on the protection of the dignity of women and men at work in 1991,[104] including calls for the establishment of a code of conduct for its implementation. The institutional backing of the European institutions[105] legitimised the

---

103    Alison Woodward, *Building Velvet Triangles: Gender and Informal Governance* (Cheltenham: Edward Elgar, 2004).

104    Commission Recommendation 92/131/EEC of 27 November 1991 on the Protection of the Dignity of Women and Men at Work, https://eur-lex.europa.eu/LexUriServ/LexUriServ.do?uri=CELEX:31992H0131:EN:HTML

105    The recommendation of the Commission on the protection of the dignity of women and men at work and the code of conduct for its implementation were supported by a Council Resolution of 19 November 1991.

issue and helped executives, trade unions and workers to make the workplace safer for women.[106] It also encouraged Member States to adopt legislation and recognise sexual harassment as an obstacle to equality of treatment at work. More than 25 years later, sexual harassment has been massively denounced by the #Metoo movement and it is recognised by courts with a definition and legal sanctions. This was the first EU initiative in the wider field of gender-based violence which previousy had not been within the EU's competence.

## The 1990s: Parity democracy and gender mainstreaming

Changes in the labour market brought new issues, which the European Commission sought to address, bolstered by the support of this closely-knit community driven by shared objectives.

In the early nineties, the *Third medium term Community action Programme for Equal Opportunities between women and men (1991-95)*[107] marked a turning point. Under the combined influence of the European Parliament's women's rights committee and the benefit of Nordic experience (see below), the scope of the policy widened considerably. The recognition that equal pay and equality on the labour market were not going to happen unless other issues pertaining to the sexual division of roles were addressed, encouraged members of the *velvet triangle* to introduce a chapter of measures to "improve the status of women in society" including unequal representation in the political sphere.

As for the Nordic experience, the Danish official who wrote the first drafts of the new programme introduced the concept of *gender mainstreaming*. In Denmark, Sweden, and Norway, a political choice

---

106    For a detailed analysis, see Kathrin Zippel, *The Politics of Sexual Harassment: A Comparative Study of the United States, the European Union, and Germany* (Cambridge: Cambridge University Press, 2006).

107    Third Programme on Equal Opportunities (1991-1995), https://eur-lex.europa.eu/legal-content/EN/TXT/?uri=LEGISSUM%3Ac10915

was made in the 1960s to draw women to the labour market rather than relying on immigrant workers (which was the choice opted for in most of Western Europe) to fill the new labour market demands. A longer experience of women's equal participation on the labour market had convinced social democratic governments that equality and anti-discrimination policies would have to deal with education and family policy, but also research, politics, the economy, as well as social policy. To bear results, gender equality had to be taken as a *transversal* issue across all policies. Therefore, both the participation of women in decision-making and 'gender mainstreaming' featured in the new EU programme.

Before going into more details about these two major shifts in the policy approach to gender policy in the EU, we must recall that at the beginning of the decade, European integration was finally gaining traction again, which offered a fertile ground for pushing for a progressive gender equality policy framework. The completion of the single market was successful with governments who welcomed the removal of administrative puzzles, businesses whose products could circulate more freely across borders, and social actors who were looking for Europe-wide solutions to promote employment; post-1989 enlargement to the East was on the cards giving even more prospects to the single market; a more generous budget was agreed, and in his 1994 white paper[108] Jacques Delors had pointed to the common challenges in facing the economic transition. Still, economic achievements had not conquered the hearts and minds of citizens.

## No democracy without parity

The time was ripe to promote a people-oriented policy approach. Harnessing the support of women was crucial to fight the democratic deficit.

---

108    European Commission Secretariat-General, Growth, competitiveness, employment, "White paper on growth competitiveness and employment" in *The challenges and ways forward into the 21st century* (Luxembourg: Publications Office, 1994).

In that same period, the OECD published a milestone report of its high-level group of experts on "women and structural change", presided over by Maria de Lourdes Pintasilgo.[109] Its recommendations included having more women in decision-making positions. Earlier, the Council of Europe had published a first report on *parity democracy*, a new concept which was brought onto the EU agenda in the first European Summit of Women in Power held in Athens in November 1992. Eliane Vogel Polsky (who was then a member of the European Expert Network on women in decision-making) saw in this concept a radically new approach to promote gender equality where the correction of past discrimination (with *positive action*) was promoted as a concrete solution:

> [*The*] *construction of the right to equality as it has been developed so far is difficult to implement because it is subject to legal systems created without women. If parity representation is recognised to be a necessary condition of democracy rather than a remote consequence, then the rules of the game and social norms will have to change. This could radically transform society and allow for gender equal relations.*[110]

The Athens Summit, hosted by one of the first female European Commissioners[111] **Vasso Papandreou**, was organised by women's organisations in the European Women's Lobby, together with experts of the network on women in decision-making. For the first time, this summit gathered women ministers or ex-ministers of the Member States who agreed that the quasi absence of women from high-level decision-making positions constituted a severe democratic deficit. They signed the *Athens declaration*[112] which proclaimed the need for

109    OCDE, *Conduire le changement structurel: le rôle des femmes*, Report to the Secretary General by the high-level group presided over by Maria de Lourdes Pintasilgo.

110    Eliane Vogel Polsky, "Les impasses de l'égalité ou pourquoi les outils juridiques visant a l'égalité doivent être repensés en termes de parité," *Parité-infos*, no. hors serie, 1994.

111    in the post of Commissioner for Employment, industrial relations and social affairs, representing Greece

112    Athens Declaration (1992),https://eurogender.eige.europa.eu/posts/athens-declaration-1992

the equal participation of women and men in political and public decision-making to renew democracy. The arguments upholding the declaration are:

- Formal and informal equality is a fundamental human right;
- Women represent more than half of the population, they represent half the potential talents and qualifications so their underrepresentation is a loss for society as a whole;
- Women's interests and needs are not properly taken into account if they are underrepresented;
- A balanced participation of women and men in decision-making could generate different ideas, values and behaviours likely to produce a fairer and more balanced world for all.

For the first time, the transformative power of gender equality was established in an official text. Women at the highest level had collectively and publicly signalled that promoting equality was not to make women catch up with men but to create a more equal society starting from scratch.

## Changes towards gender mainstreaming

The 1990s can be described as golden years for women as far as attention to equality between women and men in Europe is concerned.[113] Many factors converged to draw this considerable increase of attention, as if gender equality had become a recognised asset for European integration.

The surge of women's participation in the European (formal) labour markets had finally deconstructed the misconception that wo-

---

113    This golden age is revolving around what some third feminist wavers may consider a binary approach classifying gender into two distinct, opposite forms of masculine versus feminine, men versus woman, boys versus girls. For more on this, see for instance Judith Butler, *Gender Trouble: Feminism and Subversive Identity* (New York/London: Routledge, 1999); and *Bodies that Matter: On the Discursive Limits of Sex* (New York/London: Routledge, 1993).

men are a marginal part of the labour force.[114] However, research by the European network of experts on the situation of women in the labour market showed that the changes taking place with the growth of the service economy were creating new lines of segregation. In the wake of the drive towards the completion of the single market, European authorities started to be convinced that women's employment required a new political attention – in compliance with the double objective of fulfilling the commitment to equal pay for equal work, but also reaping the benefits from this educated but apparently more flexible workforce.[115] From the "objective 92 program" (how can the completion of the single market benefit – or at least not penalise – women) to the European integrated employment strategy (Essen 1994)[116] and the European Employment strategy (launched after the Amsterdam Treaty), the situation of women on the labour market was therefore to be a priority on the European agenda.

The third community action programme for equal opportunities between women and men (1991-95)[117] proposed by the European

---

114 Unlike most contemporary narratives presenting how women first entered the labour market in the 1960s, feminist research indicates that women have, in fact, always worked, not least in the 19th century in industrial times, even if their contribution was often made invisible due to a lack of traces and in some cases their participation to the workforce tended to fluctuate or be subsumed under the umbrella of family businesses (eg in handcraft or agriculture), not to mention that once they were present in industrial factories, they were asked to return to the domestic spheres after the realisation of the falls in fertility rates coupled with the introduction of increased wages 'for the family' in the 1940s. For more on women's labour throughout history, see, for instance, Jane Jenson, Jacqueline Laufer and Margaret Maruani, ed., *The Gendering of Inequalities: Women, Men and Work* (London: Routledge, 2017); or Silvia Federici, *Le capitalisme patriarcal* (Paris: La Fabrique, 2019).

115 M. van Hemeldonck, *Report drawn up on behalf of the Committee on Women's Rights on the 1992 Single Market and its implications for women in the EC, Part B: Explanatory statement. Session Documents 1990 (Document A3-0358/90/Part B, 15 January 1991)*, http://aei.pitt.edu/48229/

116 European Council Meeting, 9-10 December 1994 in Essen, *Presidency Conclusions*, https://www.europarl.europa.eu/summits/ess1_en.htm

117 EU Commission, Third programme on equal opportunities (1991-1995), https://eur-lex.europa.eu/legal-content/PT/TXT/?uri=LEGIS-

Commission, had allowed developments in new fields like politics, the fight against stereotypes and the general status of women in society. In 1995, its last year, the resources for equality had increased in an unprecedented way;[118] the work of the EU's nine expert networks as well as the close relationship with the newly formed European Women's Lobby allowed for a better grounding of the policy amongst the main stakeholders.

The face of EU institutions changed: following a campaign for having more women in the European Parliament, the proportion of elected women members after the 1994 election reached 27.6% (from 19%); in 1995, the enlarged college of Commissioners[119] for the first time counted 5 women out of 20 and its president, Jacques Santer (to resolve a potential conflict between commissioners) created a "group of commissioners for equality" which would meet three to four times per annum for 10 years, acting as a strong stimulus for the promotion of equality in the EU.

In the European Council, changes were also noticeable: the proportion of women ministers in the three new Member States was significant, and in seven out of the twelve old Member States, new women ministers came into office following elections and ministerial reshuffles in 1992-1994.[120] This introduced changes, noticeably in the Employment and Social Affairs portfolio where proposals from the Commission on equality found a more positive welcome. This was the case in particular for the 1996 Council Recommendation on the balanced participation of women and men in decision-making

SUM:c10915

118 In 1992-95, the staff of the unit responsible had increased from 15 to 25 and the dedicated budget from €4.8 to 8.5 million. Moreover, the European Social Fund had created a 'New Opportunities for Women' initiative which mobilised financial resources to promote the creation of enterprises by women and assist with their proper integration in the labour market.

119 Including EU commissioners from three new Member States (Finland, Sweden and Austria)

120 Figures from the Network of women in decision-making which monitors moves in governments of the Member States.

processes which was adopted under the presidency of Simone Veil, French minister for social affairs and health.[121]

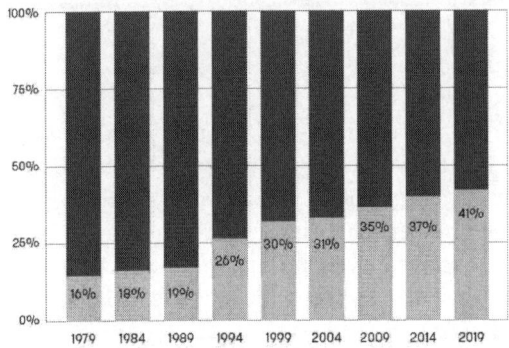

**MEPs' gender balance by year since 1979**
Source: European Parliament (2019). «European election results», availalbe from: https://www.europarl.europa.eu/election-results-2019/en/mep-gender-balance/1979-1984/

Fig. 4

## Fourth World Conference on Women in Beijing (1995)

World conferences in the nineties have been landmarks in their field, be it the environment in Rio 1992, demography in Cairo 1993, or human rights in Vienna 1994. The Beijing conference on women 1995 is no exception to the rule. It gathered officials and politicians, industrialists and civil society actors, academics and social workers, countries at war and in peace from around the world to discuss the situation of women and to explore ways to improve it.[122]

---

121    Council Recommendation of 2 December 1996, 96/694/EC, on the balanced participation of women and men in the decision-making process (OJ L 319 10.12.1996) 11, https://eur-lex.europa.eu/legal-content/EN/TXT/?uri=CELEX:31996H0694)

122    It is notably in this context that Hillary Clinton (then First Lady of the United States) gave a landmark speech where she famously declared that "human rights are women's rights and women's rights are human rights" (Beijing, 5 September 1995), https://www.youtube.com/watch?v=L7evFMipVZE&ab_channel=ClintonFoundation

The long preparatory process which precedes such conferences involves research, the production of data, publications and statements by governments, academics, and civil society organisations in all the Member States of the UN as well as regional organisations like the European Union and all the UN organisations.[123] As had been the case in previous World Conferences on Women such as Mexico in 1975 and Nairobi in 1985, the sum of information and international discussion raised public awareness on issues like violence against women or discrimination against the girl child. Most governments wished to showcase progress made since the last conference and the resources deployed in the preparatory process of the conference were higher than usual.

Fig. 5

Hillary Clinton, then First Lady, delivers a historic speech at the UN Conference on Women in Beijing, China, on Sept. 5, 1995.

Governments were the main actors in the conference expected to adopt new policies in its wake to comply with their commitments

---

123    Before Beijing, a remarkable Human Development Report was produced by the UNDP which gave a first measure of the weight of the informal economy: UNDP Human Development Report 1995 https://doi.org/10.18356/152cdfb3-en
Similarly, UNESCO, the World Food Programme, the ILO, the World Bank and the Council of Europe significantly upgraded their research efforts on and by women for the conference.

in the agreed final text: the *Beijing Declaration and Platform for Action* adopted at the end of the conference.[124] In a parallel forum organised in Huairou (China) NGOs from all over the world exchanged views on their priorities and practical experience. In the 1995 conference, world-famous feminist icons like Betty Friedan[125] (author of *The Feminine Mystique*) would meet with young feminists from Africa, India or (Latin) America – the latter being involved in concrete day-to-day concerns for many women around the world, such as the provision of infant feeding, help centres, reproductive rights, loans for women, computer literacy, water access,[126] or their survival struggle against men's alcohol consumption leading to violence against women.[127]

While the European Union does not usually play a big part in these conferences where states are the members, Beijing was an exception to the rule for a number of reasons. The EU 15 Member States arrived in Beijing with positions which had been discussed at length during the preparatory process; its new members, in particular Sweden and Finland, were keen to see progress; and the EU delegation was chaired by Cristina Alberdi, a feminist socialist minister for social affairs from Spain.

Notably, the Beijing Conference also saw the first emergence of the term *gender* – meaning the social construction of inequalities, but also widening its scope to women's rights, sexual orientation and gender stereotypes – in international human rights discussions and legal texts. This was met with contestations raised by the Va-

---

124    *Beijing Declaration and Platform for Action* (1995), https://www.un.org/womenwatch/daw/beijing/platform/

125    According to a famous anecdote, when Betty Friedan heard the term *mainstreaming* her reaction was "we do not want to get ourselves dirty in their 'men-stream', we want to use our clear and pure mountain streams."

126    For instance, a geologist from Cyprus led a group of women of different confessions to look for water sources on the Arabian Peninsula.

127    Jain Devaki, "Reworking Gender Relations, Redefining Politics: Nellore Village Women against Arrack," based on the report from *Anveshi, Hyderabad Economic and Political Weekly* (16-23 January 1993).

tican and religiously influenced governments.[128] The use of gender was radically rejected by Iran, Argentina, Burkina Faso and the Vatican (which holds UN observer status). This brought on fierce public controversy between the EU, lead by Spain, and these objecting states. The mandate agreed by the EU ahead of the conference was to introduce 'gender mainstreaming' as a commitment of all stakeholders at the end of each of the 12 chapters of the Platform for action, which eventually materialised as attested in article 56 of the Beijing Declaration and Platform for Action.[129] Further action would follow suit with the introduction of gender mainstreaming two years later in the Treaty of Amsterdam.

## A legal backlash

Despite the positive progress for gender equality brought about in Beijing (1995), a severe blow was forced on the European gender equality policy as soon as the conference ended, threatening to neutralise some of its basic principles and proving that gender equality can never be taken for granted. In its *Kalanke v Freie Hansestadt Bremen* judgement in October 1995,[130] the European Court of Justice, which had so far adopted a rather progressive stance in interpreting the European provisions on equality (see the Defrenne judgement)

---

128    see for instance Marija Antić and Ivana Radačić, "The evolving understanding of gender in international law and 'gender ideology' pushback 25 years since the Beijing conference on women," *Women's Studies International Forum*, 83 (November 2020), 102421.

129    "The success of policies and measures aimed at supporting or strengthening the promotion of gender equality and the improvement of the status of women should be based on the **integration of the gender perspective in general policies relating to all spheres of society** as well as the implementation of positive measures with adequate institutional and financial support at all levels" (Art 56, Beijing Declaration and Platform for Action, emphasis added).

130    Bundesarbeitsgericht Germany, Judgment of the Court of 17 October 1995. Eckhard Kalanke v Freie Hansestadt Bremen - Reference for a preliminary ruling: *Equal treatment of men and women, Directive 76/207/ EECArticle 2(4), promotion, equally qualified candidates of different sexes, priority given to women.* Case C-450/93 https://eur-lex.europa.eu/legal-content/EN/TXT/HTML/?isOldUri=true&uri=CELEX:61993CJ0450

condemned the "absolute and unconditional priority" given to a female candidate shortlisted by the administration of the town of Bremen for the promotion over her male colleague applying for the same position. This decision severely limited the scope of *positive action* as an instrument to compensate for indirect discrimination, promote gender equality and achieve a better balance of women in managerial positions. The only positive actions allowed in the terms of the advocate general's opinion were "training and occasional childcare". This judgement, applauded by the press in the first instance, generated strong reactions on the side of gender equality actors from Member States, European Parliament, the European Women's Lobby. The European Commission adopted an interpretative communication. In fact, the resulting shock in gender equality circles, particularly in Germany, created a remobilisation of civil society which would last until the Amsterdam Treaty. Shortly after the intense reactions to the Kalanke judgment, the court partially re-established the legality of a wider understanding of positive action, in November 1997, in the *Marschall v Land Nordrhein-Westfalen* judgement,[131] recognising that even where male and female candidates were equally qualified, male candidates tended to be promoted in preference to female candidates due to prejudices concerning the role and capacities of women in working life. Accordingly, "*a national rule that contains a saving clause is acceptable if the male candidate is guaranteed an objective assessment, which can override the priority given to the woman candidate*".[132]

## Gender mainstreaming in the Treaty of Amsterdam

Following the Kalanke and Marschall judgements and controversy about the combination of positive action and gender mainstrea-

---

131    Verwaltungsgericht Gelsenkirchen Germany, Judgment of the Court of 11 November 1997. Hellmut Marschall v Land Nordrhein-Westfalen - Reference for a preliminary ruling: Equal treatment of men and women, equally qualified male and female candidate, priority for female candidates, saving clause. Case C-409/95, https://eur-lex.europa.eu/legal-content/EN/TXT/?uri=CELEX%3A61995CJ0409

132    Ibid. Footnote 127

ming,[133] the European Commission, supported by the Advisory Committee for equality between women and men,[134] produced a Communication to explain the need for a 'double approach' associating gender mainstreaming and positive action[135] for the promotion of gender equality. The intergovernmental conference (IGC) to prepare the Treaty of Amsterdam started shortly thereafter. The European Women's Lobby, stimulated by the remobilisation of the women's movement, worked with a group of experts from the Member States on recommendations for the new treaty which included: *"consultation and participation of civil society in European policy making, provisions to avoid economic, political, social and cultural exclusion of women and other disadvantaged groups and the integration of the concept of gender mainstreaming in European policies."*[136]

They were inspired by an article written by Eliane Vogel-Polsky on European citizenship and women, where she argues that the concept of European citizenship incorporated in the Treaty of Maast-

133    Maria Stratigaki, "Gender mainstreaming vs positive action: an ongoing conflict in EU gender equality policy," *European Journal of Women's Studies* 12, no. 2 (2005): 165-186

134    As per Commission Decision 82/43/EEC of 9 December, 1982, an Advisory Committee on Equal Opportunities for Women and Men, composed of 20 gender experts from Member States, was set up to advise the Commission on the formulation and implementation of its policy to promote women's employment and equal treatment and ensure the continuous exchange of information on experience gained and measures undertaken in the Community in the fields in question. Since 2008, the Committee is ruled by Commission Decision 2008/590/EC and is composed of 68 members representing Member States' officials and equal opportunity bodies as well as employers and workers organisations at Community level: https://eur-lex.europa.eu/legal-content/en/TXT/?uri=CELEX%3A32008D0590

135    EU Commission, *Communication on Incorporating Equal Opportunities for Women and Men into all Community Policies and Activities,* COM (96) 67 final (21 February 1996).

136    See the full text [in French] https://ec.europa.eu/dorie/fileDownload.do;jsessionid=udm5YNw__H1KLnUCBfGA1m79I3BsIimqxNtgcMQE8q-cyxrFj3OK0!1939

richt which created some new rights,[137] should be supplemented by the fundamental right to equality of women and men.[138] As European integration badly needed the support of its citizens, an opinion survey conducted amongst decision-makers supported this new right to increase the legitimacy of the European project.

For the first time in its history, 50,000 European citizens, among them a large group of women, protested in the streets of Amsterdam on June 16-17, 1997, as heads of states and governments were trying to adapt a politico-institutional structure originally conceived for six Member States to the future 28 – while filling the democratic deficit which had haunted decision-makers over the last ten years. Unanimity, where all Member States have to agree when voting, and which locks up the decision-making process, was questioned (in particular for policies most responsive to citizens). So was the need to add more substance to the concept of European Citizenship, new competences to the fight against criminality without borders, and a stronger defence of fundamental rights.

Most of the new provisions agreed in the Treaty of Amsterdam on the challenges identified (institutional provisions, a common foreign and security policy, transparency, and human rights policies close to citizens) were limited. Yet they opened the door for further advances in the 2001 Treaty of Nice and in the forthcoming Convention on the Future of Europe.[139] While sincerely willing to make Europe more sustainable, once again, the heads of state and government remained bound by domestic politics.

---

137    the right of residence and free movement within EU territory, the right to vote and stand for local and European elections in the Member State of residence, the right of protection for diplomatic and consular authorities from third countries, the right to petition before the European Parliament, and the right to have recourse to the European mediator

138    Éliane Vogel-Polsky, "La citoyenneté européenne et les femmes," *Les Cahiers du Grif* no. 48 (1994), 9-43, https://www.persee.fr/doc/grif_0770-6081_1994_num_48_1_2054#grif_0770-6081_1994_num_48_1_T1_0028_0000

139    For more information about the Treaty of Nice and the Convention see, for instance, https://www.europarl.europa.eu/factsheets/en/sheet/4/the-treaty-of-nice-and-the-convention-on-the-future-of-europe

As far as gender equality is concerned, Article 2 of the Treaty of Amsterdam[140] confirms equality between women and men to be a mission of the community.

# 2000: The new millennium, a new Europe

The new millennium started for the European Union with the most ambitious prospect in its decades of existence: its enlargement to ten Central and Eastern European countries,[141] and Cyprus and Malta.

The 'Agenda 2000: for a stronger and wider Union'[142] had almost completed its programme in 1999. It comprised a single complete framework for the integration of the *acquis* in the new Member States, infrastructure projects, and a strict financial framework. The concern of most Eastern European governments was first and foremost to adapt to the market economy.

### Enlargement: what is in it for women?

Taking stock at the end of the Cold War following the fall of the Berlin Wall and the collapse of the Soviet Union, this new enlargement was conceived first as a political administrative exercise to reunite a continent which had been divided for 50 years, leaving little place for interaction with stakeholders. As far as the role of women

---

140   Article 2 "The Community shall have as its task, by establishing a common market and an economic and monetary union and by implementing common policies or activities referred to in Articles 3 and 3a, to promote throughout the Community a harmonious, balanced and sustainable development of economic activities, a high level of employment and of social protection, equality between men and women, sustainable and non-inflationary growth, a high degree of competitiveness and convergence of economic performance, a high level of protection and improvement of the quality of the environment, the raising of the standard of living and quality of life, and economic and social cohesion and solidarity among Member States."

141   Czech Republic, Estonia, Hungary, Latvia, Lithuania, Poland, Slovakia, Slovenia in 2004 followed suit by Bulgaria and Romania in 2007

142   European Commission, *Agenda 2000*, https://eur-lex.europa.eu/legal-content/EN/TXT/?uri=LEGISSUM%3Al60001

was concerned, experiences on the two sides of the Iron Curtain had been radically different: while in the West, equality was a conquest of women by means of women's lib movements and a massive (re-)entry into the labour market to acquire financial autonomy, the ex-communist states were in essence grounded on the principle of equality of women and men, having used women's labour force to fulfil the needs of their industrialisation. Women in Central and Eastern Europe (CEE) had also reached political offices in parliaments to a much greater extent, and childcare was provided by most employers, making Western Europe look backward. This *prima facie* impression of equal treatment explains the low interest for parity democracy or child care facilities amongst women from the CEE region. As a result of these different historical experiences, the very term of equality had very different meanings from Europe's East to West. A limited effort was made to better understand the different forms of patriarchy and to develop common strategies. The implicit idea that some countries' attachment to the traditional nuclear family model could be framed as a way to rebuild the nation and oppose former rulers, led to deep misunderstandings which continue to blur the development of common objectives to this day. At the time, the PHARE programme[143] designed to prepare enlargement did not take the measure of this deep-seated misunderstanding with so many implications for gender equality. The governments of acceding Member States were in charge of translating the *acquis* into national le-

---

143    The term "PHARE" - Poland and Hungary Assistance for the Restructuring of the Economy - initially described as the international efforts to provide economic support to the emerging Polish and Hungarian democracies - is the EU's main financial instrument for accession of the Central and Eastern European countries. It was launched as a specific EC programme, initiated by Council Regulation No. 3906/89. Its funding is used to channel technical, economic and infrastructural expertise and assistance to recipient states. The aim is to help these countries achieve market economies based on free enterprise and private initiative. More information in "Briefing No 33: The PHARE Programme and the enlargement of the European Union," (Brussels: European Parliament, December 1998), PE 167.944, https://www.europarl.europa.eu/enlargement/briefings/33a1_en.htm

gislation, which they did. "A detailed analysis reveals that candidate States significantly changed their domestic policies and established institutions on gender equality to comply with EU accession requirements",[144] but the process was formal and in the post-accession period, only in countries where civil society organisations created alliances with governments, could progress be achieved. More contacts between NGOs, academics and feminist activists on both sides, before accession, could have expanded the 'velvet triangle' with a less Western-centric perspective and opened the eyes of western feminists on some of the historic realities and different forms of patriarchal hegemony.

At the beginning of the century however, in the European Commission, internal EU policies like employment, social affairs and gender equality were concerned with existing Member States only. The dedicated PHARE[145] programme financed institutional reform and infrastructures as priorities with little consideration for gender equality. The European Women's Lobby, with few resources, helped to aggregate NGOs into national coordination networks as it had been done in other Member States. Furthermore, occasional contacts between women advocates for gender equality were initiated by MEPs.

## A programme and a strategy

In 1999, a Greek politician, member of PASOK (Panhellenic Socialist Movement) Anna Diamantopoulou, was appointed European Commissioner for Employment and Social Affairs. As the commissioner responsible for equality between women and men, she proposed the adoption of the Fifth Action Programme for equality between women and men as one of her very first initiatives in office. Two complementary documents were presented to the college: first, a

---

144    Olga Avdeyeva, *Defending Women's Rights in Europe: Gender Equality and EU Enlargement* (New York: State University of New York Press, 2015).

145    "Briefing No 33: The PHARE Programme and the enlargement of the European Union," (Brussels: European Parliament, December 1998), PE 167.944, https://www.europarl.europa.eu/enlargement/briefings/33a1_en.htm

Community framework strategy, intended as an overall design for actions towards equality in all relevant policies and programmes (gender mainstreaming)[146] and second, a programme to assist, support and fund specific action and transnational projects to promote gender equality[147] with a dedicated budget. The strategy was a coordination and guidance document which encompassed action for equality under other programmes like STOP,[148] the DAPHNE initiative,[149] MEDA,[150] the Sixth Framework Programme for Research (FP6)

---

146     Commission Communication of 7 June 2000: "Towards a Community framework strategy on gender equality (2001-2005)," COM(2000) 335 final, https://eur-lex.europa.eu/legal-content/EN/TXT/?uri=LE-GISSUM%3Ac10932

147     Council Decision 2001/51/EC of 20 December 2000 Establishing a Programme Relating to the Community Framework Strategy on Gender Equality (2001-2005), https://eur-lex.europa.eu/legal-content/EN/ALL/?uri=CELEX%3A32001D0051

148     to prevent and combat trade in human beings and the sexual exploitation of children, including child pornography

149     The Daphne Initiative was launched in May 1997, as a one-year funding line to fund NGO projects that support victims of violence and combat violence against women, children and young people. The one-year Daphne Initiative of 1997 struck a chord with NGOs and response to the two calls for proposals was high. As a result, funding for the Initiative was renewed in 1998 and in 1999. The Daphne Programme 2000-03 continued the work of the Initiative, with funding of €20 million over four years. It was followed by the Daphne II Programme 2004-06 with an average annual budget of €10 million and then by the Daphne III programme (2007-13) with an average annual budget of €16,7 million. The Daphne programme continued in the period 2014-20, as one part of the Rights, Equality and Citizenship Programme. EU Council, *The Daphne Toolkit: An active resource from the Daphne Programme* (2021), https://wayback.archive-it.org/12090/20210927084648/remote-office.novacomm-europa.eu/daphne-toolkit/justice/grants/results/daphne-toolkit/daphne-toolkit--active-resource-daphne-programme_en.html See also Decision No 293/2000/EC of the European Parliament and of the Council of 24 January 2000 adopting a programme of Community action (the Daphne programme, 2000-2003) on preventive measures to fight violence against children, young persons and women (OJ L 34), 09 February 2000.

150     The MEDA programme was created in July 1996 to finance bilateral and regional cooperation projects within the Euro-Mediterranean part-

and structural funds programmes like EQUAL, Urban, and Leader. Actions to promote equality were presented under four headings: economic life, participation and representation, and social rights and civil life (mainly actions focusing on the fight against gender-based violence).

Within the mandate of Anna Diamantopoulou, violence against women became a salient issue on the European agenda. While the European Parliament had already produced a resolution on the issue in 1984,[151] it had then been deemed outside the field of legislative competence of the European Economic Community. The new civil and criminal rights competences introduced by the Amsterdam Treaty had therefore opened the door for actions against criminal activities and violence against women. The programmes STOP (against trafficking) and DAPHNE (prevention measures to fight violence), adopted under the pressure of the European Parliament and the European Women's Lobby, opened up a new field of action on the eve of the new millennium. Thanks to the production of surveys, data and analysis, violence against women (VAW) has become an issue where the added value of the European Union has become undeniable.

This was a very positive move for European women, pushed by the new interest for human rights that had been sparked by the Charter of Fundamental Rights of the European Union (signed in Nice in December 2000) and the subsequent Convention on the Future of Europe. The rest of the decade, however, would be marked by a slow dismantling of the gender equality policy.[152]

Enlargement took place in 2004 with ten new Member States which had formally transposed the *acquis* and were not necessarily

---

nership. The first programme covered 1996-2000 and was replaced by a second for 2000-06.

151    European Parliament, *Resolution on Violence against Women* (1986), https://www.europarl.europa.eu/EPRS/PE2_AP_RP!FEMM.1984_A2-0044!860001EN.pdf

152    The term 'dismantling' is used by Sophie Jacquot in *Transformations in EU Gender Equality: From Emergence to Dismantling* (Bakingstoke: Palgrave, 2015).

willing to push equality further. One must admit that the first text which the new ministers were presented with in the European Council were technical, bureaucratic and unlikely to mobilise stakeholders' interest: the 'recast directive' was, for the sake of simplification (and making judicial reference easier), a mere regrouping of existing legal texts adopted earlier. The so-called Article 13 directive[153] (used for implementing the principle of equal treatment between men and women in the access to and supply of goods and services) was supposed to mark an enlargement of EU competences awarded by the Treaty of Amsterdam. Then, however, it came to the attention of the insurance sector, which lobbied for a weakening of the original text – without any counterbalance, as civil society activists took no interest in an issue considered too technical.[154] Though the object of the directive could have been a transformative move as it initially included addressing discrimination in the image of women in the media, a leak followed by vicious personal attacks on the Commissioner by the British tabloid press, convinced Anna Diamantopoulou to postpone issues related to the media to another opportunity,[155] which has not materialised yet.

## To a mere 'road map': how dismantling happens

Subsequently, the first move of the new Commission that took office in 2005 was to downgrade the 'framework strategy' (2000-05), which had entailed clear objectives and coherence, to a 'road map' approach (2006-11). With no objectives or indicators and a poor assessment of the situation, it showed a weak commitment to driving

---

153    Council Directive 2004/113/EC of 13 December 2004 implementing the principle of equal treatment between men and women in the access to and supply of goods and services, https://eur-lex.europa.eu/legal-content/EN/TXT/?uri=celex%3A32004L0113

154    Barbara Helfferich and Felix Kolb, "Multilevel Action Coordination in European Contentious Politics: The Case of the European Women's Lobby," in *Contentious Europeans: Protest and Politics in an Emerging Polity*, ed. Douglas Imig and Sydney Tarrow (Washington DC: Rowman & Littlefield Publication, 2001).

155    It was originally meant to be dealt with in the 'Television without borders' directive.

the gender equality agenda forward with Member States and other actors. This was severely assessed by the European Parliament: "the Roadmap does not include a single new legislative proposal and it fails to specify the responsibilities of the Commission and the Member States as regards implementation and information to citizens, or the funds that will be allocated to implement its recommendations."[156] Even Members of the European Council got concerned and adopted a European Pact for Gender Equality in 2006, to renew EU commitment to "promoting women's empowerment in economic and political life and taking steps to close gender gaps, combat gender stereotypes and promote better work-life balance for both women and men."[157]

In 2005, the former group of commissioners for gender equality (which had, amongst others, given the political impetus to the development of a 'women and science' policy in research and education, a high-level group on gender equality to monitor actions in the structural funds) was transformed into a 'group of commissioners on fundamental rights' which formally put gender on its agenda, once a year, on international women's day.

The last unfortunate event of this decade was the transfer of the antidiscrimination directorate, which included the gender equality unit, from its first home DG Employment,[158] to DG Justice, for reasons disconnected from the interest of the policy. Not only did this move physically cut out the mainstreaming of gender in employment

---

156   Amalia Sartori (EP Committee on Women's Rights and Gender Equality), *Report on a Roadmap for equality between women and men 2006-2010* (2006/2132(INI)), https://www.europarl.europa.eu/doceo/document/A-6-2007-0033_EN.html

157   European Pact for Gender Equality, https://www.eurofound.europa.eu/observatories/eurwork/industrial-relations-dictionary/european-pact-for-gender-equality

158   The Commission is organised into policy departments, known as Directorates-General (DGs), which are responsible for different policy areas. DGs develop, implement and manage EU policy, law, and funding programmes. In addition, service departments deal with particular administrative issues. Executive agencies manage programmes set up by the Commission.

and social affairs, but it gave rise to huge delays in the development of the policy as the budget had to be cut out of the social programme PROGRESS.[159]

Meanwhile, the financial crisis, which started in September 2008 with the collapse of Lehman brothers, was going to have a dire impact on women.

# 2010: A decade of austerity begins

The decade starting in 2010 was doomed by austerity following the financial crisis of 2008 which started in the US but had a long-lasting impact on the EU economy and social cohesion. As far as gender equality is concerned, the period starting with the Treaty of Lisbon (2007) is categorised as the "crisis period"[160] when the policy is dismantled step by step.

## Precarious employment

Firstly, the administrative splitting of the employment and social policies has been messy and unnecessary. Labour markets are increasingly segregated as most of the jobs created since the turn of the century have been low-quality, low-paying jobs. The result has been the emergence of the 'working poor', ie those, mainly women, who despite having a job, have an income below the poverty line. This would have needed specific attention within the frame of the gender equality policy. Instead, the Lisbon Strategy (2000-2010) which aimed at making the EU "the most competitive and dynamic knowledge-based economy in the world, capable of sustaining economic growth with more and better jobs and greater social cohesion" en-

---

159　In preparation of the 2007-14 financial perspectives, the approach had been to merge budget lines, starting with the dedicated budget line for equality between women and men.

160　Sophie Jacquot (*Transformations in EU Gender Equality,* 2015) describes three policy stages in the trajectory of European gender equality policy: the genesis period till the mid-nineties, the established period until the first decade of the new millennium, followed by the crisis (and dismantling) phase from the Lisbon Treaty onwards.

ded with disappointing results,[161] in particular because of lacking attention to the situation and needs of women. Even within the *social investment* paradigm they were sidelined in favour of children. [162] 'Europe 2020', the ten-year growth strategy launched in 2010, aimed "to promote smart, sustainable, and inclusive growth across EU Member States", barely addressing the specific inequalities faced by women[163] or gender equality.

Secondly, under the leadership of Viviane Reding, a former journalist and Commissioner for Justice and citizenship, the gender equality unit (having moved to DG Justice) was instructed to focus mainly on two issues during the first part of the decade: a women-on-boards directive project to deal with the considerable underrepresentation of women in economic decision-making at the highest levels, and an EU framework to tackle female genital mutilation (FGM) under the heading of violence against women. The questions of female poverty, women's employment and work life balance concerns were therefore neglected at the height of the crisis. The preparation of the women-on-boards exercise absorbed much time and energy as it started with a long phase of consultation with the CEOs of large companies who made promises which were not delivered. In 2012, the Commission eventually submitted a draft directive aiming to reach a minimum of 40 percent of non-executive members of the under-represented sex (mainly women) on company boards. In the meantime, a number of

---

161    Bea Cantillon, "The Paradox of the Social Investment State: Growth, Employment and Poverty in the Lisbon Era," *Journal of European Social Policy* 21, no. 5 (14 December 2011), 432-449, https://doi.org/10.1177/0958928711418856

162    Jane Jenson, "Lost in translation: The social investment perspective and gender equality." *Social politics* 16, no.4 (2009), 446-483.

163    The term "women" did appear in the document but only in conjunction with the expression "women and men", which were added to the employment objective of 75% upon the insistence of the Spanish presidency of the European Council. As such it was still allowing more progress for men's employment that for women due to the persisting gender unbalances on labour markets. See EU Commission, *Europe 2020: a strategy for smart, sustainable and inclusive growth* (03 March 2010), https://eur-lex.europa.eu/legal-content/EN/ALL/?uri=celex-:52010DC2020

Member States did adopt national legislative measures to address the issue, but the proposal remained blocked in the European Council until March 2022. The second item of concern for EU gender equality policy at the time, FGM, also constituted a time-consuming exercise on what still remained a rather underexplored issue which was at the time scarcely discussed in public. While important work was done on FGM, it kept the Commissionner away from the more politically controversial domestic violence or sexual harassment issues on the violence-against-women agenda. The European Commission produced a communication towards the elimination of FGM in 2013,[164] calling for action in its internal and external policies. This includes raising awareness, advocating for better legal protection and improved access to support for victims, instilling social change and capacity building of practitioners and dialogue with survivors and community-based activists. FGM is also to be made unlawful under the Istanbul Convention, a legally binding and more comprehensive text on all forms of violence against women (initiated by the Council of Europe, opened to signature in 2011). In a similar way, the Gender Action Plan for EU external action 2021-25 (GAP III)[165] as well as in the EU Action Plan for Human Rights and Democracy 2020-24[166] advocate for the elimination, prevention and protection from all forms of sexual and gender-based violence, including FGM.

164    High Representative for Foreign Affairs and Security Policy, Communication from the Commission to the European Parliament and the Council towards the Elimination of Female Genital Mutilation (COM/2013/0833 Final), https://eur-lex.europa.eu/legal-content/EN/TXT/?uri=COM:2013:0833:FIN

165    Joint Communication to the European Parliament and the Council: The EU Gender Action Plan (GAP) III: an Ambitious Agenda for Gender Equality and Women's Empowerment in EU External Action. (SWD: 2020, 284), https://ec.europa.eu/international-partnerships/system/files/join-2020-17-final_en.pdf

166    EU Action Plan on Human Rights and Democracy 2020-24.

## Inadequate attention

The twenty-tens would end on a fairly negative evaluation report stressing the inadequate attention to some policy issues, starting with the lack of attention to the quality of employment of women, the non-existent monitoring of the funding going to gender equality, the limited coordination with the European Semester (which had become the overall policy framework to manage austerity), a lack of focus on fighting stereotypes and promoting cultural change. Lastly, it underlines that important commitments of the Strategy for Gender Equality 2010-2015, such as the production of a report on gender mainstreaming, had simply never been met.

Meanwhile, in 2014, the first attempt to identify how the economic crisis and the subsequent austerity policies were affecting women in Europe was published by two eminent researchers, Jill Rubery (Professor of Comparative Employment Systems, University of Manchester) and Maria Karamessini (Professor of Labour Economics and Economics of the Welfare State, Panteion University). In "Women and Austerity: The Economic Crisis and the Future for Gender Equality", the authors traced the consequences of the crisis and of austerity measures for gender equality in employment and welfare systems in nine case studies from countries facing the most severe adjustment problems. Their analysis stressed the low attention given to gender equality in the first phase of the crisis which struck mainly the male dominated sectors (construction, manufacture, finance). In a second phase, however, the impact was mainly on women via the shrinking of public employment, the tightening of public budgets (assistance to single parents families, to ageing and disabled persons, etc) and the privatisation of public services under the triple rule of austerity, fiscal consolidation and the neoliberal doctrine. The gender gap had narrowed only due to the deterioration of men's incomes. This happened to such a severe extent that the bad working conditions formerly reserved for women were now generalising to the whole labour force. After a thorough analysis of what had happened since 2008 in the nine countries, the authors conclude "*the pursuit of sex equality must be considered as an integral part of the solution to the endemic current crisis rather than a luxury to be addressed only in times of economic growth."*

## A strategic engagement

When the Juncker Commission took office in 2015, it was meant to be a "chance commission" expected to reset the legitimacy of social policy at European level. The signing of the European Pillar for Social Rights by the EU Parliament, the Council and the Commission in Gothenburg in 2017 was a real breakthrough. Gender equality but also work-life balance feature amongst the 20 key principles of the pillar. However, the Juncker Commission will also unfortunately be remembered for having further degraded gender equality policy by transforming the five-year gender equality strategy into a mere 'strategic engagement' for the period 2015-19. Although the actual commitments and the monitoring process of the engagement did draw lessons from previous evaluation exercises,[167] it lacked accountability and legitimacy: a mere 'document of the services', it was not even adopted by the college of Commissioners, which means that many commitments were not met – without accountability. For instance, the top-level dialogue planned for 2018 never materialised, and nor did the report on gender mainstreaming planned for 2017. This blemished the image of the gender equality policy in Member States as well as within the stakeholder community.

# 2020: A fresh start

The slow dismantling of EU gender equality policy, the increasing inequalities, the severe magnitude of sexism brought to light following the #Metoo movement, and the rise of the far-right and anti-gender movements laid the ground for the 2019 European election galvanising the widespread mobilisation of European feminists. Indeed,

---

167    The strategic engagement comprised objectives, timelines, indicators and even funding indications for its 5 priority areas (economic independence, closing the pay and pension gap, balanced representation in decision-making, fighting violence, and external policy).

a truly unprecedented scale of mobilisation around feminist stakes marked the months ahead of the election: the European Women's Lobby published their *Manifesto for a Feminist Europe*;[168] Young Feminist Europe declared that "Europe needs feminism";[169] the Irish Council of Women published a *Feminist Manifesto*; the European feminist think tank G5+ argued for parity democracy; in the Member States, a trio of equality ministers and state secretaries, Carmen Calvo (Spain), Helena Dalli (Malta) and Franziska Giffey (Germany) called for putting feminism in "the soul of Europe";[170] progressive political groups such as PES Women, chaired by Zita Gurmai, conducted feminist Europe campaigns; and the European Greens (as a dou) and the Liberals put forth the only women *spitzenkandidaten* in the race. This situation brought together diverse sets of actors and organisations – from the women's grassroots movements to think tanks and top political spheres – all gearing up the race for equality.

## Breaking the glass ceiling in EU institutions

The turnout of voters was higher than usual for all groups of the population (with a much larger turnout among young people and first-time voters) but according to the Eurobarometer post-electoral survey, men were still more likely than women to turn up to vote. However there were more women candidates that ever before, and the proportion of elected women rose from 36.4 to 41% (38% after Brexit).

This increase in women's representation was also mirrored in the appointments to EU top jobs:[171] Out of the four posts available, half were taken up by women. Ursula von der Leyen was appointed President of the European Commission and Christine Lagarde was

---

168    European Women's Lobby 2019 election campaign, https://www.womenlobby.org/WomenForEurope?lang=en

169    Young Feminist Europe, https://www.youngfeminist.eu/

170    Carmen Calvo, Helena Dalli, and Franziska Giffey, *It's time for feminism at the European elections* (Falkensee: Social Europe Publishing & Consulting, 23 May 2019), https://socialeurope.eu/feminism-at-the-european-elections

171    President of the Council, President of the Commission, EU High Representative for external affairs, President of the European Central Bank

nominated the same day to preside over the very male-dominated European Central Bank (ECB). Both are the first women in EU history to hold their respective posts. These two leaders obviously went through similar experiences in their careers and are both concerned to support women and gender equality. On the occasion of a podcast recorded by the ECB, they offered some telling insights about gender bias experience in their own careers.[172] Have times changed? As EU Commission President, Ursula von der Leyen recalls in this podcast, some 15 years ago when she was appointed Minister in the first Merkel cabinet, the first question of a journalist was: "have you already decided...are you going to be a bad mother or a bad minister?"

Ahead of her formal election as the head of the EU executive by the European Parliament, Ursula von der Leyen vowed to ensure parity in her College of Commissioners although the nominations still lay in the hands of Member States. On 9 September 2019, she presented 12 women and 14 men as European Commissioner nominees. Gender balance in the Commission was only one of the significant announcements she made. In her inaugural speech, Ursula von der Leyen made gender equality a cornerstone of her case to be appointed as the first female EC President, strongly appealing to the role of women and equality. This commitment subsequently translated into the appointment of the first EU Commissioner for Equality, a post filled by socialist Helena Dalli from Malta. Soon after, the new Gender Equality Strategy 2020-2025 was presented by the Commissioner in charge, ahead of International Women's Day 2020. It was the first significant practical step of the new Commission to upgrade the EU gender equality policy. The text was positively welcomed by the EP, the EWL and the community of gender experts as finally "recognising and addressing the structural nature of inequalities and

---

172    Interview with Christine Lagarde and Ursula von der Leyen, *The ECB Podcast: Fighting biases and empowering women* (Frankfurt: European Central Bank, 04 Mach 2021), https://www.youtube.com/watch?v=tVH-9kKHLN6w

focusing on care as a central issue."[173] This was a very good start for a decade of progress.

## Care is central

On March 15, the pandemic was declared and most EU Member States started implementing strict lockdown rules, entering a public health crisis already spanning over two years at the time of writing.

So far, coping with the impact of the covid-19 crisis on the EU, on gender equality, on European societies and globally, is 'work in progress' but we can already identify contradictory trends when looking at a few facts. The EU has been able to negotiate the largest deal of solidarity ever, the planned initiatives for gender equality are on their way (pay transparency directive presented in March 2021, initiative on violence in March 2022); European societies and in particular the most precarious in society (parents and especially those in lone-parent families, young people, migrants, and mainly women in all these categories) have suffered disproportionately but the welfare systems are holding.

Major questions are being asked about the future of our (health-) care systems, and about climate change. Ideas are being put forward for a society caring for people and the environment, rooted in new growth indicators, new governance structures based on parity, etc. At this point, not much radical change is on the way but small transformations, often led from the grassroots, could be signs that we might be leaving the world of 'business as usual'.

---

173    Barbara Helfferich (FEPS), *Does Europe Care?* Progressive Post, https://progressivepost.eu/does-europe-care-about-care/

# Part III: Making it happen with institutions, agents and tools

While the Treaty of Rome (signed in 1957) only featured *a single* article concerning equal pay, five decades later the Treaty of Lisbon and the EU Charter of Fundamental Rights enshrine women's rights in *eight* articles. This development is both symbolically and legally significant as it enhanced the status of the EU's gender equality policy. On this foundation, the policy has branched out in many directions, using all EU institutions and instruments available and harnessing the support of its stakeholder community. A newcomer, approaching the policy today, may feel overwhelmed by the abundance of bodies, networks, measures, institutions and tools dedicated to the promotion of gender equality in the EU. In this chapter, we will map out this maze, point out linkages to the current and historical context, and describe the convergence of interests which created this elaborate policy framework.

## The EU Gender Equality Strategy: the overall framework

*With the gender equality strategy, we are anchoring gender equality at the core of EU policy development. We aim to ensure that women do not have to surmount additional hurdles to achieve what men have as a given and are instead able to reach their full potential.*
– Helena Dalli, Commissioner for Equality, Press Release 5 March 2020

Every five years since 1986, the European Commission has been taking stock of where the EU and its Member States stand on gender equality, and designed a multiannual plan of actions to be implemented and objectives to be reached within that time period. This has been a guiding framework for all the different actors to work together to promote gender equality: the European Commission, Member States, the European Parliament, the European Women's Lobby and its national coordination networks, as well as social partners. The Gender Equality Strategy[174] presented in March 2020 sets out policy objectives and key actions for the period 2020-25, using all policy instruments and tools at their disposal: legislation, communication, funding programmes and gender mainstreaming.

The "multiannual programmes for equality between women and men" became strategies at the turn of the century to take into account the commitment of Member States, introduced in the Treaty of Amsterdam, to "eliminate inequalities and promote equality between women and men in EU policies" (Art 3). Also, priorities have changed overtime as the women's education levels improved significantly (now they outperform men at school and university), changes occurred on the labour market and new issues like women's deficit in decision-making positions and gender-based violence emerged as big issues on the EU agenda. The progressive improvement of *gender disaggregated statistics* by the ESS (European Statistical System) and data from specific surveys improved experts' knowledge on existing differences between women and men and persisting discrimination against women according to their social status, their race, and their sexual orientation. Finally, the assistance of EIGE helped the Commission to access new knowledge and evidence on which to base its policies.

Many expectations were raised by the EU Gender Equality Strategy 2020-2025, presented just a few days before the first national decisions to 'lock down' to limit the spread of covid-19. The previous strategy had been demoted to a mere 'strategic engagement' at

174   Communication from the Commission to the European Parliament, the Council, the European Economic and Social Committee and the Committee of the Regions: a Union of Equality – Gender Equality Strategy 2020-2025, https://eur-lex.europa.eu/legal-content/EN/TXT/?uri=CELEX%3A52020DC0152

**Population with tertiary education**
25-34 year-old men / 25-34 year-old women / 55-64 year-old men / 55-64 year-old women,
% in same age group, 2020 or latest available

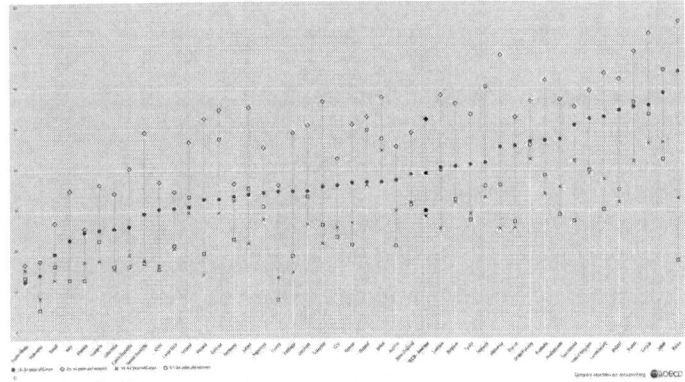

**Fig. 6**  Population with tertiary education. 2020 or latest available. Source: OECD 2020 (data available from: https://data.oecd.org/chart/6vNq).

a time when backsliding on women's rights was becoming a reality[175] under the combined influence of the impact of the financial crisis and the rise of right-wing radicalism. Also, Ursula von der Leyen, the first woman president of the European Commission had made a clear commitment to gender equality in her inaugural speech. She made it concrete by establishing the first dedicated European Commissioner for Equality, a role to which Helena Dalli was appointed.

Also, the 2021 edition of the European Gender Equality Index confirmed that progress towards effective equality 'moves at a snail's pace': with 68/100 (where 100 means full gender equality), the EU's score for gender equality had gained just 4.9 points since 2010 and 0.6 points since 2020.[176] To quote the European Institute for Gen-

---

175    European Parliament: *Backlash in Gender Equality and Women's and Girls' Rights* [Study requested by the FEMM committee] (Brussels, Strasbourg: EP, 2018), https://www.europarl.europa.eu/RegData/etudes/STUD/2018/604955/IPOL_STU(2018)604955_EN.pdf

176    European Institute for Gender Equality (EIGE), *Gender Equality Index 2021: Health*, (Vilnius: EIGE, 2021), 44, https://eige.europa.eu/publications/gender-equality-index-2021-health

der Equality (EIGE), "with gender equality inching forward by only 1 point every 2 years, it will take nearly three generations to achieve gender parity at the current pace".[177]

Will the new Gender Equality Strategy results in 2025 live up to present expectations? The strategy itself was well received when it was presented in March 2020. The president of the European Women's Lobby (EWL) hailed it as "a great first step to accelerate progress on the rights of all women and girls throughout the EU."[178] The European Parliament "[welcomed] the positive measures included in the EU's new Gender Equality Strategy but [called] for additional actions and specific and binding targets", and S&D MEP and FEMM committee coordinator Maria Noichl declared that "its proposed actions are a faster route to equality between men and women. It also strengthens our position on the backlash against women's rights taking place in several Member States. Rule of law in Europe can only exist with gender equality – without it, democracy is lagging behind."[179]

That was until the covid-19 pandemic shook the globe with full force and a clearly disproportionate impact on women. As a result, there are stronger reasons than ever before to uphold the promotion of gender equality as a necessity to overcome the crisis. Whilst the Gender Equality Strategy has potential on many fronts, it also has its weaknesses. Gender policy tends to hold a marginal stand in the EU Council of Ministers despite recurrent calls from progressive actors and civil society organisations for a *Council configuration* on

177    see *Gender Equality Index* in glossary
178    European Women's Lobby (EWL), "European Women's Lobby's reaction to the launch of the European Commission's 'A Union of Equality: Gender Equality Strategy 2020-2025'," 5 March 2020,  https://www.womenlobby.org/European-Women-s-Lobby-s-reaction-to-the-launch-of-the-European-Commission-A
179    European Parliament, "Gender Equality Strategy 2020-2025: Parliament's reaction and input," 21 January 2021, https://www.europarl.europa.eu/news/en/press-room/20210114IPR95617/gender-equality-strategy-2020-2025-parliament-s-reaction-and-inputn

gender equality:[180] Wheareas, in comparison, ministers for fishery meet three to four times a year, there is no meeting of ministers responsible for gender equality. Moreover, there are huge differences between Member States[181] and the backsliding due to anti-gender opposition is fierce, as best exemplified by the blockage around the Istanbul Convention.[182]

## Strength and weaknesses

The Strategy's affirmed goal is to create "a Union where women and men, girls and boys, in all their diversity,[183] are free to pursue their chosen path in life, have equal opportunities to thrive, and can equally participate in and lead our European society". Its key objectives address similar themes as previous strategies: from the fight against gender-based violence, gender stereotypes, the gender pay and pension gaps to the promotion of equal participation across

180    Euractiv, "PES ministers for gender equality reaffirm commitment to accelerate women's rights for a truly feminist and equal Europe," 09 July 2020, https://pr.euractiv.com/pr/pes-ministers-gender-equality-re-affirm-commitment-accelerate-women-s-rights-truly-feminist-and

181    EIGE's Gender Equality Index best exemplifies these discrepancies with scores ranging from 83.9/100 in with Sweden to 53.4 and 59.2 in Hungary and Greece at the other end of the index, measuring each Member State's advancement towards full gender equality.

182    Currently, six Member States (Bulgaria, Czech Republic, Hungary, Latvia, Lithuania and Slovenia) advance 'ideological' reasons for their refusal to ratify the Istanbul Convention. Often misleading arguments are made in this regard linking the Convention's real purpose (ie the elimination and prevention of gender-based violence) with public incentives for women to return to traditional gender roles, dismissing "false emancipation" – to quote the Hungarian minister in charge of family affairs ("The latest storm: Family Minister's video on women", Budapost, 19 December 2020) – or with measures jeopardising women's organisations and LGBTQI rights.

183    The expression 'in all their diversity' is used in the strategy to express that, where women or men are mentioned, these are a heterogeneous categories including in relation to their sex, gender identity, gender expression or sex characteristics. It affirms the commitment to leave no one behind and achieve a gender-equal Europe for everyone, regardless of their sex, racial or ethnic origin, religion or belief, disability, age or sexual orientation.

different sectors of the economy, gender balance in decision-making and in politics, and gender equality in the EU's external policy. Moreover, the Strategy reaffirms the dual approach of gender mainstreaming combined with positive actions, whilst applying intersectionality as a horizontal principle for its implementation.

Where it differs from previous strategies is in its approach. In particular, it recognises and addresses the *structural* nature of gender inequalities and discrimination, stating that policies "should not perpetuate structural gender inequalities based on traditional gender roles in the realms of work and private life."

A year later, on the occasion of International Women's Day 2021, the European Commission's annual report on gender equality in the EU[184] took stock of where the EU and its Member States stood following the adoption of the strategy in the unexpected context of the covid-19 crisis which exacerbates existing inequalities in almost all areas of life.

Concrete actions are underway on the major commitments, such as the pay transparency directive, strengthening the framework to fight gender-based violence, and engagement in the tracking and tracing expenditure to make the EU budget *gender responsive*. However, considering the disappointing record of gender mainstreaming so far and the still marginal status of gender equality, observers fear that the strategy will not be up to the challenges of the period.[185]

### The key areas of the Strategy

Actions under the strategy are organised in the following key areas: violence, the economy, decision-making, gender mainstreaming (including in funding) and intersectionality as transversal issues, and external policy.

---

184    European Commission "2021 Report on Gender Equality in the EU: Free, Thrive, Lead," (Luxembourg: European Union, 2021), https://ec.europa.eu/info/sites/default/files/aid_development_cooperation_fundamental_rights/annual_report_ge_2021_en.pdf

185    R. Guerrina, "From Amsterdam to Lisbon and beyond: reflections on twenty years of gender mainstreaming in the EU" in *Social policy in the European Union 1999-2019: the long and winding road* (Trade Union Institute, 2021).

Fig. 7

## 1) **Being free from violence and stereotypes**

According to figures available when the strategy was adopted, one in three women aged 15 and over, in the EU, was subject to physical or sexual violence, one in two has been sexually harassed, two in five has endured psychological violence and one in ten has been subject to online harassment.[186] After one year of covid-19, however, there has been an explosion of gender-based violence, and of domestic violence in particular.[187] In its 2021 study on the pandemic's impact

---

186    European Union Agency for Fundamental Rights, "Violence against women: an EU-wide survey" (2014), https://fra.europa.eu/en/publication/2014/violence-against-women-eu-wide-survey-main-results-report – A new survey conducted by Eurostat has been launched in 2020 whose results will be available in 2023.

187    World Health Organization, "The rise of interpersonal violence: an unintended impact of the Covid-19 response on families" (New York: WHO, 2020), https://www.euro.who.int/en/health-topics/disease-prevention/violence-and-injuries/news/news/2020/6/the-rise-and-rise-of-interpersonal-violence-an-unintended-impact-of-the-covid-19-response-on-families. See also European Parliament (2020), "Report on the gender perspective in the Covid 19 crisis and post crisis

on intimate violence against women[188] EIGE provides an overview of national measures to support victims of violence during the covid outbreak, identifies examples of promising practices and makes recommendations on how to better support victims during crises. Another EIGE study published in September 2021 presents an estimate of the economic cost of gender-based violence across the EU at €366 billion a year.[189]

Early in the crisis, the European Commission called on Member States to focus their emergency response to the needs of groups in disadvantaged situations such as victims of domestic violence, while pursuing its efforts to support shelters, helplines and relevant protection services.

Against this backdrop, the priority given to fight violence in the new strategy is more forcefully needed and addressed than ever before. It is seen as an issue to be pursued by all the means available: The European Commission does not give up on the objective of completing the EU's accession to the Istanbul Convention.[190] Considering

---

period." Retrieved from https://www.europarl.europa.eu/doceo/document/A-9-2020-0229_EN.html

188   European Institute for Gender Equality (EIGE), "The Covid-19 pandemic and intimate partner violence against women in the EU" (Luxemburg: Publications Office of the European Union, 2021), https://eige.europa.eu/publications/covid-19-pandemic-and-intimate-partner-violence-against-women-eu

189   The breakdown of the different costs is the following: physical and emotional impact (56 %), criminal justice services (21 %) lost economic output (14 %). Other costs can include civil justice services (for divorces and child custody proceedings for example), housing aid and child protection. See EIGE, "Gender-based violence costs the EU €366 billion a year" (Luxemburg: Publications Office of the European Union, 2021), https://eige.europa.eu/news/gender-based-violence-costs-eu-eu366-billion-year

190   New developments may occur if the Court of Justice of the European Union follows the advice of its advocate general who in March 2021 declared: "The EU's decision to conclude the Istanbul Convention would be compatible with the Treaties if it were adopted in the absence of a common agreement of all Member States to be bound by that convention. However, it would also be compatible with the Treaties if that decision were adopted only after such common agreement had

the slow pace of talks in the EU Council of Ministers,[191] the Strategy announced measures to prevent violence, protect the victims and prosecute perpetrators as provided by the Convention.[192] The Strategy also foresees complementary initiatives, such as extending the areas of crime with a cross-border dimension to include crimes like human trafficking and the sexual exploitation of women, as well as additional measures and legislation to prevent specific forms of gender-based violence such as *female genital mutilation*, *sexual harassment*, *honour killings* and *forced marriages*. The strategy also stresses the importance of *preventive measures* and *education*, including teaching gender equality to children from a young age and reinforcing public service and the criminal justice system. In addition to combatting specific forms of gender-based violence, the Commission recently adopted the *victims rights strategy* (2020-2025)[193] to provide a safe and supportive environment for victims to report crimes and be protected. EU funding available for fighting gender-based violence is through the Daphne programme with a budget of €200 million for the next seven years starting in 2021.

As *online violence* against women has emerged as an increasing form of gender-based violence in recent years, the strategy foresees (as was announced by President von der Leyen in her state of the Union letter of intent) to extend the list of EU crimes in accordance with article 83 of TFEU to cover all forms of hate crimes and hate

---

been established. It is exclusively for the Council to decide which of these two solutions is preferable." See Court of Justice of the European Union, Press release No. 37/21: Advocate General's Opinion in Avis 1/19: Istanbul Convention (11 March 2021), https://curia.europa.eu/jcms/upload/docs/application/pdf/2021-03/cp210037en.pdf

191  At the time of writing, 21 Member States have ratified it, 6 have not, and one Member State (Poland) expressed its intention to withdraw.

192  For more details, see the EU gender equality report of March 2021.

193  "Communication from the Commission to the European Parliament, the Council, the European Economic and Social Committee and the Committee of the Regions: EU Strategy on Victims' Rights (2020-2025)," (COM/2020/258 final).

speech. Already in December 2020, the Digital Service Act (DSA)[194] created stronger public oversight of online platforms through transparency reporting. This should impose supervised risk management on large platforms and empower users in their interaction with the platform systems.

The EU Gender Equality Strategy 2020-2025 did not announce the presentation of a binding framework directive to prevent and combat all forms of gender-based violence. That, however, is strongly demanded by the European Parliament (in its resolution on the strategy) as well as by civil society (see in particular the G5+ policy document on "ending VAW, the Istanbul convention and beyond").[195]

## 2) **Thriving in a gender equal economy**

In order to achieve a gender equal economy, the strategy set out its aim to offer "women and men equal opportunities to thrive, be paid equally for work of equal value and equally share caring and financial responsibilities." This was far from the case even prior to the pandemic, as missing care facilities, gender stereotypes and sexism hamper women's participation in the labour market. In 2019, women still remain underrepresented in the labour market with 79 percent of men in employment, compared to only 67 percent of women.[196]

The situation has worsened since, mainly due to the overrepresentation of women in lower-paid, unprotected jobs in sectors primarily exposed in the crisis (hospitality, retail and personal services).[197]

---

194    Proposal for a Regulation of the European Parliament and of the Council on a Single Market For Digital Services (Digital Services Act) and Amending Directive 2000/31/EC (COM(2020)825final), https://eur-lex.europa.eu/legal-content/en/TXT/?uri=COM:2020:825:FIN

195    https://docs.wixstatic.com/ugd/530efa_315962b25b7647798eb0b-c259f25f5b5.pdf

196    European Commission, "2021 Report on Gender Equality in the EU: Free, Thrive, Lead" (European Union, 2021), https://ec.europa.eu/info/sites/default/files/aid_development_cooperation_fundamental_rights/annual_report_ge_2021_en.pdf

197    European Institute for Gender Equality, "Gender equality and socio economic consequences of the COVID crisis: EIGE research note to

The *European pillar of social rights* (EPSR) is the main compass of the strategy to address the gender-unequal labour market by calling for "equality of treatment and opportunities for women and men in the labour market, terms and conditions of employment, in career progression and the right to equal pay" (principle 2). The strategy plan to implement the EPSR sets out the aim "to half the gender employment gap compared to 2019, to increase the provision of formal early childhood education and care and to support stronger female labour market participation".

As far as pay is concerned, two most important initiatives were presented by the European Commission in November 2020 and March 2021: first, a proposal for a *directive on adequate minimum wage in the EU*.[198] As the majority of minimum wage earners are women, this proposal indirectly supports the reduction of the gender pay and pension gap by setting a framework for minimum wages. Second, as was announced by the Commission's President in her political guidelines and in the gender equality strategy, a proposal for a *directive on pay transparency* with enforcement mechanisms was presented by the Commission on March 4, one year after the adoption of the strategy. The objectives are to encourage employers to ensure that their pay-setting mechanisms are free from gender bias, to prevent the under-evaluation of women's work, and to empower workers to claim their right to equal pay.

Both directives are currently being scrutinised in the European Parliament and the Council of Ministers. So far, on the fair minimum wages directive, the Presidency of the Council is trying to move the negotiations forward but nine Member States would rather opt for a recommendation rather than a directive. As to the pay transparency

---

support the Portuguese presidency of the EU and Gender Five Plus 'Towards a gendered recovery in the EU: Women and Equality in the aftermath of the Covid19 pandemic'", https://www.genderfiveplus.com/covid19-gender-equality-eu

198    European Commission, "Press Release: Advancing the EU social market economy: adequate minimum wages for workers across Member States" (28 October 2020), https://ec.europa.eu/commission/presscorner/detail/en/ip_20_1968

directive, it has so far yielded support from social partners. The EP's relevant committees (FEMM et EMPL) would favour a stronger text, whereas the employment ministers and heads of state and government welcomed the proposal when meeting for the Social Summit in Porto on 8 May 2021. On the positive side, the president of France (the country holding the EU presidency in the first term of 2022) has announced his commitment to see these texts adopted (as well as the directive on women on boards).[199]

What is unprecedented in this Strategy is its focus on *care* 'as a central issue'.[200] It simultaneously addresses inequalities built into national taxation systems affecting second earners and the question of equal pay, all in order to encourage women to find their place in the labour market (including carers who are most often unpaid, undeclared, or on low pay as was made visible under the pandemic). As explained by Annick Masselot and Eugenia Caracciolo di Torella,[201] the EU could further the use of its competence, especially based on the free circulation of workers, to address one of the most pressing needs in all Member States today. As documented by EIGE, the care sector (both childcare and long-term care) faces severe staff shortages as challenging working conditions and low pay fail to attract a large enough labour force.[202] With an ageing population, attention to carers and their working conditions is not a luxury – it is a societal issue.

---

199   "EU Presidency: France's Macron Set to Detail Plans Ahead of January 1 Takeover," France24.com (09 December 2021), https://www.france24.com/en/video/20211209-eu-presidency-france-s-macron-set-to-detail-plans-ahead-of-january-1-takeover

200   Barbara Helfferich (FEPS), "Does Europe care about care?" *Progressive Post*, https://progressivepost.eu/does-europe-care-about-care/

201   Eugenia Caracciolo di Torella and Annick Masselot, *Caring Responsibilities in European Law and Policy: Who Cares?* (Abingdon: Routledge, 2020), https://doi.org/10.4324/9780203795828

202   European Institute for Gender Equality (EIGE), "Gender equality and long-term care at home" (Luxemburg: Publications Office of the European Union, 2020), https://eige.europa.eu/news/europe-needs-care-more-about-care

Practically, the new EU directive on work-life balance for parents and carers adopted in June 2019[203] was a first milestone for a better sharing of house tasks by parents and carers in general. It deals with paternity leave, parental leave, carers' leave, and flexible working arrangements for workers who are parents or carers. The Strategy's transposition and implementation will be monitored and receive support (including financial support by the structural funds of the recovery funds). This entails, in particular, measures favouring the uptake of paternal leave to encourage fathers to share the unpaid caring work which weighs dramatically on women's working conditions. On average, EU working women spend around 22 hours per week in unpaid work compared to 9 hours for men.[204] Unequal time use often forces women to take up part-time work, which concerns 31 percent of women but only 8 percent of men.[205] It has been widely documented that insufficient access to quality and affordable formal care services is also a key driver of gender inequality in the labour market.

In the Strategy, encouraging the sharing of family responsibilities and investing in care services is framed as a labour market issue to support women's participation in paid work and their professional development.[206] It also carries the potential for decent job creation for both women and men in the care sector.

203  Directive (EU) 2019/1158 of the European Parliament and of the Council of 20 June 2019 on work-life balance for parents and carers and repealing Council Directive 2010/18/EU, https://eur-lex.europa.eu/legal-content/EN/TXT/?uri=celex%3A32019L1158

204  European Commission DG Employment, "Work-Life Balance for All: What are the Benefits?" (Luxembourg: Publications Office, 2019), https://data.europa.eu/doi/10.2767/1525

205  For a more detailed gender-impact assessment of part-time work, see Janna Besamusca and Mara Yerkes, "Part-time work: risk of opportunity?" (Brussels: Foundation for European Progressive Studies & Friedrich Ebert Stiftung, 2021) https://www.feps-europe.eu/attachments/publications/211012_part_time_work_policy_brief_care4care.pdf

206  80% of care in the EU is currently provided by informal carers, 75% of them are women, most of them have a migrant background.

The way the EU takes care of care is also seen as foundational to address future challenges such as the demographic shift and the future of work.

Incremental policies to address care issues are important but will ultimately not suffice. The EU's new gender strategy points in the right direction by offering important building blocks to put care more solidly at the centre of economic activity. The future will tell if it is a move towards the development of a 'reproductive economy' built around co-operation and care, rather than competition and inequality.

### 3) Leading equally throughout society

In EIGE's 2021 gender equality index,[207] it is the domain of 'power' which scores lowest with 55/100 points towards full equality. Yet, it is also where most progress has been registered (+13.1 since 2010 and +1.9 from 2018-2019 alone). Results are uneven amongst Member States. While the question of the deficit of women in politics and the importance of gender balanced participation and representation as conditions for effective democracy and good governance have been on the EU agenda for 30 years, progress has been slow and irregular in space and time. As to gender-balanced management and leadership functions, while it has been widely documented that a gender balance can boost innovation, competitiveness and productivity,[208] progress is very unequal, with some Member States even showing a

---

207    The domain of *power* measures gender equality in *political* decision-making positions (representation of women and men in national parliaments, government and regional/local assemblies), in *economic* decision-making (proportion of women and men on corporate boards of listed companies and national central banks) and *social* power, which includes research-funding organisations, media and sports. See EIGE (European Institute for Gender Equality), Gender Equality Index 2021 (Luxembourg: Publication Office of the EU, 2021), https://eige.europa.eu/publications/gender-equality-index-2021-health

208    International Labor Office Bureau for Employers' Activities, *Women in business and management: the business case for change* (Geneva: International Labour Organization, 2019), https://www.ilo.org/wcmsp5/groups/public/---dgreports/---dcomm/---publ/documents/publication/wcms_700953.pdf

regression, as demonstrated by the negative figures for Slovenia and Romania since 2017, and in the Czech Republic, Hungary and Poland since 2010 in *Figure 8* below.

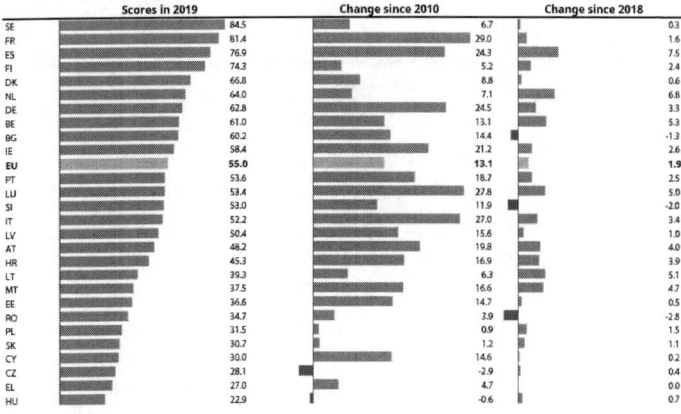

| | Scores in 2019 | Change since 2010 | Change since 2018 |
|---|---|---|---|
| SE | 84.5 | 6.7 | 0.3 |
| FR | 81.4 | 29.0 | 1.6 |
| ES | 76.9 | 24.3 | 7.5 |
| FI | 74.3 | 5.2 | 2.4 |
| DK | 66.8 | 8.8 | 0.6 |
| NL | 64.0 | 7.1 | 6.8 |
| DE | 62.8 | 24.5 | 3.3 |
| BE | 61.0 | 13.1 | 5.3 |
| BG | 60.2 | 14.4 | -1.3 |
| IE | 58.4 | 21.2 | 2.6 |
| **EU** | 55.0 | 13.1 | 1.9 |
| PT | 53.6 | 18.7 | 2.5 |
| LU | 53.4 | 27.8 | 5.0 |
| SI | 53.0 | 11.9 | -2.0 |
| IT | 52.2 | 27.0 | 3.4 |
| LV | 50.4 | 15.6 | 1.0 |
| AT | 48.2 | 19.8 | 4.0 |
| HR | 45.3 | 16.9 | 3.9 |
| LT | 39.3 | 6.3 | 5.1 |
| MT | 37.5 | 16.6 | 4.7 |
| EE | 36.6 | 14.7 | 0.5 |
| RO | 34.7 | 3.9 | -2.8 |
| PL | 31.5 | 0.9 | 1.5 |
| SK | 30.7 | 1.2 | 1.1 |
| CY | 30.0 | 14.6 | 0.2 |
| CZ | 28.1 | -2.9 | 0.4 |
| EL | 27.0 | 4.7 | 0.0 |
| HU | 22.9 | -0.6 | 0.7 |

**Fig. 8**   Scores in the domain of power and its subdomains (2018), and changes over time.

The factors that discourage women in politics and public life as well as the economy and social sectors, range from harassment in the workplace to stereotypes about gender roles and an unequal sharing of family responsibilities.

While quotas have shown to be effective measures to encourage women to take leadership positions,[209] this is still depicted as a controversial measure, hence the very slow and sometimes reversing progress.

So far, the European Commission has been treading very carefully in this field: after years of 'trying other means', a fairly weak directive for increasing the proportion of 'women on boards' was proposed in 2012.

---

209    Notably, in 2020, women made up 37.6% of the board members of the largest listed companies in the 6 Member States with binding quotas. *European Gender Equality Report* (March 2021), 39.

Compared to the bold example of Norway,[210] the proposed directive is very moderately ambitious, suggesting improving the gender balance only in non-executive positions in publicly listed companies, and by means of transparency and the use of objective criteria in the selection process of board members. Today, the directive is still blocked in the Council. Its adoption, announced under the French presidency of the European Union in the first semester of 2022, would help confront hidden blockages to women's entry into many 'boys' club' business circles in Member States. What would trigger action to correct the shamefully low number of women in executive and leadership positions of companies? In 2020, merely 1 in 10 CEOs was a woman and 1 in 5 held an executive position, with vast differences between Member States who had already adopted legislation and those who had not.

The European Commission, led by a woman president and a gender-balanced college, is certainly a better place than ever to promote gender-balanced public and private assemblies and organisations. This objective, in line with the Sustainable Development Goals, is even more necessary to address the consequences of the covid-19 crisis in a balanced, inclusive and efficient way.

The European Commission has been leading by example in showing that rapid progress towards a gender balance was possible with political will and high-level commitment. The College of Commissioners is composed of 13 women and 14 men, and the Strategy commits the Commission to reach a gender balance of 50 percent of all its management functions[211] by 2024[212] through a series of binding measures, targets and monitoring. It will also promote a "no women no panel" policy to ensure a balanced participation of women as speakers and panellists in conferences.

210     Aagoth Storvik and Mari Teigen, *Women on Board: the Norwegian experience* (Berlin: Friedrich Ebert Stiftung, 2010), https://library.fes.de/pdf-files/id/ipa/07309.pdf

211     including the management of EU agencies

212     As of 2021, there were 41% women among senior managers and 43% among middle managers. European Commission, *2021 report on gender equality in the EU*, (Luxembourg: Publications Office of the European Union, 2021), ://op..//just/2021-report-gender-equality/en/

The strategy also proposes to make use of the means available at EU level to promote a gender-balanced participation in Member States, in political parties, in the media, in sport and in the private sector, including:

- *Legislation*, eg the women on boards directive
- *Policy measures*, eg the European Democracy Action Plan which fosters inclusiveness and equality in democratic participation, gender balance, and proactive steps to counter anti-democratic attacks seeking to dissuade women and minority groups from being politically active
- *Funding* (structural reform programmes to help Member States develop strategies to promote women politicians at local level
- *Facts and figures*, eg the Gender Equality Index and the Women in Decision-Making Database managed by EIGE[213]

A special case is made for promoting the participation of women as voters and candidates in the 2024 European Parliament elections through funding and promoting best practices. A high-level meeting with European political parties will take place in 2022 to promote gender balance and a greater diversity of candidates.

## 4) Gender mainstreaming and intersectionality

*"In all its activities, the Union shall aim to eliminate inequalities, and to promote equality, between men and women."*

– Article 8 of the Treaty on the Functioning of the European Union (TFEU)

When this article was introduced in the Treaty of Amsterdam in 1997, Eliane Vogel Polsky, one of the chief academic contributors to the European gender equality policy (and a shrewd lawyer), welcomed the commitment to eliminate inequalities but also the *positive* obligation made on the Union to *actively* promote equality between women and men in its policies. This was, in her view, a giant step towards a completely new approach to equality: not only would positive ac-

---

213    EIGE, Gender Statistics Databas: Women in Decision-Making, https://eige.europa.eu/gender-statistics/dgs/browse/wmidm

tions (initiated in the early 1980s) continue to correct inequalities resulting from the past, but the introduction of *gender mainstreaming* opened a new era in which women and their historic experience would be taken into account in order to actually change the design and substance of policies to fit both women and men.

As a matter of fact, this article was effectively used, under the impulse of two women commissioners to integrate gender into regional policy, and research and education policy in the 1990s.[214] However, the declarations of intent in most of the previous roadmaps and strategic engagement did not have the intended impact, neither at EU nor at national levels. Data from the European Institute for Gender Equality (EIGE) shows that the performance of EU Member States in gender mainstreaming has been *decreasing* from a rating of 8.4 in 2012 to 7.4 in 2018,[215] with a decreasing availability of mainstreaming structures and use of gender mainstreaming tools.

Will the EU, armed with the Gender Equality Strategy 2020-2024, actually manage to better embed a gender perspective into new policies? The positive signs for success under this strategy are:

- the manifest commitment of the President and the Commissioners in charge to deliver on gender equality
- the creation of a task force on equality[216] and the appointment of equality coordinators in all European Commission services, and
- the European Pillar of Social Rights and its action plan providing a basis to integrate gender across socio-economic policies

---

214   Agnès Hubert and Maria Stratigaki, "Twenty years of EU gender mainstreaming: Rebirth out of the ashes?" *Femina Politica, Zeitschrift für feministische Politikwissenschaft* 25, no. 2 (2016): 7-8.

215   EIGE, "H3 Gender Mainstreaming" in Gender Statistics Data Base (2020), https://eige.europa.eu/gender-statistics/dgs/indicator/genmain_cont_bpfa_h3__bpfa_h3/line/year:2018

216   Previous progress in regional policy and research happened within the group of commissioners for equality between women and men created by President Santer in 1995 which was diluted in 2005 and disappeared in 2010.

- New funding should be available under the Next Generation EU recovery plan of €750 million, which puts an obligation on Member states to explain how they intend to mainstream gender equality[217] with the money available. The same obligation applies to the Recovery Assistance for Cohesion and the Territories of Europe (REACT-EU) operational programmes.

- Technical expertise has been developed by EIGE, not only to monitor progress in gender mainstreaming but also via a 'gender mainstreaming platform' which provides methods for gender mainstreaming implementation, an online toolbox, as well as sector-specific analysis on gender equality issues, contributing to knowledge-based development and capacity building. This expertise is used in particular to monitor progress towards the objectives of the gender equality strategy.

The Commission has started to integrate a gender perspective into many of its policy areas, although with uneven success: Health, the European Green Deal, the new European Research Area, Erasmus+ and the Digital Education Action Plan 2021-2027, Horizon Europe, ie the Framework research programme for 2021-2027 which has considerably strengthened its gender equality provisions.[218]

The most significant impact may come from provisions for the implementation of the seven-year budget framework, known as the *Multiannual Financial Framework* (MFF). Within the MFF, the European Commission is working on a 'methodology to track expenditure related to gender equality at programme level' to reinforce the gender dimension of its *impact assessments*, whilst drafting guidelines

---

217     Art 18.4(o) of regulation (EU) 2021/241; and commission guidance to Member States SWD (2021)12 final, p.11.

218     Where an assessment has been made by external bodies like the European Environment Bureau for the European Green Deal, the mainstreaming efforts are deemed somewhat limited. See European Environmental Bureau (EBB) and Women Engage for a Common Future (WECF), "Why the European Green Deal needs ecofeminism" (Brussels: EBB. 16 July 2021), https://eeb.org/library/why-the-european-green-deal-needs-ecofeminism/

on *socially responsible public procurement* to fight discrimination and promote equality between women and men in public tenders.

Other institutions like the European Parliament have traditionally shown much interest in gender mainstreaming and gender budgeting.[219] The European Court of Auditors (ECA), which acts as the guardian of the EU budget, recently published an audit report on "gender mainstreaming in the EU budget: time to turn words into action"[220] in which it recalls:

*"Gender-responsive budgeting is not just about funding explicit gender-equality initiatives. It is about understanding the impact of budgetary and policy decisions on gender-equality goals, and using this information to adjust for inequalities by introducing changes to public expenditure and revenue."*

The ECA report concludes by urging the Commission, "to rigorously apply gender budgeting in its 2021-27 budget cycle but also in the Next Generation EU Instrument". This, in addition to factors mentioned above, could mark a turning point in the way gender mainstreaming, supported by gender budgeting, is implemented under the new strategy.

This presentation of the main processes at work within the EU-GES would not be complete without mentioning the transversal principle for all the actions and initiatives: *intersectionality*. EIGE defines 'intersectionality' as an "analytical tool for studying, understanding and responding to the ways in which sex and gender intersect with other personal characteristics/identities, and how these intersections contribute to unique experiences of discrimination."[221] These characteristics include discrimination based on racial or ethnic origin, religion or belief, disability, age or sexual orientation. The intersectional approach to gender equality is reflected, for instance,

---

219 The first EU study on gender budgeting by the Commission in 2006 was conducted upon a request of the European Parliament

220 European Court of Auditors, "Special Report 10/2021: Gender mainstreaming in the EU budget – time to turn words into action" (26 May 2021), https://www.eca.europa.eu/en/Pages/DocItem.aspx?did=58678

221 European Institute for Gender Equality (EIGE), "Glossary & Thesaurus: Intersectionality," https://eige.europa.eu/thesaurus/terms/1263

in the "EU Roma strategic framework for equality, inclusion and participation", which includes targeted measures for women and girls, or in the "European Commission Action plan on integration and inclusion 2020-27" which provides specific attention, measures and funding for migrant women.

## 5) Promoting gender equality and women's empowerment across the world

This chapter of the strategy is crucial for ensuring a coherence between internal and external EU action and the implementation of the Sustainable Development Goals (SDGs). External action for gender equality, including EU enlargement, has traditionally been programmed in its own multiannual action plan but faithfully reflects the objectives of the Strategy. The former action plan on gender equality and women's empowerment in external relations for 2016-2020 (GAP II) focused on ending violence against women and girls, promoting women's economic and social empowerment and ensuring the fulfilment of their human, political and civil rights. Building on the achievements and lessons learned, GAP III (2021-25)[222] adopts a comprehensive approach based on five pillars:

1. The principle of gender mainstreaming is to be enforced in all sectors, including infrastructure, digital, energy and agriculture. A set of objectives and indicators are available to monitor the progress of its implementation and measure its results at country, regional and international levels.

2. A common approach for all EU actors, focusing on selected strategic issues, will be deployed at country level. Careful gender analysis and close consultation with Member States, civil society organisations, women's rights activists, and young Europeans, will provide a firm foundation for actions on the ground.

---

222    EU High Representative for Foreign Affairs and Security Policy, "EU Gender Action Plan III: an Ambitious Agenda for Gender Equality and Women's Empowerment in EU External Action [JOIN(2020) 17 final]"(Brussels: Commission, 25 November 2021), https://ec.europa.eu/commission/presscorner/detail/en/IP_20_2184

3. Accelerating progress in the fight against gender-based violence and promoting the economic, social and political empowerment of women and girls. A renewed emphasis is put on universal access to healthcare, sexual and reproductive health and rights, and gender equality in education, as well as on promoting equal participation and leadership. It also fully integrates the EU policy framework on Women, Peace and Security, and brings the gender perspective into new policy areas, such as the green transition and the digital transformation.

4. The current gender action plan (GAP III) also calls for the European Union to lead by example, including by establishing gender-responsive and gender-balanced leadership at top political and management levels.

5. It also introduces a new approach to monitoring, evaluation and learning, with a stronger focus on measuring results. The EU will set up a quantitative, qualitative and inclusive monitoring system to increase public accountability, and ensure transparency and access to information on its assistance to gender equality worldwide.

The transformative approach of the new action plan involves the participation and leadership of girls and women (to be promoted through governance programmes and public administration reforms); women, girls and young people being empowered to use their rights and increase their participation in political, economic, social, and cultural life; and gender being mainstreamed in all policies and actions.

GAP III also aims to address structural causes of gender inequality and gender-based discrimination, for instance by actively engaging men and boys in challenging gender norms and stereotypes. Finally, to leave no one behind, the action plan seeks to tackle all intersecting dimensions of discrimination, paying specific attention for example to women with disabilities, migrant women, and discrimination based on age or sexual orientation.

In the first year of the plan's implementation, the EEAS (European External Action Service) has stepped up its actions against gender-based violence both within its partnership with the UN Spotlight Initiative (the world's largest initiative to eliminate all forms of violence against women and girls by 2030),[223] and through new actions to support women and girls in vulnerable positions in conflict or hard to reach areas (deployed within the Instrument contributing to Stability and Peace (IcSP). Further, access to health and the impact of covid on women in the labour market (with ILO) have been at the forefront of the policy.

## The velvet triangle: agents and networks

*For those who care passionately about (...) gender justice, the problems still need to be addressed by actors from different places in the political world. The velvet of passion for gender justice is still the appropriate glue, even if it is no longer a triangle being held in place.*[224]
– Alison Woodward

If it is to make progress, gender equality requires more change of convictions and persuasion than any other policy as it touches on deeply ingrained beliefs and behaviours. Hence the crucial importance of the connections between those who, by function and/or conviction, contribute to spreading the word in different contexts: the academics who produce transformative analysis to support policies, civil society activists who relay the needs for change, and policy makers who transpose these needs into policies.

The *velvet triangle* is a heuristic concept coined by Alison Woodward[225] to describe the interactions between policy makers and politicians, feminist academics and experts, and the women's movement in European Union policymaking. This unusual and informal structure, which reached its peak of influence in the nineties (see part II), has been at the origin of a very rapid development of the policy.

---

223    The programme covers 26 countries and 6 regions with a regional initiative for Central Asia and Afghanistan launched in 2020.

224    Alison Woodward, "Travels, triangles and transformations: implications for new agendas in gender equality policy," *Tijschrift voor Genderstudies* 18, no. 1 (2015): 5-18.

225    Alison Woodward, "Building Velvet Triangles: gender and informal governance," in *Informal governance and the European Union,* ed. Thomas Christiansen and Simona Piattoni (London: Edward Elgar, 2003): 76-93.

These unorthodox, dynamic but 'uncontrolled' contributions to policymaking did not always please the 'bureaucracy' which undertook to break the informal networks by a wave of 'professionalisation'.[226] Still, not only did these velvet triangles survive and travel[227] but – despite the streamlining of the policy in the name of gender mainstreaming[228] and the new constraints imposed on feminist actors by one-size-fits-all obligations[229] – the spirit of the velvet triangle re-emerges regularly as a reaction to possible attacks on the policy and under the influence of the increased number of women and feminists in decision-making positions.

Amongst the official bodies concerned by the velvet triangle, we will consider:

- the European Commission, which plays a central role having the main power of initiative and a dedicated service,
- the European Parliament with its emblematic Women's Rights and Gender Equality (FEMM) committee,
- the European Women's Lobby and social partners representing civil society, and
- equality bodies in the EU and Member States like Equinet, the EU Advisory Committee on equal opportunities for women and men[230] and the European Institute for Gender Equality (EIGE).

---

226   For an academic analysis of the *velvet triangle* and attempts to its dismantling, see chapter 4 in Sophie Jacquot, "Transformations in EU gender equality: from emergence to dismantling" *Power and politics* (2015).

227   Alison Woodward, "Travels, Triangles and Transformations: Implications for New Agendas," in *Gender Equality Policy* (Amsterdam University Press, 2015).

228   Maria Stratigaki "Gender Mainstreaming vs Positive Action: an Ongoing Conflict in EU Gender Equality Policy," *European Journal of Women's Studies* 12, no. 1 (May 2005): 165-186.

229   There are many examples but one significant one is the standardisation of reporting obligations and administrative procedures of EU agencies imposed on EIGE, which has by far the smallest budget of all agencies.

230   The *Advisory Committee on equal opportunities for women and men* helps the European Commission prepare and implement activities aimed at

We will leave aside the Council of the European Union and its 'high level group on gender equality indicators' which has not yet made its mark on the policy. A formally dedicated *Council configuration* for gender equality where ministers in charge would meet would certainly make a difference in the way gender equality is dealt with by the Council. In spite of the repeated calls made by progressive actors[231] and the European Parliament,[232] gender equality issues are still debated on an *ad hoc* basis in the Employment, Social Policy, Health and Consumer Affairs (EPSCO) formation of the Council. This means that gender policy is mostly discussed by ministers present for other issues. In other words, the ministers specifically in charge of this portfolio are left without a dedicated forum to ensure a better integration of gender equality into EU policy processes. This unsatisfactory situation is partly responsible for the blockages seen in the last 15 years on the *maternity* directive, the *women-on-boards* directive and the *Istanbul Convention* ratification process. The EU being the seat of compromises between the different positions of 27 Member States, a dedicated forum to discuss positions and options is what brings a policy to life.

## The European Commission

The European Commission (EC), though it is more open to change than most national executives – comprising diverse languages and cultures – has traditionally been a patriarchal institution. The slowly

---

promoting equal opportunities for women and men. This platform facilitates ongoing exchanges of relevant experience, policies and practices between EU countries, social partners at EU level and NGOs. See Advisors Committee [E01238] website https://ec.europa.eu/transparency/expert-groups-register/screen/expert-groups/consult?do=groupDetail.groupDetail&groupID=1238&NewSearch=1&NewSearch=1

231   PES Women, "It is time to create a formal Council configuration for Gender Equality" (2020), https://pes.eu/en/news-events/news/detail/PES-Women-It-is-time-to-create-a-formal-Council-configuration-for-Gender-Equality/

232   "European Parliament resolution of 17 December 2020 on the need for a dedicated Council configuration on gender equality (2020/2896(RSP))," https://www.europarl.europa.eu/doceo/document/TA-9-2020-0379_EN.html

Fig. 9
Commission
Hallstein
(1958–76)

Fig. 10
Commission Delors II (1989-94)

Fig. 10a
Vasso Papandreou

Fig. 11    The European Commission 2019-24 (13 women and 14 men).

changing composition of the College of Commissioners (the political level of the decision-making body of the EC) is a good indicator. For many years (1957-89), the College was a men's club (see Fig. 9 of the Hallstein commission, p.119).

The very first not exclusively male College was appointed in 1989 (Fig. 10, p. 119) when Vasso Papandreou (Greece, see Fig. 10a, p.119) and Christiane Scrivener (France) became the first female commissioners. It would take another 30 years to have a gender-balanced college, on the insistence of the first female President of the EC, Ursula von der Leyen (Fig. 11, p. 119).

The EC staff has followed a similar pattern. The first alarm bell was rung by the staff committee in 1986, giving rise to the first *positive action* programme. At the time, women represented 50 percent of the staff but only 14 percent of the personnel in executive positions (recruited with a university degree).Despite successive positive action programmes and an EU gender equality policy advocating for parity democracy since 1992 (see the Athens summit in part II), progress was very slow until successive enlargements (first to the Nordic and then the Eastern Member States) brought a cultural change. Finally, one of the achievements of the Commission chaired by Jean-Claude Junker (2015-20), with Kristellina Gieorgeva in charge of human resources, female managers at all middle and senior levels reached 41 percent, up from 30 percent within five years. In 2020, 42 percent of middle managers and heads of units are women but the most impressive progress has been achieved at the very top of the organisation where female Directors-General now make up 38 percent of the total. Similarly, at Deputy Director-General level, women currently hold 40 percent of the posts. In five years, progress has been faster than in the last 50 years. These achievements now place the EC amongst the public administrations around the world with the highest share of women in leadership positions. This should be a driving factor for a change in the way gender equality is mainstreamed.

Coming back to the velvet triangle, the femocrats[233] were traditionally to be found in the dedicated units: the women's information unit,[234] ie the 'equal opportunities for women and men' unit in DG Employment and the (on and off) 'equal opportunities' unit in DG for Personnel. Most other Directorates General had, at best, one or two dedicated officials dealing with equality issues in their policy area and in their personnel. Changes came in the nineties with the disappearance of the Women's Information Bureau and the emergence of the 'women and science' unit in DG Research.[235] These changes, added to the transfer of the main 'equal opportunities policy' unit from DG employment to DG Justice, have made the velvet triangle more dispersed in the EC. The question today is how the commitments to gender justice made by the new structure of the von der Leyen Commission will materialise into a real empowerment of a truly feminist Commissioner for Equality and Task Force for Equality.[236]

---

233   A term coined in Australia in the eighties to describe feminists bringing women's policy positions into government. Later, the term became used neutrally to refer to feminists in official bodies at various levels of governance from regional to national and supranational. See for instance: Anna Yeatman, *Bureaucrats, technocrats, femocrats: essays on the contemporary Australian state* (Sydney: Allen & Unwin, 1990), 180-191; or Marian Sawer, "Femocrat," in *The Wiley Blackwell Encyclopedia of Gender and Sexuality Studies* (Oxford: Wiley Blackwell, 2016), 1-2.

234   Created and headed by Fausta Deshormes, the Women's Information Bureau published *Femmes d'Europe*, a quarterly magazine in which national correspondents (generally members of the women's movement) would exchange news on the situation of women in each Member State.

235   Which has been downgraded to a 'sector'.

236   With the support of the Task Force on Equality created at the beginning of the mandate, the Commission aims at integrating an equality perspective in all EU policies and majors initiatives. In addition to supporting Commissioner Dalli in her daily work and contributing to the delivery of concrete initiatives promoting equality, the Task Force plays a key role in mainstreaming equality in all policies, from design to implementation. It is composed of representatives of all Commission services and the European External Action Service. See: European Commission, "Union of equality: the first year of actions and achievements" (2020), https://ec.europa.eu/commission/commissioners/2019-2024/

## The FEMM committee of the European Parliament

The European Parliament, despite its multinational composition and its subsequent openness to diversity in cultures and languages, is no exception to the rule of patriarchal institutions either. Both its seats and its staff positions have been largely filled by men, with only one MEP in seven being a woman in the first directly elected European Parliament in 1979. The first significant change came in the 1994 EP election where a wind of change was brought. A campaign to "vote for women" financed by the European Commission and progressive political parties resulted in an increased share of female MEPs with 1 in 4 members being a woman. Moreover, the Athens Declaration (see part II, disseminated throughout Europe and beyond in the form of postcards by a reinvigorated feminist movement)[237] and the upcoming enlargement to Nordic countries were major contributing factors to more women in the EU Parliament. Subsequent progression towards parity was then constant up to the last EP election of June 2019 where it was almost reached with 40.4 percent (38.8 in 2021 as a consequence of Brexit). A special effort has occurred in this parliament to have an equal representation in decision-making posts of Parliament as a whole (8 vice presidents and 12 committee chairs). All political parties but one are chaired by men (the Socialists and Democrats group being the exception), and one party has a co-presidency shared by a woman and a man (the Greens/EFA).[238]

Right from the first directly elected parliament in 1979, solidarity between the few elected women guaranteed the situation of women would find its place in the new democratic assembly. The Committee

---

dalli/announcements/union-equality-first-year-actions-and-achievements_en

237  The European Women's Lobby took an active part not only in the Athens Summit but also in the new policy for having more women in power positions.

238  For more characteristics of party politics and women's representation in the EP, see https://www.tandfonline.com/doi/full/10.1080/00344893.2021.1898458

on Women's Rights[239] was eventually given the status of a permanent committee in 1984. Before that, female MEPs had obtained the creation of an *ad hoc* committee, chaired by socialist MEP and French feminist Yvette Roudy. Its mission was to analyse the situation of women within the European Community. This committee's work led to the adoption in February 1981 of a resolution on 'the situation of women in the European Community'. In June 1981, the EP set up a *committee of inquiry* to monitor the achievement of the objectives set by the 1981 resolution. This committee proposed, in a resolution of January 1984, setting up a permanent committee. Its responsibilities[240] included "the definition and evolution of women's rights in the EU, the implementation of directives relating to women, social and employment policy, female unemployment, women's role in the family, the situation of women in the EU institutions and the problems of migrant women."

Since its inception, the Committee on Women's Rights has confirmed its role as a forum for debating gender inequalities. It has played a decisive role in defining and promoting women's rights within the EU. It has made a major contribution to strengthening the provisions on equal opportunities and non-discrimination in the Amsterdam and the Lisbon Treaties, and during the Convention on the Future of Europe. It has fought for the implementation of gender mainstreaming (including in the European Parliament, ie in presence of women and content of the work of all the other committees and ruling instances),[241] for positive action and for the implementation

---

239    The name of the committee changed to committee on women's rights and gender equality, now familiarly called the FEMM committee.

240    laid down in Annex VI, point XIX of the Rules of Procedure of the European Parliament

241    Since 2003, when Parliament formally launched gender mainstreaming activities within the institution, its FEMM Committee has regularly prepared monitoring reports on the state of gender mainstreaming in the EP. The subsequent resolutions, adopted in 2007, 2009, 2011, 2016 and 2019, are part of a whole series of activities over the past two decades to support and intensify gender mainstreaming in the EP, notably the adoption of a new Gender Action Plan (July 2020) and a roadmap for its implementation (April 2021).

of the principles of the Beijing Platform for Action. Over the years, it has contributed to widen the scope of the gender equality policy via its successive programmes and strategies. In the context of the 1998 employment guidelines, it helped make equal opportunities one of the pillars of the new strategy. Since the first *annual report on gender equality* in 1996 it has closely monitored progress as reported by the EC. As its legislative competences are limited, this committee has made extensive use of its right to initiate reports on new and/or controversial issues, and to push the Commission to adopt a more ambitious approach. When the committee was formally set up in 1984, violence against women (VAW) became one of its focal points. Long before this issue made its way into public debate, the Dutch socialist MEP Hedy d'Ancona produced a report on violence against women, which led to the EP resolution on VAW presenting it as a gender equality problem deeply rooted in structural inequalities between women and men.[242] Yet, the labour market focus of the EU has posed a major barrier for the velvet triangle to achieve an EU-coordinated approach to address VAW, resulting in a fourfold focus:

1) sexual harassment,
2) trafficking in human beings,
3) domestic violence and
4) VAW in external relations.

More recently, the FEMM Committee has played its role in alerting public opinion and the Institutions to the impact of the pandemic on domestic violence, and to the general backsliding of gender equality alongside the worrying regression of sexual and reproductive health across the EU. The backlash against abortion rights and access to comprehensive sex education, but also LGBTIQ+ rights in Poland and Hungary severely jeopardise gender equality advancements. MEPs called for a continuous monitoring of these rights and of regressive initiatives and disinformation in all Member States, for an alarm sys-

242    European Parliament Resolution A2-44/86 on violence against women, https://www.europarl.europa.eu/EPRS/PE2_AP_RP!FEMM.1984_A2-0044!860001EN.pdf

tem to highlight when rights are taken away and for sanctions to be enforced. Concerned by the reticence of some Member States concerning the Istanbul convention, the Committee similarly pushed for an EU framework directive to prevent and combat all forms of gender-based violence and called for binding measures to define and prohibit violence and harassment at work. Following the pandemic, MEPs also called for levelling up wages and working conditions in female dominated sectors such as care, health and retail sale.

It is worth mentioning that the FEMM committee has consistently been chaired by progressive MEPs with two exceptions (see list of chairs and their political groups below).

**List of FEMM Committee Chairs**
Committee on women's rights
1984–1987 **Lenz Marlene** Germany / EPP
1987–1989 **d'Ancona Hedy** Netherlands / PES
1989–1992 **Crawley Christine M.** United Kingdom / PES
1992–1994 **Crawley Christine M.** United Kingdom / PES
1994–1997 **van Dijk Nel B. M.** Netherlands / Greens Group
1997–1999 **van Dijk Nel B. M.** Netherlands / Greens Group
              **Hautala Heidi** Finland / Greens Group

Committee on Women's Rights and Equal Opportunities
1999–2002 **Theorin Maj Britt** Sweden / PES
2002–2004 **Karamanou Anna** Greece / PES

Committee on Women's Rights and Gender Equality
2004–2007 **Záborská Anna** Slovakia / EPP
2007–2009 **Záborská Anna** Slovakia / EPP
2009–2012 **Gustafsson Mikael** Sweden / GUE–NGL
              **Svensson Eva–Britt** Sweden / GUE–NGL
2012–2014 **Gustafsson Mikael** Sweden / GUE–NGL
2014–2019 **García Pérez Iratxe** Spain / S&D
2019–2022 **Regner Evelyn** Austria / S&D
2022–2024 **Robert Biedron** Poland / S&D

## The European Women's Lobby (EWL)[243]

The EWL was created in 1989. Its creation was linked to the emergence of new forms of interaction between citizens and political officials at European level. It provides information to decision-makers to ensure that women's rights and needs are taken into account in the preparation of policies and legislation whilst promoting the participation of women's organisations at EU level, and providing them with the information they need to be proactive. It has played a major role in bringing together the women's movement in Europe and to promote women's interests in the construction of Europe.

With very limited means[244] but with the informal support of the velvet triangle and the strength of national coordination networks of women's organisations, it has brought together and influenced both European Institutions and the general public in support of women's human rights and equality between women and men. Being the largest European umbrella network of women's associations, it represents more than 2000 organisations in 27 EU Member States, three candidate countries, Iceland, and the United Kingdom.

Over its 30 years of existence, the contribution of EWL has been particularly crucial in the Athens summit in 1992, the Beijing Conference in 1995, the Amsterdam Treaty in 1997, and the enlargement process in 2004. Each EU election is an occasion to call for gender balance in the EP through its '50/50 campaign. Members of the EWL have been very proactive campaigning on violence against women campaigning at all levels. Since 2018, the League has been advocating for a 'purple pact' which frames 'a feminist approach to the economy'.[245]

Through its network of good and continuous relations with academics, politicians, and policy makers involved with gender equality; the EWL is at the core of the *velvet triangle* community.

---

243    https://www.womenlobby.org/Mission-vision-and-values-588

244    It gets the smallest grant of all social and human rights interest groups which get regular support from the European Commission.

245    European Women's League (EWL), "Purple Pact: it's Time for a Feminist Approach to the Economy", https://www.womenlobby.org/Purple-Pact-It-s-Time-for-a-Feminist-approach-to-the-Economy

## The European Institute for Gender equality (EIGE)

In 1999, inspired by the dynamism of the Nordic council model, the Swedish minister for social affairs and gender equality suggested the creation of a European Agency for Gender Equality. The European Commission financed a feasibility study without drawing any conclusions. It was only in 2004 that the European Parliament decided to launch another study[246] – with the support of the Irish presidency of the Council of the EU – and called for the establishment of an EU agency to support the promotion of gender equality in Europe.

The process got entangled into a difficult political context where the proliferation of agencies with different sets of rules and objectives had raised concerns in the institutions which undertook to negotiate a complex interinstitutional agreement on agencies[247]. The European Gender Institute, a rather small institution when compared to other agencies (eg the European Environment Agency or the Fundamental Rights Agency) was chosen to set an example of rigour in the ongoing controversies, having to accept disproportionate administrative and reporting obligations, gender balance in its board, and a seat away from institutions headquarters – when assisting the institutions of implement gender mainstreaming would have required a constant dialogue with policy makers.[248]

Despite these adverse circumstances, the Institute was created by a council regulation agreed in 2006[249] with headquarters in Vilnius (Lithuania) and became fully operational in 2010. In its ten years of existence, it has become a worldwide resource and reference centre for gender equality, in particular thanks to its work on gender

---

246  Yellow Window Management Consultants, "Study: Role of future European Gender Institute" [PE 358.898], (Brussels: European Parliament / DG General Internal Politics, 2004).

247  https://eur-lex.europa.eu/legalcontent/EN/TX-T/?qid=1484571761943&uri=CELEX:52008DC0135

248  Agnès Hubert, and Maria Stratigaki, "The European Institute for Gender Equality: a Window of Opportunity for Gender Equality Policies?" *European Journal of Women's Studies* 18, no. 2 (2011), 169-181.

249  https://eur-lex.europa.eu/legal-content/EN/TXT/?uri=CELEX-%3A32006R1922

mainstreaming and gender budgeting but also on data and its annual flagship Gender Equality Index measuring the EU's advancement towards full gender equality.

## Other bodies

A number of other bodies can be considered as part of the *velvet triangle* for their commitment to gender equality and their networking and coordination with other actors in the field.

First, both **ETUC** (the European Trade Union Confederation) and **Business Europe** (the employers' representative body in Brussels) have been active in informing and influencing gender equality policy – be it officially when they had to negotiate two milestone directives (ie the reversal of the burden of proof and parental leave) under the rules of the European social dialogue, but also when consulted on legislative proposals or significant initiatives, representing employers and workers.

**National gender equality bodies** also intervene in many different forms in the preparation and implementation of gender equality policy – individually when answering consultations or receiving project grants for the citizen's programme but also collectively in **Equinet** and the **Advisory Committee on equality between women and men**. Equinet is an institution created in 1979 for anti-discrimination policy led by the national equality bodies which assist victims of discrimination, monitor and report on discrimination issues, and contribute to an awareness of rights and a societal valuing of equality. They offer legal assistance against discrimination on any of the grounds stated in Article 10 TFEU.[250] The Advisory Committee on equal opportunities for women and men was created in 1981 by a Commission decision subsequently amended in 1995 and 2006. Composed of two representatives per Member State and observers, it assists the European Commission in formulating and implementing the Community's activities aimed at promoting equal

---

250    "In defining and implementing its policies and activities, the Union shall aim to combat discrimination based on sex, racial or ethnic origin, religion or belief, disability, age or sexual orientation." (Art 10 TFEU)

opportunities for women and men, and fosters an ongoing exchange of relevant experience, policies and practices between the Member States and the various parties involved. Over the years, the Advisory Committee has produced multiple progressive opinions on important issues for the policy.[251]

Also forming part of the velvet constellation, two networks, mainly of academics, assist the Commission in the implementation and evaluation of the policy: the **European network of *legal* experts in gender equality and non-discrimination** and the **European network of experts on gender equality**. The former is consulted on legal issues and the latter can offer advice on the policy in context. Under contract for the duration of the EU Gender Equality Strategy, they produce advice on request as well as reports with a future oriented outlook on the policy.

### Socialist Women's and Gender Equality Organisations

Amongst the constituent organisations on a political EU level, **PES Women** plays a major role in driving gender-sensitive progressive politics forward as the Party of European Socialists' women's organisation. Under the leadership of Zita Gurmai as its president (following former presidents Karin Jons and Fiorella Ghilardotti), PES Women has been working within the party, with member organisations, civil society organisations and the general public on gender equality and women's rights issues. Activities span the political scene across of Europe and across the world in order to secure fundamental rights, ensure political will, and push for concrete policies that improve the lives of women and girls in all their diversity. Similarly, **Rainbow Rose**, headed by President Camilla Garfias, promotes LGBTI rights in Europe by bringing together people from Socialist, Labour and Social Democratic parties across Europe. From a youth perspective, **YES** (Young European Socialists, formerly ECOSY) has also played a major part, not only defining feminist values but also implementing

---

251    https://ec.europa.eu/info/publications/list-previous-opinions-advisory-committee-equal-opportunities-women-and-men_en

them inside their own structure since 2005 when Ania Skzrypek was elected as the organisation's first female secretary general. Following her two consecutive mandates, women continued entering into leadership positions with Secretary General Ana Pirtshkalava and President Alicia Homs Ginel breaking the glass ceiling into pieces.

# The scales of justice

The EU has over the years developed a solid and progressive legal framework for gender equality: it consists of obligations under the Treaties and the Charter of Fundamental Rights, of a set of directives[252] and case law of the European Court of Justice (ECJ), renamed the Court of Justice of the EU (CJEU) in the Lisbon Treaty, which has played a very important role in the field of equal treatment between women and men. It has delivered important judgments interpreting EU equality legislation and relevant Treaty provisions but has also ensured that individuals can effectively invoke and enforce their right to gender equality.

## The Treaties

Since the entry into force of the Lisbon Treaty on 1 December 2009, provisions that are relevant to the field of gender equality feature in the Treaty on European Union (TEU), the Treaty of the Functioning of the European Union (TFEU), and the Charter of Fundamental Rights of the EU which has the same legal value as the two Treaties.

The TEU declares that *one of the values* on which the EU is based is equality between women and men (Article 2 TEU). The promotion of equality between men and women throughout the European Union is one of the *essential tasks of the EU* (Article 3(3) TEU). Since the entry into force of the Lisbon Treaty, Article 8 TFEU specifies that

---

252    A directive is a legal act of the European Union which requires Member States to achieve a particular result without dictating the means of achieving that result. Directives first have to be enacted into national law by Member States before its laws are ruling on Individuals residing in their countries.

"[in] all its activities, the Union shall aim to eliminate inequalities, and to promote equality, between men and women."

Article 10 TFEU contains a similar obligation for all the discrimination grounds mentioned in Article 19 TFEU, including sex: "In defining and implementing its policies and activities, the Union shall aim to combat discrimination based on sex, racial or ethnic origin, religion or belief, disability, age or sexual orientation." This provision lays down the obligation of gender mainstreaming. It means that both the EU and the Member States shall actively take into account the objective of equality between men and women when formulating and implementing laws, regulations, administrative provisions, policies and activities. These provisions impose obligations on both the EU and the Member States.

In addition, the Charter of Fundamental Rights of the EU "prohibits discrimination on any ground, including sex" (Article 21); it "recognises the right to gender equality in all areas, and is thus not limited only to employment, and it also recognises the possibility of positive action for its promotion" (Article 23). Furthermore, it also "defines rights related to family protection and gender equality. The Charter guarantees, inter alia, the 'right to paid maternity leave and to parental leave" (Article 33). [253]

## The directives

The development of EU gender equality law has been a step-by-step process, starting with the principle of equal pay between women and men for equal work enshrined in the Treaty of Rome in 1957. Since then, the following directives have been adopted which prohibit discrimination on the grounds of sex:

> • the *Directive on **equal pay** for men and women* (75/117/ EEC, replaced by the recast directive 2006/54/EC below),

---

[253] On the Charter establishing *gender equality* as a fundamental right, see the Lisbon Treaty and the EU Charter of Fundamental Rights, analysed by Sophia Koukoulis-Spiliotopoulos, "The Lisbon Treaty and the charter of fundamental rights: maintaining and developing the acquis in gender equality," *European Gender Equality Law Review* 1 (2008), 15-24.

- the *Directive on equal treatment of men and women in employment* (76/207/EEC, amended by Directive 2002/73/EC and now repealed by Recast Directive 2006/54/EC),
- the Directive on equal treatment of men and women in statutory schemes of social security (79/7/EEC),[254]
- the *Directive on equal treatment of men and women in* occupational social security schemes (86/378/EEC, amended by Directive 96/97/EC and now repealed by Recast Directive 2006/54/EC),
- the Directive on equal treatment of men and women engaged in an activity, including agriculture, in a self-employed capacity (86/613/EEC, repealed by Directive 2010/41/EU),[255]
- the Pregnant Workers' Directive (92/85/EEC),[256]
- the Parental Leave *Directive* (96/34/EEC, repealed by Directive 2010/18/EU),[257]
- the Directive on equal treatment of men and women in the access to and the supply of goods and services (2004/113/EC),[258]
- the so-called Recast Directive (2006/54/EC) which updates the content of all the directives repealed,[259] and, finally,
- the work-life balance *Directive* (EU) 2019/1158 of 20 June 2019 on work-life balance **for parents and carers.**[260]

254 https://eur-lex.europa.eu/legal-content/EN/TXT/?uri=celex-%3A31979L0007

255 https://eur-lex.europa.eu/legal-content/EN/TXT/?uri=celex-%3A32010L0041

256 https://eur-lex.europa.eu/legal-content/EN/TXT/?uri=celex-%3A31992L0085

257 https://eur-lex.europa.eu/legal-content/EN/TXT/?uri=celex-%3A32010L0018

258 https://eur-lex.europa.eu/legal-content/EN/TXT/?uri=celex-%3A32004L0113

259 https://eur-lex.europa.eu/legal-content/EN/TXT/PDF/?uri=CELEX-:32006L0054&from=EN

260 https://eur-lex.europa.eu/legal-content/EN/TXT/?uri=celex-%3A32019L1158

These directives have progressively set common legal standards across Europe, ensuring a duty to promote equality between women and men and a broad protection from discrimination.

## Case law

From the epoch-making Defrenne cases (see part II), well over 200 cases related to gender equality have been brought to the European Court of Justice strengthening the principle of equality and delivering justice for victims of discrimination.

Both directives and the case law have helped to clarify core concepts such as direct and indirect discrimination, or sexual harassment; they have firmed up the rights to equal pay and equal treatment at work; established rights to maternity, paternity, parental and other types of care leaves; created equal treatment in occupational pension schemes and statutory schemes of social security; created rights for self-employed workers; set standards for equal treatment in relation to goods and services, mainly in the insurance sector; case law is on course to setting common standards for preventing violence against women within and beyond the Istanbul Convention. For women in the Member States, this has generally upgraded their rights.

How is European law used by the courts or by gender equality actors? The European network of legal experts in gender equality and non-discrimination (EELN) monitors the implementation of European law by the courts of the Member States in an *annual report*. Its members also hold legal seminars where they review the latest cases and lessons to draw, the use of positive actions,[261] strategic litigation, etc. Their discussions are based on expert reports[262] thus providing

---

261    In a telling presentation to the network, Christopher McCrudden, a longstanding expert of gender equality and non-discrimination, deplores the lack of proper understanding of positive action as a key instrument to promote women's equality in employment and suggest a directive on positive action.

262    European Equality Network, "2019 Seminar: Update on CJEU case law, Positive action in gender equality and non-discrimination [...]," https://www.equalitylaw.eu/seminars/95-2019-legal-seminar-up-

an important source of information for equality lawyers, policy makers and civil society activists who participate in these conferences.

In its latest seminar in 2019, the network noted a persistence of barriers in the access to justice and a lack of judicial mobilisation[263] and strategic litigation by women's organisations in most Member States, deploring the low number of cases and poor use of the EU gender equality law.

## The measure of gender inequalities: work, money, time, power, education and health

Public policies are based on evidence: facts, figures and analysis of the reality they are due to impact. Let's remember, at the end of 1961, governments decided to skip their commitment on equal pay for equal work between women and men made in Article 119 of the Treaty of Rome because of the lack of comparable figures on pay. They appointed a group of experts to work on it but it was not before the nineties that Eurostat and then later the European Statistical System (ESS) started to regularly produce sex disaggregated statistics. These statistics are now widely used and where necessary complemented (eg by the data base on women and decision-making by the European Institute for Gender Equality).

---

date-on-cjeu-case-law-positive-action-in-gender-equality-and-non-dis-crimination-racial-discrimination-in-education-and-eu-equali-ty-law-strategic-litigation-in-gender-equality-and-non-discrimination-religious-ethos-in-employment-and-access-to-goods-and-services-bur-den-of-proof-in-cases-of-gender-equality-and-non-discrimination

263   See also this homage to Eliane Vogel Polsky by Sophie Jacquot, "Activisme juridique: Pourquoi les arrêts Defrenne sont-ils restés orphelins? Ou, pourquoi le Lobby Européen des Femmes n'a-t-il jamais déployé de stratégie d'activisme judiciaire?" *E-Legal, Revue de droit et de criminologie de l'ULB*, no. 3 (April 2019), http://e-legal.ulb.be/volume-n03/hommage-a-eliane-vogel-polsky/axe-3-activisme-juridique-pourquoi-lesarrets-defrenne-sont-ils-restes-orphelins-ou-pourquoi-le-lobby-europeen-des-femmes-n-a-t-il-jamaisdeploye-de-strategie-d-activisme-judiciaire

It all started with employment statistics in the Labour Force Survey (LFS), then came statistics on population, and on income and living conditions (SILC), structure of earnings and labour cost surveys.

Specific gender analyses were made in the nineties by the European Network on women and employment[264] One of the first major reports produced by the network in 1992 was ground-breaking in the revealing new patterns of activity of women, from the 'M' *curve* interrupting employment to raise children to the inverted 'U' *curve* of continuous employment; also surveying reconciliation of work and family and working time of women and men, a further report of the network established that a 32-hours working week would be the perfect match for work-life balance.

The very first comprehensive analysis of sex-disaggregated statistics commissioned by Eurostat was its *Statistical portrait of women and men in the EU*, published in 1995 for the UN Beijing Conference on women. It provided knowledge on activities, employment, education, paid and unpaid work, leisure and resources of women and men in the three stages of life: youth, adulthood and beyond retirement. Two editions of this statistical portrait would follow in 2008 and 2020, allowing for comparisons over time.

Another important source of information for gender equality policy is the *time use surveys* which have been conducted by 18 Member States.[265] Using national data, Eurostat has so far published two rounds of harmonised European Time Use Surveys. The next publication, which starts in 2020, integrates data from those 18 Member States, Norway, Albania, Serbia, Turkey and the United Kingdom.

The next major breakthrough in the use of sex-disaggregated data for policy making is the Gender Equality Index (GEI), which came with the creation of the European Gender Institute (EIGE).

The idea of a European gender equality index was first mentioned in the European employment strategy in 2003 when a feasibility

---

264    which became the Expert Group on Gender and Employment (EGGE) in 1996 and came to an end in 2003

265    Austria, Belgium, Bulgaria, Estonia, Finland, France, Germany, Greece, Hungary, Italy, Latvia, Lithuania, Luxembourg, the Netherlands, Poland, Romania, Slovenia, Spain

study was commissioned,[266] based on the universal care-giver model outlined by Nancy Fraser[267]. This study served as a reference for the elaboration of the current gender equality index of EIGE by a brilliant in-house team of statisticians and gender specialists. The first GEI was published 2013, then biannually, and annually from 2019. The idea was to have a tool to measure progress on gender equality in the EU and its Member States, to highlight areas that need improvement, and ultimately to support policy makers in the EU and Member States to design more effective gender equality measures. The Gender Equality Index entails 31 indicators in the six core domains *work, time, power, money, education* and *health* and the two additional domains *violence against women* and *intersecting inequalities.*

An audit led recently by the European competence centre on composite indicators and the European Joint Research Centre (JRC) concluded positively on the conceptual and statistical coherence of the framework, the quality of the data, and the impact of modelling assumptions on the results. It suggests that meaningful inferences can be drawn from the Gender Equality Index. It confirms that the 2020 GEI meets the quality standards for statistical soundness and acknowledges it as a reliable composite indicator to measure gender equality in the European Union. [268]

The list of useful data for gender equality policy makers, politician and activists would not be complete without a mention of *She Figures* publications,[269] the main source of pan-European, comparable statistics on the state of gender equality in *research and innovation.*

---

266    Janneke Plantenga & al., "Towards a European gender equality index," *Journal of European Social Policy* 19, no. 1, http://dx.doi.org/10.1177/0958928708098521

267    Fraser, Nancy. Justice Interruptus: Critical Reflections on the "Postsocialist" Condition. New York, NY: Routledge, 1997.

268    For a critical review of the strengths and weaknesses of indexes also consider Anne-Laure Humbert and Agnès Hubert, "Gender Equality Index" in *Handbook on Diversity and Inclusion Indices: a Research Compendium*, ed. Eddy Ng et al. 2021, (Cheltenham/Northhampton: Edward Elgar, 2021), 117-132.

269    https://op.europa.eu/en/web/eu-law-and-publications/publication-detail/-/publication/61564e1f-d55e-11eb-895a-01aa75ed71a1

The data, presented throughout six chapters, follow the chronological journey of women, from graduating from doctoral studies to participating in the labour market and acquiring decision-making roles, while exploring differences in women's and men's working conditions and research output. Looking at the evolution over the editions, the reader can see positive changes in certain themes. For instance, there is almost gender parity among doctoral graduates at the earliest career stage. However, in other themes, such as women's representation in decision-making positions and in inventorship, progress remains slow and uneven across the EU. *She Figures* has been released every three years since 2003, and the report constitutes a key evidence base for policies in this area.

The Eurobarometer, a policy making instrument to survey European public opinion, published by European institutions since 1974, is the source of information on what citizens think about gender equality. In its 2017 edition, which entailed questions about gender equality, 9 respondents in 10 answered that "promoting gender equality is important for society, the economy and for [them] personally". For half of respondents, "there should be more women in political decision-making positions", and 7 in 10 are "in favour of legal measures to ensure parity between men and women in politics". More than 8 in 10 respondents said that "a man should do an equal share of household chores, or take parental leave to take care of his children". 90 percent of respondents say that "it is not acceptable for women to be paid less than men", and 64 percent are "in favour of salary transparency as a way to empower change".

A previous Eurobarometer on *violence against women* revealed a great awareness of the topic among European citizens: The survey showed that 1 European in 4 knows a woman among friends and family who has been a victim of domestic violence. 1 in 5 of the EU citizens surveyed said they know someone who commits domestic violence in their circle of friends and family. 87 percent of those surveyed believed that the EU should be involved in the fight against domestic violence.

As analysed by Sophie Jacquot and Celine Belot,[270] "Eurobarometer surveys and the appeal to the 'voice of the citizens' have always had a legitimising function for gender equality, but the purposes of this legitimisation have changed over time. Recently, in a context of low citizen support for the European Union political system, surveys have been integrated into the day-to-day routine of gender equality."

## The double approach: positive action and gender mainstreaming

We have seen earlier the genesis and some of the controversies around the concept of *gender mainstreaming* but also its importance as a tool to advance gender equality. We also have seen that gender mainstreaming did not replace *positive action* for women but was another complementary  tool to be used, as it was firmly established[271] by the Commission Communication on "Incorporating equal opportunities for women and men into all Community policies and activities" in 1996.

In the following section, we will not consider the controversies but how these tools are implemented and what obstacles are to be overcome for proper implementation.

### Positive action

The concept of positive action came on the European agenda in the early eighties as a way to translate *de jure* equality into reality by giving advantages to women (or any underrepresented, disadvantaged group) in order to compensate for their past disadvantages.[272]

---

270    p. 332 in Céline Belot, and Sophie Jacquot, "Eurobarometer Surveys: Another History of European Gender Equality Policy?" *European Journal of Politics and Gender* 3, no.3 (March 2020): 331-347.

271    As it resulted from a difficult internal debate see Maria Stratigaki, "Gender Mainstreaming vs Positive Action: An Ongoing Conflict in EU Gender Equality Policy." *European Journal of Women's Studies* 12, no. 2 (2005): 165-186.

272    The concept was imported from the US where *affirmative action* denotes "positive steps taken to increase the representation of women

In 1984, a Council Recommendation on the Promotion of Positive Action for women[273] proposed that Member States adopt the policy

*to eliminate existing inequalities in working life and to promote a better balance between the sexes in employment, comprising appropriate general and specific measures, within the framework of national policies and practices, whilst fully respecting the spheres of competence of the two sides of industry.* (p.1)

When recalling the Kalanke (1995) and Marshall (1997) cases, we understand that the serious legal debates about positive actions came, years after the introduction of this concept into European texts. In the Kalanke case, the city of Bremen had given priority to a woman with equal qualification for the post, over the male candidate. This measure was meant to compensate for the under-representation of women in decision-making positions in the administration of the city of Bremen but was felt to be discriminatory against the male candidate who went to court. According to the advocate general the only positive action measures allowed would have been offering training (but the female candidate already had equal qualification) or offering childcare (she had no children). This decision of the court was later watered down in the Marshall case, establishing a rule for the implementation of positive action. Yet bitter feeling about positive action persisted. In the European Commission Human Resources policy, the term 'quota' (a sort of specific, temporary measure, generally binding, to create a gender balance in decision-making positions) was replaced by 'targets'. These had with little effect until in the Juncker Commission (2015-20) when political will created binding objectives equivalent to quotas.

---

and minorities in areas of employment, education, and culture from which they have been historically excluded."
See Robert Fullinwider, "Affirmative Action," in *Stanford Encyclopedia of Philosophy*, ed. Edward Zalta, Uri Nodelman et al. (Standford University: Metaphysics Research Lab, 2018), https://plato.stanford.edu/entries/affirmative-action/

273    Council of the European Communities, *Council recommendation of 13 December 1984 on the promotion of positive action for women*, 84/635/EEC https://op.europa.eu/en/publication-detail/-/publication/2c756080-da95-498c-b11d-ee26443f2281/language-en

While quotas are now increasingly seen as one of the best (if not the only) way to create a gender balance in decision-making positions, individuals can rightly feel unfairly treated and contest a breach in a policy of equal treatment – if they do not consider the big picture.

The concept of positive action is still contested in some Member States in the name of universalist rights (including in Eastern European Member States where the principle of equality under communism did not suffer differential treatment).

In the EU gender equality policy, positive action does not only apply to a gender balance in decision-making positions but refers to any specific action dedicated to the achievement of gender equality (it can be specific budgets, campaigns, training, etc.). It warrants that specific attention is paid to the needs of the underrepresented and/or disadvantaged sex.

## Gender Mainstreaming

The idea that gender inequalities would not be corrected only by positive action had gained ground in the Nordic countries in the eighties. Women had been on the labour market since the sixties[274] when the concept of integrating a gender perspective into other instruments of public policies was perceived as necessary. Gender equality was stalling as the effect of positive action was being cancelled by decisions made in mainstream policies which did not account for the specific situation of women. Hence the concept of integrating a gender perspective into all policies was perceived as a way to go forward.

Often, when considering gender equality policies, the effect of programmes and projects is to give with one hand what is going to be taken away by mainstream policies conceived without women's interests in mind. An example could be decisions to apply budget restrictions to social services, cancelling the provision of childcare facilities.

---

274    When other Member States called on migrants in the sixties, the social democratic governments in Nordic countries attracted women on the labour market to fulfil the needs of a growing economy.

Still, even if it was initially welcomed by those who wanted to advance gender equality in a more structural way, there is a lot of evidence to prove that the concept of gender mainstreaming has been met with resistance. The first resistance came from those who saw it as an opportunity to dilute gender equality policies and dismantle specific measures and institutions. The affirmation of the *double approach* (mainstreaming plus positive action) by the European Commission came as a welcome reaction. The second source of resistance was linked to the perceived lack of legitimacy of gender equality. Hence the 'maieutic method'[275] conceived by the Commission in its first communication on gender mainstreaming.[276] Unfortunately, this was not followed up on, and with no specific introduction of the new policy, the very concept of integrating a gender perspective into 'their' policy domain, when it was not lost in translation, was raising different forms of resistances from managers in institutions.[277] The third form of resistance came from the complexity of the concept of gender mainstreaming which discouraged most policy makers. The definition of gender mainstreaming as coined by the Council of Europe is:

"The(re)organisation, improvement, development and evaluation of policy processes, so that a gender equality perspective is incorporated in all policies at all levels and at all stages, by the actors normally involved in policy making."[278] This implies many layers of

---

275    Maieutic comes from the Greek word for midwifery. In one of Plato's dialogues, Socrates applies *maieutikos* to his method of bringing forth new ideas and conceptions previously latent in one's mind by reasoning and dialogue. The technique was compared to that of a midwife delivering a baby.

276    This communication was never presented to the College. By the time it was ready, the Commission's priority was the mainstreaming of employment into policies, side-lining gender equality. This episode is related by Sophie Jacquot, "L'égalité au nom du marché? Emergence et démantèlement de la politique européenne d'égalité entre les femmes et les hommes," (Bruxelles: Éditions P.I.E. Peter Lang, 2014), 153-155.

277    From a number of interviews with managers in the European Commission, Sophie Jacquot created a typology of resistance to gender mainstreaming ("L'égalité au nom du marché?" 2014, 189-194).

278    definition by the Council of Europe, which is the most frequently used

action which require knowledge, expertise and resources. None of these elements are widespread.

## Gender mainstreaming: A personal anecdote

When I was appointed head of the unit for 'equal opportunities for women and men' in the European Commission with the task of implementing the Third Action Programme, I found the word 'mainstreaming' for the first time in my life. The European Commission had to produce *a* "communication on gender mainstreaming". When trying to understand what was required, I imagined having to convince my colleagues in DG Transport (a male bastion) that all the railway gauges would have to be changed on all the rail networks because medical research had found that the existing width of the gauge was creating vibrations which were dangerous for pregnant women. When I further imagined the reaction of my colleagues in transport...I was about to refuse the post.

This was an illustration of the possible scope (and costs) of integrating a gender perspective into a policy area.

There is an abundant literature on the 'stop-an-go' implementation of gender mainstreaming in the EU.[279] As a general rule, however, progress has been disappointing so far in light of the expectations and efforts deployed.[280] However, the context is changing...

First, as already mentioned, the current European Commission presided over by Ursula von der Leyen, assisted on gender equality by

---

279    Agnès Hubert and Maria Stratigaki, "Twenty years of EU gender mainstreaming: rebirth out of the ashes?" *Femina Politica, Zeitschrift für feministische Politikwissenschaft* 25, no. 2 (2016), 7-8.

280    For both efforts and some early results, see "Progress report from the Commission on the follow-up of the Communication: 'Incorporating equal opportunities for women and men into all Community policies and activities'" [COM(1998) 122 final].

two commissioners,[281] is showing determination to achieve results. In particular, the special task force for equality under the responsibility of Commissioner Dalli is in charge of gender mainstreaming.

Second, the European Gender Equality institute EIGE (whose tasks include "to develop, analyse, evaluate and disseminate methodological tools in order to support the integration of gender equality into all Community policies and the resulting national policies and to support gender mainstreaming in all Community institutions and bodies")[282] has now reached maturity and offers concrete methodologies, tools and processes to help decision makers at all levels with understanding and implementing gender mainstreaming.

Third, one would hope that gender equality has, at least amongst progressive actors, gained legitimacy.

Fourth, the context is changing in the field of budgeting. Following the commitment to *gender-responsive budgeting* in the Gender Equality Strategy, it was also mentioned in the interinstitutional agreement accompanying the Multiannual Financial Framework 2021-26, as well as the European Court of Auditors's report on gender mainstreaming. The Commission (DG Budget) is now engaged in updating its impact assessment guidelines, in developing a methodology to track gender expenditure considering dedicated programmes (like Daphne), in creating a systematic data catalogue, and in developing specialised training programmes for the staff with EIGE and the European University Institute. This could mark the beginning of a landslide change in the implementation of gender mainstreaming.

## How to mainstream gender in your policy area

The concept definition having been agreed upon, EIGE now outlines its different *dimensions* to ensure the gender mainstreaming of policies. Firstly, it looks at the representation of women and men in the policy area (as policy beneficiaries, in the labour force and in the de-

---

281    Vice president Jourova and Commissioner Dalli

282    Regulation (EC) No 1922/2006 of the European Parliament and of the Council of 20 December 2006 on establishing a European Institute for Gender Equality

cision-making processes). Secondly, it consider the gender-responsive content of the policies (Are the needs of all citizens adequately addressed?). The *enabling conditions* include proper preparation and having people with the power to introduce change). Then, the *policy process* is presented as a **4-stage cycle**, namely the *defining*, *planning*, *implementing*, and *checking* (monitoring and evaluating) stages.

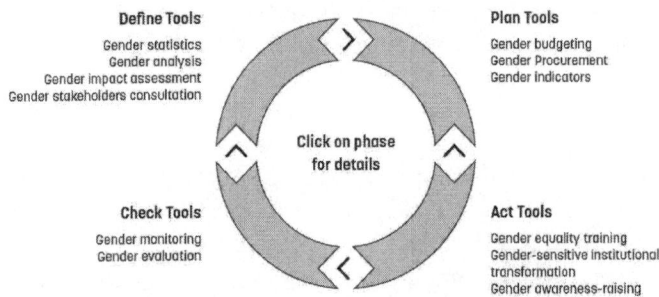

Fig. 13

## Communicate on what gender equality is doing for Europe and vice versa

"Why 81% of the members of the European Parliament shave in the morning" – this sentence is one of the slogans[283] used in the Europe wide campaign "vote for women" launched with the European Network on women in decision-making, in the preparation of the 1994 European elections. In fact, within a convergence of other favourable circumstances, the percentage of women in the EU Parliament elected in 1994 climbed from 19 to 27 percent (and that of men decreased from 81 to 73 percent). It may not be enough to prove

---

283 Another slogan was "Can you imagine a world with 81% Romeos and 19% Juliets?"

that communication and humour always work when trying to change deeply ingrained stereotypical perceptions about the role of women and men, but it is worth trying.

Recently, the European Women's Lobby has understood the power of communication to convince women to take an interest in the European Union. It is however a vain struggle without stronger institutional backing and substantial resources to reverse the male-dominated, competition-oriented image of the European Union.

The European Council, the body that features most regularly in national news, is not likely to help women identify with Europe (see Fig. 14). Hence the symbolic importance to have women like the President of the European Commission at the wheel, even if she is most often surrounded by men or even instrumentalised to show a supposed inferiority of women – as happened in the widely mediatised 'sofagate' when she was refused a seat with her male counterparts during a meeting hosted by the Turkish prime minister in Istanbul.[284]

Against this backdrop, it is regrettable that the European Commission has not maintained a specific department dealing with the information interaction with women's organisations in the Member States (eg its former 'Service Information Femmes' which in the seventies and eighties was doing just that as reflected inter alia in the *Femmes d'Europe* publications.[285] Occasionally, a Europe-wide campaign on violence against women or equal pay is commissioned. It is never connected to an overall communication strategy on what Europe is doing for women.

Gender equality and the EU would have a common cause in upgrading the way they interact with the wider public.

This said, the role of *institutions* and *interest groups* is important in passing on the message of how women and Europe could gain from

---

284    "Von der Leyen says 'sofagate' shows the need to tackle sexism" (27/04/201). Euractiv. Retrieved from: https://www.euractiv.com/ section/non-discrimination/news/von-der-leyen-says-sofagate-shows-need-to-tackle-sexism/

285    Historical Archives of the European Union, *Femmes d'Europe* (Brussels: EC Commission Directorate-General for information, communication and culture, 1977-92), https://archives.eui.eu/en/isaar/46

each other. To this end it would be helpful to have both a dedicated service for women's information in the European Commission, and increased resources for actors (EWL and women's organisations) to develop a continuous flow of information on gender in the EU. Let us now consider now *ideas*, the third element in the triad *Institutions, Interests and Ideas* – which is so crucial if communication is to play its part in the transformative power of gender equality. This will be approached in the next chapter.

Fig. 14

# Part IV : Issues at stake

Women are the first to suffer in times of crisis. This was the case during the financial crisis in 2008,[286] and the covid-19 crisis is no exception either. The pandemic has exacerbated existing inequalities between women and men in almost all areas of life, in Europe and beyond, rolling back on the hard-won achievements of past years. According to estimates available in some countries, domestic violence has increased by 30-50 percent,[287] pushing the UN to declare the outbreak of a 'shadow pandemic' with figures of gender-based violence spiking.[288] More women than men have lost (and will still lose) their jobs. Moreover, women are overrepresented in the sectors and occupations that have been locked down, and they represent the majority of frontline workers whose essential role has suddenly been brought to light.

Alerts, evidence, and calls for action on this topic come from multiple sources. The European Commission sees the pandemic as a major challenge for gender equality and its annual Gender Equality Report,[289] presented on 8 March 2021, highlights multiple negative effects of the covid-19 pandemic on women. EIGE has presented a detailed picture of the pandemic's impact on essential workers, economic hardship, unpaid care and housework, health, gender-based

286    Maria Karamessini and Jill Rubery (ed.), *Women and Austerity: The Economic Crisis and the Future for Gender Equality* (Abingdon/ New York: Routledge, 2013).

287    https://www.undp.org/sites/g/files/zskgke326/files/publications/un-dp-gender-GBV_and_COVID-19_0.pdf

288    UN Women, "The Shadow Pandemic: Violence Against Women and Girls and COVID-19" (6 April 2020), https://www.unwomen.org/en/digital-library/multimedia/2020/4/infographic-covid19-violence-against-women-and-girls

289    European Commission, "2021 report on Gender Equality in the EU", https://ec.europa.eu/info/sites/default/files/aid_development_cooperation_fundamental_rights/annual_report_ge_2021_en.pdf

violence, and people in vulnerable situations, concluding that co-vid-19 has "derailed gender equality gains".[290] Very early on after the breakout of the crisis, UN Women summarised data, research, and policy work on the pandemic's impact on women and girls, including effects on extreme poverty, employment, health, unpaid care, and violence against women and girls. Their work brought into focus the paucity of gender data, calling for greater investment and prioritisation of data on the gendered effects of the crisis. The UN secretary general later issued a policy brief[291] which strongly outlines suggested priority measures to accompany both the immediate response and longer-term recovery efforts. As highlighted by an article drafted for McKinsey at the peak of the pandemic in Spring 2020, "given the trends we have observed over the past few months, in a gender-regressive scenario in which no action is taken to counter these effects, we estimate that global GDP growth could be $1 trillion lower in 2030 than it would be if women's unemployment simply tracked that of men in each sector."[292] The International Labour Organization (ILO) "sees the challenges and opportunities in building a transformative agenda for gender equality", and emphasises the "actions needed to support the role of women as agents of change towards a human-centred path to a more equal world of work in the Covid-19 pandemic and beyond."[293] Some analysts like Maria Jepsen[294] (deputy director of Eurofound) can imagine a positive scenario post-covid-19 "[b]ecause the measures introduced during the pandemic

290    EIGE, "Covid-19 derails gender equality gains," https://eige.europa.eu/news/covid-19-derails-gender-equality-gains

291    UN Secretary-General's policy brief: The impact of COVID-19 on women (April 2020), https://www.unwomen.org/en/digital-library/publications/2020/04/policy-brief-the-impact-of-covid-19-on-women

292    Anu Madgavkar et al., "COVID-19 and gender equality: Countering the regressive effects" (McKinsey & Company, 15 July 2020), https://www.mckinsey.com/featured-insights/future-of-work/covid-19-and-gender-equality-countering-the-regressive-effects

293    https://www.ilo.org/gender/Events/WCMS_773334/lang--en/index.htm

294    Maria Jepsen, "Good news for gender equality as we exit the Covid-19 crisis?" *Social Europe* (April 2021), https://socialeurope.eu/good-news-for-gender-equality-as-we-exit-the-covid-19-crisis

have led to a realisation that many workers – mostly women and for very different reasons – are not adequately covered, there is a general reassessment of the welfare systems in place to cover citizens who fall between the cracks. This paves the way for a largely positive outlook, in which the pay and conditions of many frontline workers are deemed inadequate, leading to structural improvements in both. Remote working does become a mainstay of working life for all, but with workplaces introducing measures to counteract potential negative impacts, enabling men and women better to share unpaid work". However, the author also identifies a darker, alternative scenario where the reverse could happen if gender issues were not mainstreamed in the recovery: "gender equality will regress as women (mostly low-paid) find it hard to re-enter the labour market, as sectors reopen in an asymmetric, modified and hesitant manner. Remote work will become a permanent feature and women will embrace it so as to continue to assume the lion's share of unpaid work – as a consequence, they will become invisible in the workplace and lose out on training and promotions. Budget constraints will bring a halt to social investment in child – and eldercare, and restrictive measures will be introduced with regard to income replacement." The European Women's Lobby (EWL) has raised awareness concerning the stark increase of violence against women, and lobbied institutions to take the situation of women into account in the distribution of recovery and new generation programme funds. EWL calls for more EU action as "[t]he current Covid-19 crisis has only made the need for coordinated EU action on women's rights clearer to everyone. It is proof that inequalities between women and men are persistent and that unpaid and undervalued care – overwhelmingly provided by women – is the backbone of our societies." Also, a number of newspaper reports have repeatedly underlined the paradox of the better performance of women in leadership positions and the small number of women amongst experts chosen by governments or the media to provide advice on strategies. "It's time to make women truly count" was the message sent out in March 2021 by a group of European socialist ministers for gender equality, composed of Mariana Vieira da Silva (Portugal), Franziska Giffey (Germany), and Tytti Tuppurainen

(Finland),[295] together calling on Europe to use recovery plans as an opportunity to enact *structural change* for gender equality. Finally, the upsurge of gender-based violence and the need to upgrade all gender equality policies, including sexual and reproductive health and rights, is raised strongly by the European Parliament in its resolution of 21 January 2021 about the gender perspective on the covid-19 crisis and post-crisis periods.[296]

## Regression or rebirth

As almost all these reports, studies, calls, articles, letters and resolutions highlight that the covid-19 crisis has increased and exposed pre-existing inequalities and discrimination, including intersectional discrimination. For instance, evidence shows that women in poverty (who often belong to other vulnerable groups based for instance on migrant or ethnic origin) are amongst the most heavily and negatively affected by the covid-19 pandemic, which acted as a magnifying glass on their vulnerability. Very often, the sort of discrimination they are confronted with is three-dimensional as their socio-economic status is closely linked to their race, age or disability. The *good news* is, as recognised by many stakeholders, that the EU Gender Equality Strategy 2020-2025 is an ambitious text, which could provide answers to compensate for the increasing disadvantage of women on the la-

---

295    Mariana Vieira da Silva is minister of state for the presidency in Portugal. Franziska Giffey was federal minister for family affairs, senior citizens, women and youth in Germany. Taina Bofferding is minister for equality between women and men in Luxembourg. Tytti Tuppurainen is minister for European affairs and ownership steering and leader of Social Democratic Women in Finland.
See Mariana da Silva, Franziska Giffey, Taina Bofferding, and Tytti Tuppurainen, "It's time to make women truly count," *Social Europe* (15 March 2021), https://socialeurope.eu/its-time-to-make-women-truly-count

296    European Parliament resolution of 21 January 2021 on the gender perspective in the COVID-19 crisis and post-crisis period [2020/2121(INI)], https://www.europarl.europa.eu/doceo/document/TA-9-2021-0024_EN.html

bour market, to fight violence against women, including domestic violence, to take measures to increase the participation of women in decision-making positions, and to boost action to promote gender equality in the EU's external policies. The *bad news* however is that the calls made by women's movements[297] for a forceful 'European Union to act in solidarity showing a strong, coordinated and brave leadership in making this Strategy a reality' only underline the perceived marginality of gender equality in EU policies. The EWL formulated concrete recommendations to the Member States[298] asking for a reinforcement of national gender equality bodies and for gender equality to be given more prominence in their recovery plans.

In a documented report on the impact of covid-19, the experts of the first European feminist think tank *Gender Five Plus* (G5+) list its challenges for gender equality in the aftermath of this public health crisis as follows:[299]

- Combatting gender-based violence and its effects
- Recognising the value of jobs in female dominated sectors and the contribution of migrant women
- Achieving a more equal sharing of care and domestic work
- Reducing gender inequalities in the labour market
- Taking back control of women's health
- Stopping the spread of anti-democratic and anti-gender politics
- Increasing the participation of women in decision-making

297 EWL. "4 reasons why the new Gender Equality Strategy (2020-2025) is key in responses to the COVID-19 crisis and its aftermath", 20 May 2020, retrieved from: https://www.womenlobby.org/4-reasons-why-the-new-Gender-Equality-Strategy-2020-2025-is-key-in-responses-to

298 EWL's recommendations to EU Member States and to the European Parliament to ensure the implementation of the Gender Equality Strategy (2020-2025) leaves no woman behind: https://www.womenlobby.org/IMG/pdf/ewl_s_recommendations_to_member_states_on_the_eu_gender_equality_strategy.docx-2.pdf

299 Nelli Kambouri, "Towards a gendered recovery in the EU, women and equality in the aftermath of the Covid 19 Pandemic" (G5+, August 2020), 2, https://f3a391c2-4245-4e49-aa95-5dc4452adce4.filesusr.com/ugd/530efa_ba5024aa406c4c309ca74f22177098c5.pdf

As mentioned earlier, some of these issues are already addressed by the EU Gender Equality Strategy but the covid-19 crisis requires its accelerated implementation, together with the gender mainstreaming of economic and budgetary policies still moving too slowly and unevenly. Some research suggests that the focus of the Recovery Plan will result in higher gender inequality in the field of employment, for instance.[300] In its above-mentioned report, G5+ formulates a set of recommendations for a more holistic approach to guide the EU's policy responses in three major interlinked directions for a paradigmatic shift towards a caring economy, parity democracy and a new model for growth in Europe. Some of the arguments upholding this three-fold approach are explained below.

## Shaping a caring economy

The report suggest "a paradigm-shift from economic activities based on competition to those based on care to secure the well-being of future generations."[301] Considering that the crisis has highlighted that "[g]rowing populations, ageing societies, changing families and the spectre of future global health issues render care-work a most significant socio-economic activity that should be at the centre of efforts to organise a sustainable post pandemic recovery,"[302] policy makers should recognise the centrality of care both as a human right and a driver of economic dynamism. The authors warn that this will require a major shift in our thinking (from a competition to a value-driven ethos) and in our investments:[303]

300    Elisabeth Klatzer and Azzurra Rinaldi, "Next Generation EU leaves women behind: Gender Impact Assessment on the EC proposal for #Next Generation EU" (June 2020), https://plataformamulheres.org.pt/site/wp-content/ficheiros/2020/10/Sumario-Gender_Impact_Assessment_NextGenEU_Klatzer_Rinaldi.pdf

301    Kambouri for G5+ (2020), 24.

302    Kambouri for G5+ (2020), 23.

303    Similar conclusions are reached by Sabine O'Hara (2014), "Everything Needs Care: Toward a Context-Based Economy". In Bjørnholt, Margunn; McKay, Ailsa (eds.).

*Major public investment is necessary to allow care facilities to respond to people's needs throughout the life cycle, supported by investments in gender sensitive public infrastructures, training and education facilities. An economy driven by a value-based care system must be supported by macro-economic tools and mechanisms including a gender sensitive tax framework and gender budgeting to ensure that public expenses and financial investments serve equality goals.*[304]

The heart of gender equality, as underlined by feminist economists, comes down "to take into account the grossly unequal burden that women carry in relation to paid and unpaid labour", which is in large part invisible. The report concludes with an idea raised by many feminist economists:[305] "As the motor fuelling future economic activities, caring for others should also extend to the environment and sustainability."

Echoing this research, the *Care4Care* project launched by the Foundation for European Progressive studies (FEPS) and the Friedrich Ebert Stiftung (FES), which was summarised in the policy brief "Towards a fairer, care-focused Europe" in 2021,[306] sets forth a 10-points action plan made of practical steps to move towards a European care deal.

## A 10-point action plan for a European care economy (FEPS-FES Care4Care)

1. Adopt an overall people-centred approach, respecting gender equality, intersectionality and generational divides, paying attention to all phases of life;

---

304    Kambouri for G5+ (2020), 24.
305    Similar conclusions are reached by Sabine O'Hara (2014), "Everything Needs Care: Toward a Context-Based Economy". In Bjørnholt, Margunn; McKay, Ailsa (eds.).
306    Barbara Helfferich, "Policy Brief: Towards a fairer, care-focused Europe. FEPS-FES: March 2021.

2. Craft sound statistical analyses and indicators to measure care, its provision and their impact on well-being, welfare and gender equality;

3. Establish 'care checks' and care-monitoring mechanisms to be included in the procedures for social and economic impact assessment required before presenting legislation (e.g. through already existing governance tools such as the European Semester). Such care checks need to include impact on gender equality and on the quality of care provision and of carers' working conditions;

4. Encourage investment in gender-proven public infrastructures, including crèches and care facilities or services for elderly family members and family members in need of care;

5. Secure sufficient public investments via the Structural Funds;

6. Apply gender budgeting;

7. Use macro-economic tools and mechanisms to put care at the centre of economic activities;

8. Re-design the tax framework and re-direct substantial public investment in and valuing of care;

9. Train and educate family carers and acknowledge the value of their work and its relevance for gender equality;

10. Promote self-care, which needs to be acknowledged for its importance rather than being undermined due to women's disproportionate unpaid care burden.

## Parity Democracy in the EU and Member States

There are at least three reasons for advocating the urgency of reaching gender parity in decision-making posts and using all existing powers to achieve it:

First, with political will, gender balance in decision-making is recognised as a precondition for an effective integration of gender equality in all EU legislation and funding. Considering the increased importance of mainstreaming gender equality into policies and programmes in the covid-19 recovery and the current lack of gender perspective in the recovery plans,[307] having more women in decision-making positions is vital. This could already justify more binding measures to reach gender parity.

Second, as illustrated in a topical G5+ report,[308] the pandemic has strengthened anti-democratic governance trends in some EU Member States, along with misogynist policies. Anti-democratic, far-right trends were evident in Europe prior to the covid-19 outbreak, but authoritarian modes of decision-making have been reinforced in some Member States during the pandemic, raising concerns about anti-equality gender discourses and policies.

Third, progress is still slow despite years of pressure from the *velvet triangle* but also commitments of EU institutions from the Gender Equality Strategy to the European Pact for Gender Equality.[309] The indicator of access to power has the lowest score of the Gender Equality Index.[310] In 2021, only 15 percent of the EU's presidents and

---

307    Economic stimuli under the recovery plan seem to be geared mainly to industries with high male employment (energy, construction, agriculture, transport and digital) neglecting care and health, education and social workers, and culture, not to mention domestic work, which employ mainly women.

308    Alazne Irigoien, "European Parliament's Elections 2019: towards parity democracy in Europe," (G5+, 2018), 9-10, https://www.genderfiveplus.com/parity-democracy

309    Member States committed to gender equality through the European Pact for Gender Equality, originally adopted in 2006. A revision of the pact was prepared under the Hungarian Presidency of the European Council in the first half of 2011, to provide fresh impetus and to support the link between the pact and Europe 2020, and the European Commission's Strategy for equality between women and men 2010–2015. In March 2011, a new European Pact for Gender Equality (2011–2020) was adopted, aimed at encouraging the EU and Member States to take measures to address gender inequality. It also reaffirms the importance of integrating the gender perspective into all policies, including external actions of the EU. Source: Eurofound (2017). European Pact for Gender Equality. Retrieved from: https://www.eurofound.europa.eu/observatories/eurwork/industrial-relations-dictionary/european-pact-for-gender-equality

310    EIGE, "Gender Equality Index 2020: Digitalisation and the future of work," https://eige.europa.eu/publications/gender-equality-index-2020-digitalisation-and-future-work

prime ministers, and 30 percent of Member State governments were women. At global level, women only govern 18 countries or 545 million people, corresponding to 7 percent of the world's population. Women have also been overwhelmingly under-represented in the decision-making bodies responding to the covid-19 crisis, both at European and national levels.[311] Their voices and especially the voices of women belonging to social groups most exposed to covid-19, were neither sufficiently represented nor considered in the responses to the pandemic. While the majority of those working in jobs critical for the response to the covid-19 crisis are women, a very limited number of women scientists and qualified medical professionals participated in the committees making decisions about the pandemic, translating a major democratic and efficiency deficit.

Measures to be considered by the makers and stakeholders of the policy are of two kinds. Firstly, *soft* tools to apply the concept of *parity democracy* in its wide meaning. Secondly, *hard* policies to impose binding measures wherever possible.

G5+ argued in favour of a parity democracy concept that "does not limit itself to increasing the number of women in politics, decision-making positions and democratic bodies but entails a transformation of our understanding of democracy, political culture and structures" (p.3). Thus, what feminist and 'mother of social Europe' Eliane Vogel Polsky pointed out in 1994 still holds true: "If parity is recognised as a critical prerequisite for democracy, then the rules of the game and social norms will have to change."[312] Achieving gender balance in decision-making is not only a matter of justice or fairness – recalling that women represent half of the European population – but also a

---

311     Zsuzsa Blaskó, Eleni Papadimitriou, and Anna Manca, "Science for Policy Report: How will the COVID-19 crisis affect existing gender divides in Europe?" (Joint Research Centre, 2020), [EUR 30181 EN], https://ec.europa.eu/jrc/en/publication/eur-scientific-and-technical-research-reports/how-will-covid-19-crisis-affect-existing-gender-divides-europe

312     Vogel Polsky, E.(1994) "Les impasses de l'égalité ou pourquoi les outils juridiques visant à l'égalité doivent être repensés en termes de parité", Parité Infos. Hors Série, 1994, no. 1, p.9

matter of having better, more effective policies developed and decisions taken as women's participation in decision-making adds "half of the talents, knowledge, skills, creativity, and ideas" (to use the words of the President of the European Commission) necessary to address challenges like the covid-19 pandemic.

This argument is largely supported by recent research conducted on leadership and crisis management during the covid-19 pandemic. Jack Zenger and Joseph Folkman carried out a notable study for the Harvard Business Review, which gives gender-segregated ratings across 19 competencies deemed essential for exerting leadership.[313] While women are rated more positively on 13 out of 19 of these indicators, men slightly outscore women (55/53) only on technical or professional expertise (see Fig. 15, p. 158). All in all, the close scores show the advantage of having mixed teams.

Other statistical data on the impact of female and male leadership in crisis management suggest that countries with female leaders had six times fewer confirmed covid-19 deaths from covid, as well as more rapid, effective 'pandemic- flattening' processes than countries ruled by male leaders.[314] It is argued that female leaders are ostensibly less likely to underestimate the risks and to delay responses; they have also relied more heavily on preventive measures and long-term social welfare benefits, rather than on short-term economic considerations.[315]

Will the Conference on the Future of Europe create an opportunity for discussing ways to secure gender parity in EU governance? Many scholars note that parity democracy would establish the right to equality between women and men as a *structural prerequisite for*

313    Jack Zenger and Joseph Folkman, "Research: Women Are Better Leaders During a Crisis" (30 December 2020), https://hbr.org/2020/12/research-women-are-better-leaders-during-a-crisis

314    Tomas Chamorro-Premuzic and Avivah Wittenberg-Cox, "Will the Pandemic Reshape Notions of Female Leadership?" Harvard Business Review (June 2020), https://hbr.org/2020/06/will-the-pandemic-re-shape-notions-of-female-leadership

315    Fioramonti, Coscieme, and Trebeck, "Women in power is a matter of life and death," *Social Europe* (1 June 2020), https://www.socialeurope.eu/women-in-power-its-a-matter-oflife-and-death

## Women Outscored Men on Most Leadership Competencies

According to an analysis of 360-degree reviews during the pandemic, women were rated higher on most competencies.

| Competencies (• — where difference is statistically significant) | Ratings: Women | Ratings: Men |
| --- | --- | --- |
| • Takes initiative | 60 | 50 |
| • Learning agility | 59 | 50 |
| • Inspires and motivates others | 59 | 52 |
| • Develops others | 58 | 49 |
| • Builds relationships | 58 | 51 |
| • Displays high integrity and honesty | 57 | 49 |
| • Communicates powerfully and prolifically | 57 | 52 |
| • Collaboration and teamwork | 56 | 50 |
| • Champions change | 56 | 51 |
| • Makes decisions | 56 | 49 |
| Innovates | 56 | 53 |
| Solves problems and analyzes issues | 56 | 53 |
| Customer and external focus | 56 | 54 |
| • Drives for results | 55 | 48 |
| • Values diversity | 55 | 45 |
| • Establishes stretch goals | 55 | 50 |
| Develops strategic perspective | 55 | 54 |
| Technical or professional expertise | 53 | 55 |
| Takes risks | 52 | 51 |

Source: Zenger Folkman, 2020 HBR Fig. 15

*democracy.*[316] This would seem important in particular to strengthen the power of the EU to end national so-called 'emergency' measures, which contravene the European gender *acquis,* with injunctions fol-

316 Rubio-Marin, R. (2012): New European Parity-Democracy Sex Equality model and why it won't fly in the
United States. The American Journal of Comparative Law, 60 (1), pp. 99-125; Gubin, E. (2007): Eliane Vogel-Polsky, une femme de conviction. Institut pour l'égalité des femmes et des hommes, pp. 1-170. D/2007/10.043/11; and Irigoien (2018) G5+ report.

lowed by sanctions. The EU must make use of its powers to stand by agreed value, force reluctant governments to rescind legislation that violates the basic rights of women and minorities, and implement gender parity in government decision-making posts. The European Union's main institutions have exhorted Member States to adopt gender quotas to increase the proportion of women in decision-making.[317] It is time for Member States to implement those recommendations.

The democratic deficit rooted in low rates of female participation in politics and decision-making should be treated as a matter of urgent concern; parity cannot be achieved without the introduction of gender quotas at EU level, no matter how politically controversial this might seem. According to the European Council's position on the Conference on the Future of Europe,[318] the conference itself "should focus on topics that truly matter to our citizens with long lasting impacts and wide outreach", suggesting a serious interest in the issue of parity democracy.

## Towards a New Model for Growth in Europe

According to G5+, the 2008 economic crisis generated calls to move major economies away from a primary focus on the financial sector and towards investing in the 'real' economy, capable of delivering security, stability, and sustainability. From a progressive standpoint, the covid-19 crisis is a further wake-up call, indicating the need for a paradigm shift, towards a just, sustainable Europe that focuses on health, care and the environment. There is a growing public demand

---

317   Shreeves R., M. Prpic and E. Claros (2019) "Women in politics in the
        EU: state of play" European
        Parliamentary Research Service.
        https://www.europarl.europa.eu/RegData/etudes/BRIE/2019/635548/
        EPRS_BRI(2019)635548_EN.pdf

318   European Council, "Conference on the Future of Europe: Council
        agrees its position" (24 June 2020),  https://www.consilium.europa.eu/
        en/press/press-releases/2020/06/24/conference-on-the-future-of-eu-
        rope-council-agrees-its-position/

for a change in course. The covid-19 crisis has been a telling indicative of the failure of the current system to deliver a healthy, safe and just environment. Angry electorates have signalled this to their leaders and will continue to do so. As described earlier, women are particularly hard-hit as workers and carers by the economy itself, the burden of care only being a side effect thereof. "It's not all about care, says Brigitte Young (emerita professor of international political economy at the university of Munster) in an indignant piece[319] about the lack of considerations on how traditional macroeconomics has fundamentally made care invisible. Together with a few other feminists and economists,[320] she suggests "analysing the care economy in the larger context of financialisation and the monopolistic extraction of value at the expense of value creation in the real economy."[321] Traditional economists, she says, ignore the care sector because the choice of data for statistical accounting, such as the Gross National Product (GNP), is based on the experience of men as the default, creating gender-blind outcomes: **"Such inadequate metrics have led to wrong policies and widened the gender gap"**. She exhorts feminists to "deconstruct the 'black box' of global finance" which is perniciously increasing inequalities, at the expense of the poorer strata of society with, on average, more women. "Feminists," she says,"need to design a concrete but ambitious strategy for social and economic well being which could be linked to the Sustainable Development Goals and the ideal of a social economy Europe".

The first step of such a strategy to secure fundamental changes in a sustainable way, would be to develop a new model of growth, based on alternative indicators that focus on a more caring (for people and the environment), gender-equal society and economy in Europe. In order to achieve their social and environmental objectives, EU institutions and Member States should seize the current opportunity to jettison the focus on the type of economic growth that has almost

319    Brigitte Young, "Covid 19, women and the economy: its not all about care," *Social Europe* (12 July 2021), https://socialeurope.eu/covid-19-women-and-the-economy-its-not-all-about-care

320    Marianna Mazzucato, Maja Göpel, Kate Raeworth and Ann Pettifor

321    Brigitte Young 2021

exclusively shaped policy making over the last 40 years. In the name of economic and financial growth, the push for constant increases in the production and consumption of poor-quality products has been fostering unlimited waste, poor health, the enslavement of workers worldwide, and ecological damage. The agenda outlined in *Beyond GDP* is not new.: following a large conference held in 2007, the European Commission produced a communication with a plan of action.[322] In February 2008, the OECD issued a report by the Stiglitz Commission on "The Measurement of Economic Performance and Social Progress".[323] These advances disappeared from the political agenda with the financial crisis of 2008 but not from the working agenda of institutions like the OECD and the European Commission. Moreover, Eurostat and the European Statistical System (ESS) made progress in generating more precise social, gender-disaggregated and environmental indicators. Today, the need to secure an equitable, sustainable recovery from the covid-19 crisis and the urgency to act on climate change make it the right moment to shift towards political decisions based on new ecological, societal and gender-balanced indicators. The European Commission could propose that both the *Gross Social Domestic Product* and the *Gross Environmental Product* be applied in addition to GDP in guiding and assessing major EU economic initiatives like the European Semester and recovery plans. Experts within European institutions have accumulated substantial knowledge regarding the use of alternative indicators (including the *Gender Equality Index* – GEI), as have members of the research community and civil society organisations, all of which should be gathered and channelled into EU policy making.

322  "Communication from the Commission to the Council and the European Parliament: GDP and beyond – measuring progress in a changing world" [COM/2009/0433 final], https://eur-lex.europa.eu/legal-content/en/TXT/?uri=CELEX%3A52009DC0433

323  Stiglitz Commission, "The Measurement of Economic Performance and Social Progress," https://ec.europa.eu/eurostat/documents/8131721/8131772/Stiglitz-Sen-Fitoussi-Commission-report.pdf

## "Our bodies, ourselves"

This is an old title from the 1970s, when a group of scholars in Boston realised that they knew and controlled very little about their own bodies and wrote an epoch-making book on women's health and sexuality which spread all over the world and was translated in 33 languages. Some five years ago, I was most surprised when a group of young feminist asked me to give a talk on the EU gender equality policy under this heading. I realised then how strongly the slogan relates to the deep trends of the current period, calling for policy interventions relating to some of the pertinent issues raised in the book, such as sexual orientation and preferences, gender identity, sexual health, birth control, abortion, pregnancy and childbirth, violence and abuse, or what is now known under the UN denomination of SRHR or Sexual and Reproductive Health and Rights.

On the positive side, violence and abuse against women and girls but also the rights of LGBTIQ+ communities feature now on the European agenda.[324]

Revitalised by the #Metoo movement, the mobilisation of women worldwide to "expose and challenge the persistence of patriarchy"[325] has never been so strong. With better knowledge of their rights and the encouragement from the digital and real-life mobilisation to create women's support groups of all sorts, victims have started to dare voice their concerns and take control of their life while challenging the patriarchal 'state'. The same goes for those who do not feel at ease with their assigned sex and wish to be free from gender stereotypical norms. They start to express their concerns, sometimes in radical ways, after years of suffering in silence.

---

324 European Commission Studies and research on LGBTIQ+ equality, https://ec.europa.eu/info/policies/justice-and-fundamental-rights/ combatting-discrimination/lesbian-gay-bi-trans-and-intersex-equality/ studies-and-research-lgbti-equality_en

325 Enloe, Cynthia. *The Big Push: Exposing and Challenging the Persistence of Patriarchy*. 1st ed. University of California Press, 2017. https://doi. org/10.2307/j.ctv1g248zv.

These emancipation movements of women with all their intersecting discriminations including sexual orientation are more visible than ever before. Individuals and Movements articulate their claims and are being listened to by policy makers.

This said, there is also a growing reaction by various vanguards of the patriarchal order against losing control. This shows what a cornerstone of the patriarchy is being shaken. This patriarchal backlash crystallises around the term 'gender', best exemplified by the blockage around the Istanbul Convention ratification process but also generally against most anti-discrimination legislation proposals presented in accordance with articles in the Treaty. These 'defenders of patriarchy' who oppose 'gender ideology'[326] have been joined by a fairly large community of 'anti-gender' actors, which has served right-wing patriotic governments to mobilise their most disadvantaged citizens against the 'others (those who contest traditional values, migrants and in general the EU). Even after Brexit, almost a quarter of the EP and a number of conservative governments in the Member states adopt discriminatory attitudes rooted in anti-EU, anti-gender views against the pursuit of an emancipatory vision for gender equality, sexual orientation, race, religion programmes and policies. At national level, they claim to protect traditional families[327] which has so far helped with their re-election, including by a good proportion of women voters.

## Backlash in Gender Equality and Women's and Girls' Rights

A 2018 report[328] commissioned by the FEMM Committee of the EP on 6 countries (Austria, Hungary, Italy, Poland,

---

326   see part I

327   See Hungarian policy on family, https://hungarytoday.hu/novak-family-policy-hungarian-minister-porto/

328   European Parliament. "Backlash in Gender Equality and Women's and Girls' Rights" (June 2018), https://www.europarl.europa.eu/RegData/

Romania and Slovakia ) underlines the following measures: restricting the space for egalitarian civil society mobilisations, defunding or otherwise marginalising gender equality institutions, redefining institutions and policies from a focus on women (or gender) to a focus on 'the family', and tacitly or overtly supporting a campaign that constructs and elevates 'the theory of gender' (also referred to disparagingly as 'gender ideology') into a *casus belli*.[329] Other recurrent features include support for 'men's rights' movements, and critiquing, including by declining to ratify or threatening to withdraw from, the Istanbul Convention on addressing violence against women and domestic violence.

At a time when the right to abortion is critically put into question from Poland to Arizona, it is fair to recall that the FEMM committee of the European Parliament has repeatedly reaffirmed its determination to defend SRHR and the victims of restrictive policies. Given the very progressive Europeanisation of Health and the fight against Violence against women, the determination of the European Commissioner for Equality on reproductive rights could find its way into strengthening women's control over their own bodies at European level.

## Engendering democracy

Women's marches for the legalisation of contraception and against bans on abortion have been in the DNA of feminist claims to equality as much as patriarchal nationalism has been against the EU from the outset. Still, moves to defend SRHR in the EU have been as feeble as the use of Article 7 (TEU) against governments "persistently breaching the EU's founding values." Linking these two causes is, as argued before, essential for the future of Europe.

---

etudes/STUD/2018/604955/IPOL_STU(2018)604955_EN.pdf

329    Peto Andrea, Weronika Grzebalska, and Eszter Kovats, "Gender as symbolic glue: how 'gender' became an umbrella term for the rejection of the (neo-) liberal order," in *Political Critique* (13 January 2017).

In the 1970s, when women's movements advocated for the dissociation of reproduction from sexuality, it was easy to exclude the issue from the EEC's agenda under the pretext that it had no competence in health policies beyond provisions related to the free circulation of citizens. However, the European Parliament has, over time, reiterated its call for the EU to use its existing competences to promote Sexual and Reproductive Health Rights (SRHR) on multiple occasions.[330] Recently, the EP issued a landmark report[331] authored by MEP Predrag Fred Matić giving a high level of political importance to SRHR at EU level. The covid-19 pandemic has further hindered women's access to healthcare, including SRH services, and has exacerbated existing structural gender inequalities and sexual and gender-based violence as denounced by the many above-mentioned reports.

In her 2021 State of the Union Address, the president of the European Commission stated her determination to build a European Health Union and, for that purpose, "to get the HERA authority[332] up and running."[333] This new authority, named after the goddess of the protection of women and reproduction, should also be a reminder of the need to integrate the protection of women's rights transversally into the new European Health Union. The care strategy recently an-

---

330    Among many other examples, the EP report of the Committee on Women's Rights and Equal Opportunities (A5-0223/2002); a resolution presented by Ann Van Lancker in 2002; the famous Estrela report and a draft resolution of 2013 which was rejected by the assembly https://www.europarl.europa.eu/doceo/document/A-7-2013-0426_EN.html; and the EP Resolution on the backlash against gender equality and women's rights in the EU, 13 February 2019. See also European Parliament resolution of 26 November 2020 on the *de facto* ban on the right to abortion in Poland.

331    Report on the situation of sexual and reproductive health and rights in the EU, in the frame of women's health.

332    Health Emergency preparedness and Response Authority

333    European Commission, "2021 State of the Union Address by President von der Leyen," 15 September 2021, https://ec.europa.eu/commission/presscorner/detail/en/SPEECH_21_4701

nounced by the president of the Commission[334] is a first step in the right direction.

It will be a test for the new initiatives of the EU in the field of health to mainstream gender and keep the commitment of the European Commission in the Gender Equality Strategy "to address gender aspects of health, including SRHR." More data on sexual and reproductive rights gathered by the European Institute for Gender Equality (EIGE) for its 2021 index[335] and the review of the Beijing Platform for Action (review +25) will be of help to argue for policy initiatives. Already, within its remit to take action to prevent and combat sexual and gender-based violence, the European Commission will promote comprehensive sexual education for "boys and girls from an early age about gender equality and supporting the development of non-violent relationships."[336] In addition, violations of women's SRHR, including the denial of access to safe and legal abortion care, have been rightly recognised as a form of gender-based violence against women and girls, and as amounting to torture in certain circumstances, including by the European Parliament[337] and international human rights mechanisms. It is noteworthy that the CEDAW Committee considers that "a restriction affecting only women from exercising reproductive choice, and resulting in women being forced to carry almost every pregnancy to full term, involves mental and physical suffering constituting violence against women

---

334     "We will come forward with a new European Care Strategy to support men and women in finding the best care and the best life balance for them." See https://ec.europa.eu/info/sites/default/files/soteu_2021_address_en_0.pdf

335     European Institute for Gender Equality (EIGE), *Gender Equality Index* (Vilnius: EIGE, 2021), https://eige.europa.eu/gender-equality-index/about

336     EU Gender Equality Strategy 2020-25

337     European Parliament resolution of 12 September 2017 on the proposal for a Council decision on the conclusion, by the European Union, of the Council of Europe Convention on preventing and combating violence against women and domestic violence

and potentially amounts to torture or cruel, inhumane and degrading treatment." This points towards the EU being competent to address these forms of gender-based violence as well.

Will these new elements and the political will which seems to sustain a more coherent and efficient approach to defending SRHR be sufficient to guarantee everyone real access to their right to decide freely on matters concerning their own body, which seems to be even more important for the younger generations?

In a telling piece, taking Poland as a case study as well as an example to argue the claims of Eastn and Central European feminists, Elena Zacharenko[338] makes a plea for moving from the human rights discourse (which puts an emphasis on individual rights and choices in a neoliberal context) towards a broader social and economic rights-for-all discourse. She argues that the "decision on whether or not to have a child can only be made freely if it is accompanied by the ability to raise children who will have access to a decent quality of life in a healthy and safe society." She thus identifies a key to challenging the radical right-wing anti-gender policies strategically providing support to poor families to maintain the subordination of women. "Progressive actors must recognise that ensuring full access to reproductive rights cannot be done without including this struggle into the fight against neoliberalism and the simultaneous promotion of inclusive and extensive social safety nets at national and European level."[339]

This is where the iconic feminist fight for the right to make decisions over one's own body meets the sustainability of democracy in the EU.

---

338     Eszter Kováts (ed.), "Reproductive rights as a social justice issue in the EU" in *The future of the European Union: feminists perspectives from East-central Europe* (Bonn/Berlin: Friedrich-Ebert-Stiftung, 2017).

339     Eszter Kováts, 2017

# Conclusion

> *It is becoming clear that the gender dimension cannot be mainstreamed due to the lack of much greater societal transformations than is now acceptable to male elites. The European experience, however, shows that loopholes in the edifice exist and that they can be exploited through a non-doctrinaire approach, a capacity to act inside and outside the formal system and a political will.*
> – Catherine Hoskyns, 1996[340]

As we reach the end of our journey through the history, means, tools, dilemmas and challenges of EU Gender Equality Policy, there is cause to rejoice, cause for optimism, *and* cause for concern.

In the first category, equality between women and men in the EU has a rich and solid history. It has solid foundations in the Treaties and the Charter, extensive legislation, sources of funding, and strong institutions including a dedicated agency (EIGE), and a motivated community of stakeholders (the velvet triangle). It has pushed the boundaries of EU competencies to address the status of women in society, recognising the structural nature of gender inequalities. It is finding ways to combat the plague of gender-based violence. Civil society organisations in the Member States have harnessed the leverage of European norms to progress towards gender equality. We should rejoice as well that this policy, which has known its good and bad days, seems to get approval from the general public, one of the most important features in a union of citizens. Public opinion, as measured by the Eurobarometer surveys, indicates a wide support for gender equality,[341] against violence,[342] for equal pay and for having women in leadership positions.

---

340    Catherine Hoskyns, *Integrating Gender: Women, Law and Politics in the European Union* (London: Verso, 1996), 209-210.

341    Special Eurobarometer 465: Gender Equality 2017

342    Special Eurobarometer 344: Domestic Violence against Women 2019

In the second category, optimism, it is having committed actors in charge in institutions which makes all the difference, especially after almost two regressive decades with no political will and worsening conditions caused by the impact of the financial crisis. The first gender-balanced college of commissioners, presided over by a committed woman president, with an equally committed commissioner for equality, has already begun to deliver on its promises with its new Gender Equality Strategy, the pay transparency proposal, the target to close the employment gap, its equality strategy for LGBTIQ equality, and upcoming measures to treat gender-based violence as a criminal offence. A task force for equality chaired by Commissioner Dalli oversees the mainstreaming of equality in all EU policies, and DG Budget is working to introduce gender budgeting into the Multiannual Financial Framework 2020-27. Gender equality has also increased in the European Parliament with a higher proportion of women MEPs. The strong institutional framework supportive of gender equality is further strengthened by a new wave of feminism drawing its collective energy from the #Metoo mobilisation against sexual harassment and gender-based violence.

In the third category, the causes for concern are serious. First and foremost, as shown by the latest edition of EIGE's Gender Equality Index, at the current pace of progress, it would take another 60 years to reach equality. This projection does not even feature in the massive toll the covid-19 crisis has taken on women in terms of added unpaid work, increased levels of domestic violence, the rise in unemployment and poverty. A lot of this backsliding is still to materialise as a lot of the precarious jobs held by women disappear, and the informal care work for elder and younger family members will remain heavy long after the crisis subsides. Another concern is the backlash into a patriarchal order which is being established in some Member States, anti-gender, pro-family movements on the rise, trying to turn women against the EU.[343] As far as the EU Institutions are concer-

---

343   The Hungarian minister of familiy affairs explains that "women have not to compete with men" and expect equal pay, See "The latest storm: Family Minister's video on women", Budapost, 19 December 2020,

ned, the larger proportion of women in the European Commission and the European Parliament is unfortunately not sufficient to get gender-sensitive proposals agreed by the Council. The Council of the EU, which has the last word in accepting or rejecting proposals, has been sitting on the *women on boards* proposal[344] since 2012. It took the Council many years to finally accept a watered-down version of *the work-life balance* directive for parents and carers,[345] not to mention the EU accession to the Istanbul convention which is at a complete standstill. The fact that the current European Council formations do not entail meetings of ministers responsible for gender equality[346] – despite repeated calls from stakeholders including *PES Women*[347] – is certainly one of the reasons for this inertia, besides the unanimity voting procedure which still applies to issues that simply aim to implement Treaty provisions. The last concern relates to most of the recent EU initiatives to overcome the pandemic and respond to the environmental and digital challenges (NextGenerationEU, the National recovery plans, the Green deal, the Digital pact). Their success or failure to integrate "a gender perspective requires close scrutiny" (Elisabeth Klatzer & Azzurra Rinaldi,[348] EEB ecofeminism

---

https://telex.hu/english/2020/12/14/minister-for-the-familes-to-women-dont-worry-about-the-gender-pay-gap-be-happy-you-get-to-take-care-of-others

344    Proposal for a Directive of the European Parliament and of the Council on improving the gender balance among non-executive directors of companies listed on stock exchanges and related measures [COM/2012/0614 final]

345    The Directive (EU) 2019/1158 of the European Parliament and of the Council of 20 June 2019 on work-life balance for parents and carers and repealing Council Directive 2010/18/EU

346    When ministers for fisheries and aqua culture meet on a very regular basis

347    PES Women, "PES ministers for gender equality reaffirm commitment to accelerate women's rights for a truly feminist and equal Europe" (8 July 2020), https://pes.eu/en/news-events/news/detail/PES-ministers-for-gender-equality-reaffirm-commitment-to-accelerate-womens-rights-for-a-truly-feminist-and-equal-Europe/

348    https://alexandrageese.eu/wp-content/uploads/2020/07/Gender-Impact-Assessment-NextGenerationEU_Klatzer_Rinaldi_2020.pdf

report)[349] as they run the risk of adopting policies that widen the existing gaps between women and men. Ongoing efforts to operationalise gender budgeting in the next seven years of EU budgets are a silver lining. This is to be welcomed, as it may structurally change the situation, if only gradually.

Most probably because the EU is presented as the most advanced gender-equal region in the world, it generates high expectations worldwide. Geopolitical realities strengthen its duty to act boldly to uphold its values by supporting resilient women leaders in their struggle against a persistent patriarchy (eg Afghan women demonstrating against the Taliban regime, the women and girls from Ukraine suffering the consequences of the war) and countering a dangerous relapse into regressive behaviours and policy moves against gender equality. This is defending part of the humanistic heritage and foundation of the EU.

Meanwhile, every election calls, to varying degrees, for new political actors, and for more attention to well-being and the environment, not only in the EU but also in its Member States. Moreover, the incumbent European Commission strives to achieve a more *inclusive* Union, "reaching our full potential by using all our talents, our ideas, our energy and raising each child, girl or boy, of whichever race religion or sexual orientation"[350] based on the conviction that the sky is the limit to one's ambitions regardless of gender.

Clearly, despite the power of habit, 'business as usual' is not a sustainable option to face the challenges created by the pandemic, an ageing society and the green and digital transitions.

In search of a bolder approach and faster progress towards a fair, sustainable Europe, the time has come to reassess the connections between European integration and the emancipation of women. These two great historical projects, which started in the second part of the 20th century, are rooted in the same aspirations, but relied on different actors and interests. It would not be out of place to hypothesise that a strong foundation for a stronger *value-based* Euro-

349   https://eeb.org/library/why-the-european-green-deal-needs-ecofeminism/
350   Ursula von der Leyen, State of the Union address 2020

pean Union with a clear priority for inclusion and fairness led by the critical spur of a gender perspective could emerge from a proactive arrangement of their complementarities.

Following spectacular progress in the 1990s, both these movements have undergone tumultuous developments. Since the turn of the century, a resurgence of nationalism and the patriarchal order has been threatening both movements in equal measure.

**Two specific needs for reframing our vision** come to mind regarding the association between gender equality and European integration.

**The first** refers to the sustainability of democracy. In the field of representation, the relationships 'women and nationalism' and 'Europe and nationalism' have been equally profound, complex, and often adverse. Unfortunately, interpreting this constellation is too often monopolised right-wing ideology, with little interference of progressive thinking.

With the analytical lens of a historian who had himself experienced totalitarianism and genocide, and then became a refugee and discovered his own minority sexual status, George Moss, the contemporary historian of the role of masculinity and virility in nation building in Europe in the 19th and 20th centuries describes the rise of fascism and Nazism as a result of an "image of man"[351] taking its strength in exclusion, racism, sexism, antisemitism and warfare. He explains that the First and Second World Wars saw a resurgence of the ideal of harsh masculinity because the challenges of feminism and androgynism both in the early years of the 20th century and in the 1920s "stiffened the ideal of normative manhood." This is the mould, including its symbolic pursuit of the fascist 'new man'[352] or

---

351    The Image of Man. The Creation of Modern Masculinity George L. Mosse New York, Oxford University Press, 1996,

352    "a 'virile' being who would put decadent bourgeoisie, cerebral Marxist and 'feminine' liberals to shame" as described by Robert Soucy in "Fascism: Volksgemeinschaft - The 'new man'." Encyclopaedia Britannica, April 13, 2021, https://www.britannica.com/topic/fascism/Volksgemeinschaft

the Third Reich conception of masculinity, from which Europe has emerged to challenge new causes of war.

There is no doubt that the persistence of gender-based violence is one of the many evils caused by remnants of this normative frame of manhood. However, when progressive thinkers recall that the very existence of the European Union relies on the elimination of abusive domination, they rarely make the link with patriarchy. We need new approaches to analyse the commonalities of the fields of European integration and gender equality as they evolve. So far, their interaction and how they relate to democracy are insufficiently explored in the academic literature.

There is no deficit of knowledge on European integration since for three generations of scholars, the subject has mobilised the attention of political science as one of its most intriguing phenomena, to the point of establishing itself as a discipline in its own right. In parallel, over the last 70 years, feminism has inspired women's studies and gender studies, and since the 1990s scholars have even taken a specific interest in the analysis of EU gender equality policy and gender mainstreaming. There is no deficit of cognitive or normative frames but a deficit of *common frames.*[353]

**The second** need for reframing our vision of gender and European integration refers to the economy. The meager results of mainstreaming gender into European policies in the last twenty years call into question the utilitarian vs. structural relationship between European integration and gender equality.

While integrating the concept of gender into research, the structural funds, and social and employment policy has known some success, matters related to macroeconomy are traditionally gender blind. In the 2019 report on "New Visions for Gender Equality",[354] the authors[355] adopt a counterintuitive approach: The instrumentali-

---

353   See a first attempt to define common theoretical frames in "Gendering European integration theory, engaging new dialogues" Gabriele Abels, Heather MacRae eds Barbara budrich publishers 2016.

354   SAAGE, ed Nial Crowley and Sylvia Sansonetti.

355   Yasmine Ergas and Annick Masselot The business case for gender equality

sation of gender equality by the economy prevents consideration of what a gender equal economy could be because gender is subsumed by the economy and not on an equal footing. Ergas and Masselot suggest using the terms of the Treaty, to use gender mainstreaming "to shift the way we measure the economy and to implement a value-based economy, where the value of gender equality could guide the EU economy rather than the other way around." The reader may imagine all the implications of such a shift, not only for progress towards gender equality but for reshaping a just and sustainable European Union.

# Glossary

**Analysis (gender)**

Gender analysis is a critical examination of how differences in gender roles, activities, needs, opportunities, rights and entitlements affect men, women, girls and boys in certain situation or contexts. Gender analysis examines the relationships between females and males and their access to and control of resources and the constraints they face relative to each other. A gender analysis should be integrated into all sector assessments or situational analyses to ensure that gender-based injustices and inequalities are not exacerbated by interventions, and that where possible, greater equality and justice in gender relations are promoted.

**Awareness raising (gender)**

Gender awareness raising is the process that aims at showing how existing values and norms influence our picture of reality, perpetuate stereotypes and support mechanisms (re)producing inequality. It challenges values and gender norms by explaining how they influence and limit the opinions taken into consideration during decision-making. (EIGE)

**Balance (gender)**

Gender balance is the term used to refer to the equal participation of women and men in all areas of work, projects or programmes. In a scenario of gender equality, women and men are expected to participate in proportion to their share in the population. In many areas, however, women participate less than what would be expected based on the sex distribution in the population (under-representation of women) while men participate more than expected (over-representation of men).

**Barcelona targets**

The Barcelona Targets on Childcare were agreed by EU Member States in 2002. Whilst the target of 33% of children under 3 in childcare has been reached across the EU as a whole, and the target of

90% of children from age 3 up until mandatory school age has nearly been reached, this conceals large differences between Member States and between different territorial units within states. Unfortunately, availability of accessible, affordable and quality childcare is not yet a reality in all countries. This has a negative impact on labour market participation of parents as well as on gender equality. In contrast, some Member States have reached and even surpassed the Barcelona targets, which means they no longer act as an incentive in such cases, whereas continual improvements remain necessary across the whole of the EU.

### Balanced participation (gender)

In a strict sense, gender-balanced participation implies equal representation often referred to as parity participation of women and men. However, the general understanding is that the representation of either women or men in any decision-making body in public and political life should not fall below 40%.

### Bias (gender)

In relation to gender, it refers to prejudiced actions or thoughts founded on the gender-based perception that women are not equal to men.

### Blindness (gender)

In relation to gender, it refers to the failure to recognise that the roles and responsibilities of men/boys and women/girls are assigned to them in specific social, cultural, economic, and political contexts. Projects, programmes, policies and attitudes which are gender-blind do not take into account these different roles and diverse needs. They maintain the *status quo* and will not help transform the unequal structure of gender relations.

### Beijing Declaration and the Platform for Action

The Beijing Declaration and the Platform for Action were adopted unanimously by 189 countries at the UN Conference on women peace and security in 1995. Considered to be the most comprehensive and progressive global policy framework for the rights of women, the Declaration recognises women's rights as human rights and sets out a comprehensive roadmap for achieving equality between women and men, with concrete actions and measurable outcomes across a range of issues affecting women and girls. These outcomes are divided into 12 interrelated areas where a need for urgent action was identified: poverty, education and training, health care, violence against women and girls, armed conflict, economic empowerment, power and decision-making, mechanisms to promote advancement of women, women's human rights, the media, the environment, and the rights of the girl child.

## Care

Care activities comprise two major categories. First, those that consist of direct, face-to-face, personal care activities (sometimes referred to as 'nurturing' or 'relational' care), such as feeding a baby, nursing a sick partner, helping an older person to take a bath, carrying out health check-ups or teaching young children. Second, those that involve indirect care activities, which do not involve face-to-face personal care, such as cleaning, cooking, doing the laundry and other household maintenance task. The latter

provide the preconditions for personal caregiving and are sometimes referred to as 'non-relational care' or 'household work'. These two types of care activities cannot be separated from each other, and they frequently overlap in practice, both in households and in institutions. (ILO)

- **child (care)**

Provision of public, private, individual or collective services to meet the needs of parents and children.

- **(care) economy**

Part of human activity, both material and social, that is concerned with the process of caring for the present and future labour force, and the human population as a whole, including the domestic provisioning of food, clothing and shelter. It is the sum of all forms of care work, both unpaid carers and care workers.

- **(care) ethics**

Ethics of care is a feminist approach to ethics. It challenges traditional moral theories as male-centric and problematic to the extent that they omit or downplay values and virtues usually culturally associated with women or with roles that are often cast as 'feminine'. Traditional proponents of feminist care ethics include 20th century theorists Carol Gilligan (b. 1936) and Nel Noddings (b. 1929). Gilligan's influential 1982 book, *In a Different Voice,* claimed that Sigmund Freud's theory of psychoanalysis and Lawrence Kohlberg's theory of moral development were biased and male-oriented.

### - (**care**) **jobs**

Care jobs or paid care work is care work performed for profit or pay within a range of settings, such as private households (as in the case of domestic workers), and public or private hospitals, clinics, nursing homes, schools and other care establishments. Care workers may be in an employment relationship where the employer is a private individual or household, a public agency, a private for-profit enterprise or a private non-profit organisation, or they may be working on their own account (self-employed).

### - (**care**) **work**

Care work always takes place within a care relationship, between a caregiver and a care receiver – between mother and child, nurse and patient, domestic worker and client, son and ailing father – and can be paid or unpaid.

### Charter of Fundamental Rights

The Charter of Fundamental Rights sets out the fundamental rights that must be respected both by the European Union (EU) and the EU countries when implementing EU law. It establishes principles and rights for EU citizens and residents that relate to dignity, liberty, equality, solidarity, citizenship, and justice. In addition to protecting civil and political rights, it covers workers' social rights, data protection, bioethics and the right to good administration. This legally binding tool has the same legal value as the EU treaties.

### Convention on the Elimination of All Forms of Discrimination against Women

The Convention on the Elimination of All Forms of Discrimination against Women (CEDAW) was adopted in 1979 by the UN General Assembly. It is often described as an international bill of rights for women. Consisting of a preamble and 30 articles, it defines what constitutes discrimination against women – addressing intersectional discrimination in one of the most comprehensive manners – and sets up an agenda for national action to end such discrimination.

**Council of Europe Convention on preventing and combatting violence against women and domestic violence (Istanbul convention)**

The Council of Europe Convention on preventing and combatting violence against women and domestic violence, better known as the Istanbul Convention, is a human rights treaty of the Council of Europe against violence against women and domestic violence, which was opened for signature on 11 May 2011, in Istanbul, Turkey. The Istanbul Convention recognises violence against women as a violation of human rights. It condemns all forms of violence against women and describes this violence as an expression of a historical imbalance of power between women and men. It remains the most comprehensive legislative instrument to date aimed at preventing and protecting women and girls from violence. All countries that have ratified the Istanbul Convention must adopt legislation on matters such as rape, sexual harassment, female genital mutilation, honour-based violence and oppression, and forced marriage. A monitoring mechanism assesses on a regular basis how the country fulfils its obligation to comply with the Convention's requirements concerning prevention, protection, prosecution and coordinated policies in the efforts to combat men's violence against women.

**Democratic deficit**

Limited legitimacy of democracy that partly results from an inadequate gender balance, ie from the overrepresentation of men and underrepresentation of women.

**Discrimination**

- **(direct) discrimination**

Direct discrimination occurs when a difference in treatment relies directly and explicitly on distinctions based exclusively on a protected ground (such as sex), which cannot be justified objectively.

- **(indirect) discrimination**

Indirect discrimination occurs when a seemingly neutral law, policy or measure bears discriminatory effects when implemented. This can occur, for example, when women are disadvantaged compared to men with respect to the enjoyment of a particular opportunity or benefit due to pre-existing inequalities (eg work-related requirements to travel, meetings scheduled late in the work day, etc).

### - (**Multiple**) discrimination

Multiple discrimination takes place when someone is discriminated against for more than one reason, for example on the basis of gender *and* religion, age *and* ethnicity.

### - discrimination (**against women**)

Any distinction, exclusion or restriction made on the basis of sex which has the effect or purpose of impairing or nullifying the recognition, enjoyment or exercise by women, irrespective of their marital status (on a basis of equality of men and women) of human rights and fundamental freedoms in the political, economic, social, cultural, civil or any other field (Article 1 CEDAW).

### Domestic Violence

Domestic violence shall mean all acts of physical, sexual, psychological or economic violence that occur within the family or domestic unit or between former or current spouses or partners, whether or not the perpetrator shares or has shared the same residence with the victim (Istanbul Convention).

### Double approach

A double (or dual) approach to gender equality refers to complementarity between gender mainstreaming and specific gender equality policy and measures, including positive measures. It is also referred to as a twin-track strategy.

### Emancipation of women

Process, strategy and a myriad of efforts by which women have been striving to liberate themselves from the authority and control of patriarchal and traditional power structures, as well as efforts to secure equal rights for women, remove gender discrimination from laws, institutions and behavioural patterns, and set legal standards that shall promote their full equality with men.

### Equal pay for work of equal value

The principle of equal pay for men and women for equal work – or work of equal value – is one of the fundamental rights and principles of the European Union. It was laid down in the Treaty of Rome and has since become enshrined in the European Pillar of Social Rights.

Equal pay for work of equal value is to be attributed, without discrimination on grounds of sex or marital status, with regard to all aspects of pay and conditions of remuneration. In 2006, this principle formed part of the recast Gender Equality Directive prohibiting direct or indirect sex discrimination concerning pay for the same work or for work of equal value. To address current gender pay gaps as a form of discrimination, the Commission's proposal for a Directive focuses on two things: access to information and access to justice.

**Empowerment of women and girls**

It concerns women's and girls' access power and control over their own lives. It involves awareness-raising, building self-confidence, expansion of choices, increased access to and control over resources, and actions to transform the structures and institutions which reinforce and perpetuate gender discrimination and inequality. This implies that to be empowered they must not only have equal capabilities (such as education and health) and equal access to resources and opportunities (such as land and employment), but they must also have the agency to use these rights, capabilities, resources and opportunities to make strategic choices and decisions (such as is provided through leadership opportunities and participation in political institutions)

**Equal opportunities**

This concept indicates the absence of barriers to economic, political and social participation on grounds of sex, gender or other characteristics. Such barriers are often indirect, difficult to discern and caused and maintained by structural phenomena and social representations that have proved particularly resistant to change. Equal opportunities as one of the gender equality objectives is founded on the rationale that a whole range of strategies, actions and measures are necessary to redress deep-rooted and persistent inequalities.

**Equal treatment**

Ensuring the absence of discrimination on the grounds of sex, gender or other characteristics, either directly or indirectly.

**Equality between women and men in the EU**

The principle of equality between men and women with regard to equal pay was established in the Treaty of Rome of 1957. Since then, a series of EU laws (directives) has broadened the principle of equality between women and men to cover working conditions, social security, access to goods and services, work-life balance, maternity protection, parental leave and equal treatment in work in a self-employed capacity. The principle of equality as one of the EU's fundamental values was set out in the Lisbon Treaty and, more specifically, Articles 2 and 3(3) of the Treaty on European Union, Articles 8, 10, 19, 153 and 157 of the Treaty on the Functioning of the European Union and Articles 21 and 23 of the EU Charter of Fundamental Rights. Gender equality, as one of the 20 key principles of the European Pillar of Social Rights, seeks to ensure: the right to equal pay for equal work or work of equal value; equality of treatment and opportunities between women and men in all areas, including in the labour market, terms and conditions of employment, and career progression. Over the years, the European Commission has adopted strategies for equality between men and women. The latest Gender Equality Strategy, which covers the 2020-2025 period, presents policy objectives and actions to make significant progress by 2025 towards a gender-equal Europe.

### Equality (gender)
In relation to gender, it refers to the equal rights, responsibilities and opportunities of women and men and girls and boys. Equality does not mean that women and men will become the same but that women's and men's rights, responsibilities and opportunities will not depend on their gender. Gender equality implies that the interests, needs and priorities of both women and men are taken into consideration, recognising the diversity of different groups of women and men. Gender equality is not a women's issue but should concern and fully engage men as well as women. Equality between women and men is seen both as a human rights issue and as a precondition for, and indicator of, sustainable people-centred development.

### Equality bodies
Formal state-supported bodies mandated to promote, analyse, monitor and support equal treatment in the national context.

### Equinet
Through Equinet (the European Network of Equality Bodies), public institutions fighting discrimination at the national level which

are members of this umbrella organisation can share their expertise at the European level. The Network ensures that information and knowledge flows as efficiently as possible between members in order to learn from the successes achieved and the challenges raised during the implementation of their mandate at national level.

**EU treaties**

The EU treaties are binding agreements between EU member countries. They set out EU objectives, rules for EU institutions, how decisions are made and the relationship between the EU and its member countries. Every action taken by the EU is founded on treaties. The **Treaty of the European Union** (**TEU**) sets out the objectives and principles of the EU. The **Treaty of the Functioning of the European Union** (**TFEU**) forms the detailed basis of EU law by defining the principles and objectives of the EU and the scope for action within its policy areas. It also sets out organisational and functional details of the EU institutions.

**European Commission**

The European Commission is the executive branch of the European Union (EU). Established in 1957, it is currently composed of 27 commissioners, including its president. It acts in the EU's general interest with complete independence from EU Member States' national governments and is accountable to the European Parliament. It has the right of initiative to propose laws in a wide range of policy areas. In the area of justice and home affairs, it shares the right of initiative with Member States. The European Parliament and the Council of the European Union may request the Commission to table legislative proposals. EU citizens may also call on the Commission to propose laws by means of the European Citizens' Initiative. The Commission may be given the right to adopt non-legislative acts, in particular delegated and implementing acts, and has important powers to ensure fair conditions of competition between EU businesses. The Commission oversees the application of EU law. It implements the EU's budget in cooperation with the Member States and manages funding programmes. It also exercises coordinating, executive and management functions, as laid down in the Treaties. It represents the EU during international negotiations, in particular in areas of trade policy and humanitarian aid. The Commission is organised into policy departments, called Directorates-General (DGs), and Services, which are mainly located in Brussels and Luxembourg.

**European network of legal experts in gender equality and non-discrimination**

The European network of legal experts in gender equality and non-discrimination is to provide reliable, expert information to enable the Commission to fulfil their role as guardian of the Treaties. The disclosure and gathering of information on gender equality and non-discrimination legislation, case law and developments at national level, that is often not easily accessible due to the specificities of national legal systems, language barriers and difficulties in finding relevant information, is one of the key goals of the new network. The dissemination of general information about the *acquis* (*communautaire* and national), the latest developments at the EU level and in the countries involved in the network, remains a vital issue both for the further implementation of gender equality and non-discrimination law and its further development.

**European Parliament**

The European Parliament is the legislative branch of the European Union and one of its seven institutions. It is directly elected and made up of 705 members (MEPs) representing all EU countries. The European Parliament decides upon **EU legislation**, including the multiannual budget, together with the Council of the European Union (EU Member State governments). The EP holds other EU institutions, like the European Commission, to account. It **elects the president of the European Commission** and plays a key role in vetting commissioner-designates through individual hearings. The College of Commissioners – as the twenty-seven commissioners are referred to collectively – must then be approved through a consent vote by the EP. Members of the European Parliament are elected in EU Member States every five years and **represent around 446 million citizens**. Over the years, and with subsequent changes to EU treaties, the Parliament has acquired substantial legislative and budgetary powers.

### European Pillar of Social Rights

In 2017, the European Commission presented a communication establishing the European Pillar of Social Rights whose purpose is to deliver improved living and working conditions in the EU. It sets out 20 key principles and rights which fall within three themes:

1. Equal opportunities and access to the labour market (eg skills, education and lifelong learning, equal opportunities, gender equality, and active support to employment);

2. Fair working conditions (eg secure and adaptable employment, wages, information about employment conditions and protection in case of dismissals, social dialogue, and work-life balance);

3. Social protection and inclusion (eg childcare, minimum income, unemployment benefits, inclusion of people with disabilities, assistance for the homeless, access to essential services, health, and long-term care). At the Social Summit in Gothenburg in November 2017, the European Parliament, the Council and the Commission adopted a common proclamation on the European Pillar of Social Rights. The Social Pillar serves as a reference framework to monitor performance of EU countries' employment and social policies by means of a Social Scoreboard and incorporates a new approach to mainstream social priorities into all EU policies. On 4 March 2021, the Commission adopted the European Pillar of Social Rights Action Plan. The Action Plan puts forward three headline targets and a set of action in the areas of more and better jobs, skills and equality and social protection and inclusion. The Action Plan is accompanied by a proposal to update the Social Scoreboard.

### European Women's Lobby

The European Women's Lobby (EWL) is the largest umbrella organisation of women's associations in the European Union, founded in 1990, working to promote women's rights and equality between women and men, and representing a total of more than 2000 organisations. EWL membership extends to organisations in 26 EU Member States, three EU candidate countries, Iceland and the UK, as well as to European-wide bodies. With a secretariat based in Brussels, Belgium, the EWL is one of the longest-standing European level NGOs, and works closely with European institutions and civil society partners. At the international level, the EWL has a consultative status at the Council of Europe, and participates regularly in the activities of the UN Commission on the Status of Women (CSW).

### Female Genital Mutilation (FGM)

All procedures that involve a partial or total removal of the external female genitalia, or other injury to the female genital organs for non-medical reasons.

### Femicide

Femicide is generally understood to involve intentional murder of women because they are women, but broader definitions include any killings of women or girls. Femicide is usually perpetrated by men, but sometimes female family members may be involved. Femicide differs from male homicide in specific ways. For example, most cases of femicide are committed by partners or ex-partners, and involve ongoing abuse in the home, threats or intimidation, sexual violence or situations where women have less power or fewer resources than their partner.

### Feminisation of poverty

Increasing incidence and prevalence of poverty among women compared to men, as a result of structural discrimination that affects women's lives and is reflected in lower salaries, lower pensions, fewer benefits, etc.

### FEMM Committee

The Committee on Women's rights and gender equality of the European Parliament is one of 20 specialised standing committees of the European Parliament. As the other EP committees, FEMM instructs legislative proposals through the adoption of reports, propose amendments to the plenary and appoint a negotiation team to conduct negotiations with the Council on EU legislation. It also adopts own-initiative reports, organises hearings with experts and scrutinises the other EU bodies and institutions. It consists of 25 full members and 29 substitutes. A chair and four vice chairs, elected by the committee, from the bureau. It is responsible for:

1. the definition, promotion and protection of women's rights in the Union and related Union measures

2. the promotion of women's rights in third countries;

3. equal opportunities policy, including the promotion of equality between men and women with regard to labour market opportunities and treatment at work;

4. the removal of all forms of violence and discrimination based on sex;

5. the implementation and further development of gender mainstreaming in all policy sectors;

6. the follow-up and implementation of international agreements and conventions involving the rights of women;

7. the encouragement of awareness of women's rights.

**Gender**

Gender refers to the social construction of power relations between sexes. It also relates to the social attributes and opportunities associated with being male and female and the relationships between women and men and girls and boys, as well as the relations between women and those between men. These attributes, opportunities and relationships are socially constructed and are learned through socialisation processes. They are context- or time-specific. Gender determines what is expected, allowed and valued in a woman or a man in a given context. In most societies there are differences and inequalities between women and men in responsibilities assigned, activities undertaken, access to and control over resources, as well as decision-making opportunities. Gender is part of the broader socio-cultural context. Other important criteria for socio-cultural analysis include class, race, poverty level, ethnic group and age.

- **(gender) analysis**

An analysis from a gender perspective helps to see whether the needs of women and men are equally taken into account and served by [a] proposal. It enables policy makers to develop policies with an understanding of the socio-economic reality of women and men and allows for policies to take (gender) differences into account.

- **(gender) expression**

Gender expression is how a person publicly expresses or presents their gender. This can include behaviour and outward appearance such as dress, hair, make-up, body language and voice. A person's chosen name and pronoun are also common ways of expressing gender. Others perceive a person's gender through these attributes.

### - (gender) identity

Gender identity is each person's internal and individual experience of gender. It is a person's sense of being a woman, a man, both, neither, or anywhere along the gender spectrum. A person's gender identity may be the same as or different from their birth-assigned sex.

### - (gender) reassignment

Set of medical measures that can, but do not have to, include psychological, endocrinological and surgical treatments aimed at aligning a person's physical appearance with their gender identity.

### Gender gap

It is the gap in any area between women and men in terms of their levels of participation, access, rights, remuneration or benefits. The concept used most frequently is the gender pay gap, which is the difference in average gross hourly earnings between women and men.

### Gender mainstreaming

This notion has been embraced internationally as a strategy towards realising gender equality. It involves the integration of a gender perspective into the preparation, design, implementation, monitoring and evaluation of policies, regulatory measures and spending programmes, with a view to promoting equality between women and men, and combating discrimination. The principle of gender mainstreaming consists of taking systematic account of the differences between the conditions, situations and needs of women and men in all Community policies and actions

### Gender budgeting

It is the application of gender mainstreaming in the budgetary process. It means a gender-based assessment of budgets, incorporating a gender perspective at all levels of the budgetary process and restructuring revenues and expenditures in order to promote gender equality.

### Gender contract

It is a set of implicit and explicit rules governing gender relations which allocate different work and value, responsibilities and obligations to men and women and is maintained on three levels – cultural superstructure – the norms and values of society; institutions – family welfare, education and employment systems, etc; and socialisation processes, notably in the family.

### Gender sensitive language

Language not only reflects the way we think; it also shapes the thinking of listeners or readers and influences their beliefs and behaviour. Gender-sensitive language relates to the use of the written and spoken language so that women and men are equally treated and considered. It requires avoiding talking in generic masculine terms, excluding women or reflecting stereotyped assumptions about gender roles. Being aware of the importance of gender-sensitive language could lead to the promotion of gender sensitivity, and also to a higher degree of precision.

### Gender studies

Academic, usually interdisciplinary, field that focuses on the complex interaction of gender and sexuality with other identity markers such as race, ethnicity, class, disability, age. It analyses of the social and cultural constructions of situations of gender relations in various aspects of life, as well as the gender dimension of all other disciplines.

### Glass ceiling

Artificial impediments and invisible barriers that militate against women's access to top decision-making and managerial positions in an organisation, whether public or private and in whatever domain. The term 'glass' is used because these impediments are apparently invisible and are usually linked to the maintenance of the status quo in organisations, as opposed to transparent and equal career advancement opportunities for women and men within organisations.

### Glass cliff

Phenomenon whereby individuals belonging to particular groups are more likely to be found in leadership positions that are associated with a greater risk of failure and criticism. According to research by the University of Exeter, women and minority groups are, for example, more likely to be appointed as CEOs of a failing company rather than a successful one, making their position risky and difficult.

### Heteronormativity

Heteronormativity is what makes heterosexuality seem coherent, natural and privileged. It involves the assumption that everyone is 'naturally' heterosexual, and that heterosexuality is an ideal, superior to homosexuality or bisexuality.

### Impact assessment (gender)

It involves examining policy proposals to see whether they will affect women and men differently, with a view to adapting these proposals to make sure that discriminatory effects are neutralised and that gender equality is promoted. It is an ex-ante procedure that should be performed before the final decision on the policy proposal is taken. It involves comparing and assessing, according to gender relevant criteria, the current situation and trends in relation to the expected outcome resulting from the introduction of the proposed policy. Gender impact assessment is used to assess the impact of a given policy proposal on women and men and on gender relations in general.

### Intersectionality

Analytical tool for studying, understanding and responding to the ways in which sex and gender intersect with other personal characteristics/identities, and how these intersections contribute to unique experiences of discrimination. It starts from the premise that people live multiple, layered identities derived from social relations, history and the operation of structures of power. Intersectional analysis aims to reveal multiple identities, exposing the different types of intersectional and multiple discrimination and disadvantage that occur as a consequence of the combination of identities and the intersection of sex and gender with other grounds.

### Intersex

Umbrella term to denote a number of different variations in a person's bodily characteristics that do not match strict medical definitions of female or male.

### Indicators (gender)

In relation to gender, such indicators are established to measure and compare the situation of women and men over time. They can refer to quantitative indicators (based on statistics broken down by sex) or to qualitative indicators (based on women's and men's experiences, attitudes, opinions and feelings). Gender-sensitive indicators allow changes to be measured in the relations between women and men in relation to a certain policy area, a specific programme or activity, or changes in the status or situation of women and men.

### LGBTIQ+

Umbrella term used to denote individuals from the Lesbian, Gay, Bisexual, Trans, Intersex and Queer/Questioning Community.

### Lone parent

Someone who lives without a partner, and who has daily caring responsibilities for a dependent child or children.

### Marginalised groups

Different groups of people within a given culture, context and history at risk of being subjected to multiple discrimination due to the interplay of different personal characteristics or grounds, such as sex, gender, age, ethnicity, religion or belief, health status, disability, sexual orientation, gender identity, education or income, or living in various geographic localities.

### Masculinities

Different notions of what it means to be a man, including patterns of conduct linked to men's place in a given set of gender roles and relations. It involves questioning the masculine values and norms that society places on men's behaviour, identifying and addressing issues confronting men and boys in the world of work, and promoting the positive roles that men and boys can play in attaining gender equality.

### Minimum wage

Wage level defined in law or by agreement, representing the lowest possible rate an employer is permitted to pay.

### Non-discrimination law

The aim of non-discrimination law is to allow all individuals an equal and fair chance to access opportunities available in a society. This means that individuals or groups of individuals which are in comparable situations should not be treated less favourably simply because of a particular characteristic, such as their sex, racial or ethnic origin, religion or belief, disability, age or sexual orientation. The Treaty on the Functioning of the European Union (TFEU) prohibits discrimination on grounds of nationality. It also enables the Council to take appropriate action to combat discrimination based on sex, racial or ethnic origin, religion or belief, disability, age or sexual orientation. In this matter, the Council must act unanimously and after obtaining the European Parliament's consent. However, in the specific area of equal treatment and equal opportunities for men and women, the ordinary legislative procedure applied, which does not require unanimity but only qualified majority (Article 157 TFEU).

### Non-governmental organisations (NGOs)

Non-profit, voluntary citizens' groups, principally independent from government, which are organised on a local, national or international level to address issues in support of the public good. NGOs are recognised as key third-sector actors in many areas of public action. Women's NGOs are best known for two often interrelated, types of activity: the delivery of services to women in need, and the organisation of policy advocacy and public campaigns in pursuit of the social transformation required to achieve gender equality. NGOs are also active in a wide range of other specialised roles such as parity democracy building, conflict resolution, policy analysis, research, and information provision. NGOs are essential partners of governments in the pursuit of gender equality. By presenting the views of their members on matters relevant to gender equality, making proposals or suggestions, cooperating in specific projects, pursuing research into substantive issues, or, in the context of the media, giving visibility and legitimacy to gender equality matters, NGOs have a role to play in the achievement of gender equality, one which must be valued and encouraged by states.

### Norms (gender)

These are ideas – often integrated early in life – about how men and women should be and act. We internalise and learn these 'rules'. This sets up a life-cycle of gender socialisation and stereotyping. Put another way, gender norms are the standards and expectations to which gender identity generally conforms, within a range that defines a particular society, culture and community at that point in time.

### Online (cyber) gender-based violence

Gender-based violence that is perpetrated through electronic communication and the internet. Although cyber violence can affect both women and men, women and girls experience different and more traumatic forms of cyber violence. There are various forms of cyber violence against women and girls, including, but not limited to, cyber stalking, non-consensual pornography (or 'revenge porn'), gender-based slurs, hate speech and harassment, 'slut-shaming', unsolicited pornography, 'sextortion', rape threats and death threats, and electronically facilitated trafficking. Cyber violence is not a separate phenomenon to 'real world' violence, as it often follows the same patterns as offline violence.

**Parity democracy**

Full integration of women, on an equal footing with men, at all levels and in all areas of the workings of a democratic society, by means of multidisciplinary strategies.

**Patriarchy**

A society, system or group in which men predominate women and have the political power, moral authority, social privilege and have control of property.

**Perpetrator**

A person who deliberately uses violent and abusive behaviour to control their partner or former partner, whether or not they have been charged, prosecuted or convicted.

**Positive action**

Positive action (also called *affirmative action*, *specific action* or *positive discrimination*) refers to measures targeted at a particular group and intended to eliminate and prevent discrimination or to offset disadvantages arising from existing attitudes, behaviours and structures. It means action aimed at favouring access by members of certain categories of people eg women, to rights which they are guaranteed, to the same extent as members of other categories, eg men. Together with gender mainstreaming, specific action is one of the two approaches to gender equality implemented by the European Union.

**Precarious employment**

Various forms of non-standard, atypical, alternative employment.

**Queer theory**

Theoretical reflection, developed in the mid 1980s against a backdrop of growing theoretical interest in sexualities, which lead to the civil movement's reclaiming of the word 'queer', which previously had a pejorative meaning, to identify all individuals who fall outside the dominant gender and sexuality norms.

### Quotas

Positive measurement instrument aimed at accelerating the achievement of gender-balanced participation and representation by establishing a defined proportion (percentage) or number of places or seats to be filled by, or allocated to the under-represented sex, generally under certain rules or criteria.

### Rape

Engaging in non-consensual vaginal, anal or oral penetration of a sexual nature of the body of another person with any bodily part or object without consent, using force, coercion or by taking advantage of the vulnerability of the victim. Consent must be given voluntarily as the result of the person's free will, as assessed in the context of the surrounding circumstances.

### Segregation (gender)

Gender segregation can manifest itself in differences in patterns of representation of women and men in labour market, public and political life, unpaid domestic work and caring, and in young women's and men's choice of education.

### Sex (biological)

Sex is the anatomical classification of people as male, female or intersex, usually assigned at birth.

### Sex-disaggregated statistics

Data collected and tabulated separately for women and men. They allow for the measurement of differences between women and men on various social and economic dimensions and are one of the requirements in obtaining gender statistics. Having data by sex does not guarantee, for example, that concepts, definitions and methods used in data production are conceived to reflect gender roles, relations and inequalities in society, therefore collecting data disaggregated by sex represents only one of the characteristics of gender statistics.

### Sex trafficking

Illegal trade in human beings, largely in women and children, for the purpose of sexual exploitation. Trafficking for sexual exploitation is the most commonly reported form of human trafficking in the European Union. It is a form of gender-based violence that disproportionately affects women. Trafficking is defined as the recruitment, transportation, transfer, harbouring or reception of persons, including the exchange or transfer of control over those persons, by means of the threat or use of force or other forms of coercion, of abduction, of fraud, of deception, of the abuse of power or of a position of vulnerability or of the giving or receiving of payments or benefits to achieve the consent of a person having control over another person, for the purpose of exploitation.

**Sexism**

Actions or attitudes that discriminate against people based solely on their gender.

**Sexual and reproductive health and rights**

Sexual and reproductive health and rights encompass efforts to eliminate preventable maternal and neonatal mortality and morbidity, to ensure quality sexual and reproductive health services, including contraceptive services, and to address sexually transmitted infections (STI), violence against women and girls, and sexual and reproductive health needs of adolescents. Universal access to sexual and reproductive health is essential not only to achieve sustainable development but also to ensure that this new framework speaks to the needs and aspirations of people around the world and leads to realisation of their health and human rights.

**Sexual harassment**

Any form of unwanted verbal, non-verbal or physical conduct of a sexual nature with the purpose or effect of violating the dignity of a person, in particular when creating an intimidating, hostile, degrading, humiliating or offensive environment.

**Sexual orientation**

Each person's capacity for profound emotional, affectional and sexual attraction to, and intimate and sexual relations with, individuals of a different gender, the same gender or more than one gender.

**Statistics**

In relation to gender, these are statistics that adequately reflect differences and inequalities in the situation of women and men in all areas of life. Gender statistics are defined by the sum of the following characteristics: (a) data are collected and presented disaggregated by sex as a primary and overall classification, (b) data are reflecting gender issues, (c) data are based on concepts and definitions that adequately reflect the diversity of women and men and capture all aspects of their lives, and (d) data collection methods take into account stereotypes and social and cultural factors that may induce gender biases.

### Stereotypes

In relation to gender, these are preconceived ideas whereby males and females are arbitrarily assigned characteristics and roles determined and limited by their sex. Sex stereotyping can limit the development of the natural talents and abilities of boys and girls, women and men, their educational and professional experiences as well as life opportunities in general Stereotypes about women both result from and are the cause of deeply engrained attitudes, values, norms and prejudices against women. They are used to justify and maintain the historical relations of power of men over women as well as sexist attitudes which are holding back the advancement of women.

### Time use survey

Measurement of the use of time by women and men, particularly in relation to paid and unpaid work, market and non-market activities, and leisure and personal time.

### Transgender (or Trans)

It is an umbrella term referring to people with diverse gender identities and expressions that differ from stereotypical gender norms. It includes but is not limited to people who identify as transgender, trans woman (male-to-female MTF), trans man (female-to-male FTM), transsexual, cross-dressers, or gender non-conforming, gender variant or gender queer.

### Velvet triangle

This is a heuristic concept designed to describe interactions between policy makers and politicians, feminist academics and experts, and the women's movement in European Union policy making.

### Violence against women (VAW)

Violence against women is understood as a violation of human rights and a form of discrimination against women and shall mean all acts of gender-based violence that result in, or are likely to result in, physical, sexual, psychological or economic harm or suffering to women, including threats of such acts, coercion or arbitrary deprivation of liberty, whether occurring in public or in private life (Istanbul Convention).

### Women's liberation Movement (or Women's lib)

It was a political alignment of women and feminist intellectualism that emerged in the late 1960s and continued into the 1980s primarily in the industrialised nations of the Western world, which effected great change throughout the world.

### Work–life balance

Work-life balance refers not only to caring for dependent relatives, but also to 'extracurricular' responsibilities or important life priorities. Work and leave arrangements should be sufficiently flexible to enable workers of both sexes to undertake lifelong learning activities and further professional and personal development, not necessarily directly related to the worker's job. The balance between work and family life is central to the principle and objectives of promoting equal opportunity. Issues related to the improvement of career opportunities, lifelong learning and other personal and professional development activities are considered to be secondary to the objective of promoting the more equal sharing between men and women of responsibilities in the family and household as well as in the workplace.

# List of Abbreviations

**CEDAW:** The Convention on the Elimination of All Forms of Discrimination against Women

**Covid-19:** Coronavirus disease

**EC:** The European Commission

**EIGE:** European Institute for Gender Equality

**EP:** The European Parliament

**EU:** European Union

**Eurofound:** European Foundation for the Improvement of Living and Working Conditions

**EWL:** European Women's Lobby

**FEMM Committee:** Committee on Women's rights and gender equality of the European Parliament

**FEPS:** Foundation for European Progressive Studies

**FGM:** Female genital mutilation

**FRA:** European Union Agency for Fundamental Rights

**G5+:** Gender Five Plus (European feminist think tank)

**ILO:** International Labour Organization

**Istanbul Convention:** The Council of Europe Convention on preventing and combating violence against women and
domestic violence

**LGBTIQ+:** Lesbian, gay, bisexual, transgender, queer, intersex and other non- dominant sexual
orientations and gender identities in society

**OECD:** Organisation for Economic Co-operation and Development

**SRHR:** Sexual and reproductive health and rights

**UN:** United Nations

**WHO:** World Health Organization

# List of some Feminist Figures

Although this list does not pretend to be exhaustively presenting all the most important contributors to EU Gender Equality policy, it provides a list of the names mentioned throughout the *Primer* for the reader to have them easy at hand.

### Anna Diamantopoulou

Anna Diamantopoulou (b. 1959) is a Greek politician and public figure who has led a distinguished career in public service in Greece and in Europe. She was a European Commissioner for Employment, Social Affairs and Equal Opportunities from 2000 to 2004. She has held several significant portfolios as a minister in the Greek government as well. She was minister of Development, Competitiveness and Shipping, and, prior to that, minister of Education, Research and technology, and lifelong learning.

### Betty Friedan

Betty Friedan (1921-2006) was an American feminist writer and activist. A leading figure in the women's movement in the United States. Her 1963 book *The Feminine Mystique* is often credited with sparking the second wave of American feminism in the 20th century.

### Charlotte Hauglustaine

Charlotte Hauglustaine (1922-2008) was a Belgian factory worker best known for having been one of the leaders of the women's strike in the FN (Fabrique Nationale) in Herstal in 1966, which lead to the implementation of the EU equal pay principle (Article 119).

### Christine Lagarde

Christine Lagarde (b. 1956) was the first woman to be appointed President of the European Central Bank. She has held this position since 1 November 2019. She had previously been the French minister of

Finance (2007-2011) and the Managing Director of the International Monetary Fund (July 2011 - September 2019).

## Cristina Alberdi

Cristina Alberdi (b. 1946) is a Spanish politician and feminist lawyer. She served as Minister of Social Affairs (1993-96) in the government of Felipe Gonzales. In that capacity, she led the EU delegation in the UN Beijing Conference during the Spanish Presidency of the Council.

## Eliane Vogel Polsky

Eliane Vogel Polsky (1926-2015) was a Belgian feminist lawyer who was committed to gender equality throughout her life. She is considered as one of the mothers of social Europe having dedicated her academic and professional career to give consistency to Article 119 of the Treaty of Rome by bringing the famous Defrenne case to the European Court of Justice in 1976. The court's judgment was a decisive turn in the EU policy for equality between women and men. She wrote and acted for a stronger European social policy, for parity democracy and European citizenship. A street in Brussels is named after her, and in 2021/22, she was chosen by the rector Federica Mogherini to be the patron of the promotion of the College of Europe.

## Evelyn Regner

Evelyn Regner (b. 1966) Has been member of the European Parliament since 2014 and chair of the Committee for Women's Rights and Gender Equality (FEMM) of the European Parliament (2019-21). She was then appointed Vice President of the European Parliament for the end of the mandature, leaving the chair of the FEMM committee to Robert Biedron, a Polish Socialist. She is an Austrian politician, former unionist, and Member of the Social Democratic Party of Austria (SPÖ). Her main interest has always been on labour-related affairs, namely the improvement of workers' rights and the reduction of unemployment.

## Evelyne Sullerot

Evelyne Sullerot (1927-2017) was a French sociologist and co-founder of the French family planning programme. In 1968, she was hired by the European Commission to make a decisive survey on women's employment in the Member States.

## Helena Dalli

Appointed in December 2019, Helena Dalli (b. 1962) is the first EU Commissioner for Equality in EU history. Her role is to deliver on the Union of Equality chapter within the Political Guidelines of President von der Leyen, by strengthening Europe's commitment to equality and inclusion in all its senses. Prior to taking her role as Commissioner, Dalli held various political roles in Malta including Member of Parliament (1996-2019), Minister for European Affairs and Equality (2017-19), and Minister for Social Dialogue, Consumer Affairs and Civil Liberties (2013-17). She was also opposition Shadow Minister for public administration, equality, public broadcasting and national investments (1998-2013) and Junior Minister for Women's Rights in the Office of Prime Minister (1996-98). Dalli holds a PhD in Political Sociology from the University of Nottingham, and lectured in Economic and Political Sociology, Public Policy, and Sociology of Law at the University of Malta.

## Henrietta Moore

Henrietta Moore (b. 1957) is a British social anthropologist. She is the director of the Institute for Global Prosperity at University College, London. In 1991 she published the first book which examines the nature and significance of a feminist critique in anthropology.

## Judith Butler

Judith Butler (b. 1956) is a philosopher based at the University of California, Berkeley and one of the very challenging thinkers of our time. She rose to prominence in 1990 with *Gender Trouble*, which caused an unexpected stir as it unearthed foundational assumptions both in philosophy and in feminist theory, namely the facticity of sex. Unmooring feminism at its basis, the book questions the assumption that there is such a thing as the unity of the experience of *women.* Controversial debate on the subject(s) extended far beyond academia to which Butler responded, in part, in *Bodies that Matter* (1993). Butler's academic rigor is pursued through innovative and critical readings of a wide range of texts in philosophy, psychoanalysis and literature, challenging the confines of disciplinary thinking.

### Kate Millett

Kate Millett (1934-2017) is a leading figure of second wave femiinism. She was an American feminist activist in the seventies. Sexual Politics, a book published in 1970, based on her PhD dissertation , is a classic of feminism and one of radical feminism's key texts. She has analysed specifically the subjugation of women in art and literature, denouncing the ubiquity of male domination in culture.

### Kristellina Gieorgeva

Kristellina Gieorgeva (b. 1953) is a Bulgarian economist and politician, managing director of the International Monetary Fund since 2019. She previously served as Vice-President of the European Commission responsible for human ressources (2014-16). In her responsibility she insisted on ambitious quotas to appoint women in high level decision-making posts in the European Commission.

### Lissy Gröner

Lissy (Liselotte Carola) Gröner (1954 –2019) was a  German politician and a  Member of the European Parliament (1989-2009) for the Social Democratic Party of Germany (SPD). She was the Party of European Socialists coordinator in the Committee on Women's Rights and Gender Equality where she became famous for her reprots on gender mainstreaming in the European Parliament and gender budgeting. she also sat on the European Parliament's Committee on Culture and Education .

### Marguerite Thibert

Marguerite Thibert (1886-1982) was one of the first female high-level civil servants in the International Labour Organization in charge of women and children work. As such she gained influence to promote equal pay in the treaty of Rome. She was also a central figure of the French comité du travail féminin (women's work committee).

## Mary Wollstonecraft

Mary Wollstonecraft (1759-97) is regarded as one of the founding feminist philosophers. Her most emblematic book was A Vindication of the Rights of Woman (1792), in which she argues that women are not naturally inferior to men, but appear to be only because they lack education. She suggests that both men and women should be treated as rational beings and imagines a social order founded on reason

## Olympe de Gouge

Olympe de Gouge (1748-93) has gained fame worldwide as  author of the Declaration of the Rights of Woman and of the Female Citizen (1791) published during the french revolution. As a French playwright and political activist , she challenged the practice of male authority and exposed the inequalities of women and men. She was executed during the Reign of Terror (1793-94) for attacking the regime of the Revolutionary government .

## Pauline Green

Pauline Green (b. 1948) is a former Labour Member of the European Parliament and the first female Leader of the Parliamentary Group of the Party of European Socialists (PES). She did two terms in the European Parliament from 1989 to 1999 when she retired to take up a position as the first female Chief Executive of Co-operatives UK . In 2009, Dame Pauline Green is the first woman President of the International Co-operative Alliance in its 117 year history.

## Simone de Beauvoir

Simone de Beauvoir (1908-86) was a French existentialist writer and philosopher who occupies a special place in the feminist movement of the seventies. "The second sex", written in 1949, gives a detailed analysis of all aspects of the domination of women by a patriarchal order. As an encyclopedist, she wanted to know everything about her subject. When it was published, the book was forbidden by the

Vatican and bitterly criticised by mainstream intellectuals. As an existentialist, she insisted that women themselves should act for their "liberation", advocating for contraception and equal access to the labour market as the two weapons for their emancipation. Beauvoir wrote a large number of novels, essays, biographies, autobiographies and monographs on philosophy, politics, and social issues. She was also a political activist who took part in large feminist demonstrations.

## Shulamit Firestone

Shulamit Firestone (1945-2012) was a Canadian-American radical feminist, writer and activist. She was a central figure in the early development of radical feminism and second-wave feminism. She was a founding member of three radical-feminist groups: New York Radical Women, Redstockings, and New York Radical Feminists. In 1970, she authored *The Dialectic of Sex: The Case for Feminist Revolution* which became an influential feminist text.

## Ursula von der Leyen

Ursula von der Leyen (b. 1958) is the first woman to hold the post of President of the European Commission. She is a German politician and physician. On 2 July 2019, she was proposed by the European Council as the candidate for President of the European Commission. She was then elected by the European Parliament on 16 July and took office on 1 December. Prior to her current position, she held ministerial positions in Germany from 2005 to 2019, holding successive positions in Angela Merkel's cabinets, serving most recently as Minister of Defence.

## Vasso Papandreou

Vasso Papandreou (b. 1944) is a Greek politician and a founding member of PASOK (the Panhellenic Socialist Movement). After serving as a minister in Greece (1986-88), she became the first female European Commissioner in the second Delors Commission in 1989. She was responsible for employment and social affairs In her responsibility for equality for women and men, she hoste the first European women in power conference in Athens in 1992. On her return to Greece, she was elected as a member of the Greek parliament and then held important ministerial posts in successive governments government.

## Zita Gurmai

Zita Gurmai (b. 1965) holds the position of President of PES Women, which promotes gender equality inside and outside the Party of European Socialists. She was a member of the Hungarian Parliament from 2002-04 where she was reelected in April 2018. In between, she was elected  Member of the European Parliament in 2004 and again in 2009. Amongst other activities, Gurmai is Vice-President of FEPS, the European Progressive Think Tank . As a member of the Council of Europe parliamentary assembly, Gurmai has been General Rapporteur on violence against women since October 2020 and drafted the report 'The Istanbul Convention on violence against women: achievements and challenges' in 2018

# Timeline

**1957**
Signature of the Treaty of Rome and its Article 119 (precursor to Art. 141 EC) which stipulates that "Each Member State shall during the first stage ensure and subsequently maintain the application of the principle that men and women should receive equal pay for equal work"

**1960**
In order to enter the second phase of integration despite non-compliance with the requirements of Article 119, the EEC creates a 'group Article 119' to overcome the equal pay deadlocks

**1964**
Equalisation of salary grids and cleaning up of collective agreements, removing discriminatory clauses

**1965**
Release of first report on equal pay implementation in Member States is beset by the first EEC constitutional crisis, the "empty chair policy" stalling progress on other matters

**1966**
Herstal strike for equal pay rallying 3,500 female factory workers for 12 weeks

**1969**
Defrenne v Belgian State case in national court (Defrenne I)

**1970s**
Women's liberation movements, legalisation of contraception, transformation of civil codes and family norms

**1973**

Report on Article 119 and infringement procedures and first enlargement of the EEC to the United Kingdom, Ireland and Denmark

**1975**

First EU directive on Equal Pay and First UN World Conference on Women in Mexico

**1976**

Defrenne II case against Sabena obtains landmark decision by the European Court of Justice (ECJ) resulting in the direct applicability of Article 119 in all Member States and recognising equality between women and men as a principle of community law
Second EU directive on Equal Treatment at work

**1979**

Council directive on the progressive implementation of equal treatment in state regimes of social security[356] (later in 1986 to become Council Directive on the implementation of the principle of equal treatment for men and women in occupational social security schemes)[357]

**1979-80**

Women's rights advances confronted with Thatcherism and Reaganism

**1981**

Mitterrand and Kohl

---

356    Council Directive 79/7/EEC of 19 December 1978 on the progressive implementation of the principle of equal treatment for men and women in matters of social security, https://eur-lex.europa.eu/legal-content/EN/ALL/?uri=celex%3A31979L0007

357    Council Directive of 24 July 1986 on the implementation of the principle of equal treatment for men and women in occupational social security schemes, https://eur-lex.europa.eu/legal-content/EN/TXT/PDF/?uri=CELEX:31986L0378

**1983**
43% of women on the labour market following their increasing levels of education and the rise of the service economy

**1984-94**
Jacques Delors Presidency in the European Commission

**1985**
First 'three-years action programme for equality between women and men' (followed by a second programme in 1988-91)

**1989**
Charter of fundamental social rights followed by a social action programme

**1991**
Recommendation on sexual harassment in the workplace
Third Community action programme for equal opportunities between women and men 1991-95 (the Commission is assisted by 9 networks)

**1992**
Treaty of Maastricht
Recommendation on Child care and Athens Declaration on parity democracy issued following the very first European Summit of Women in Power

**1995**
The Fourth UN World Conference on Women in Beijing with the landmark Beijing **Declaration and Platform for Action** adopted unanimously by 189 countries
New Commission president: Jacques Santer

**1996**
4th Community action programme for equal opportunities between women and men 1996-2000

**1997**

Amsterdam Treaty introduces the notion of Gender Mainstreaming in the scope of EU action

**2000**

5th Action Programme for gender equality and Strategy for mainstreaming gender

Daphne Programme on violence against women and children

**2004**

Enlargement to 10 new Member States

Directive article 13 on equal access to goods and services

**2005**

Adoption of the Lisbon Strategy

**2006**

Start of the #Metoo movement by sexual assault survivor Tarana Burke

Directive Recast on the implementation of the principle of equal opportunities and equal treatment of men and women in matters of employment and education

**2007**

Romania and Bulgaria join the EU

**2008**

Lehman Brothers collapse marks the start of the financial crisis

**2010**

Adoption of Europe 2020 Strategy

Second Barroso Commission moves gender equality from DG Employment to DG Justice

Strategy for Equality 2010-15

**2011**
The Istanbul convention is opened for signature

**2015**
No agreement on the Women on boards directive and a strategic engagement replaces strategy

**2019**
First woman becomes President of the European Commission (Ursula von der Leyen)
First female President of the European Central Bank (Christine Lagarde)

**2019**
Appointment of the first EU Commissioner for Equality, a post filled by Socialist Helena Dalli from Malta

**2020**
Launch of the EU Gender Equality Strategy 2020-25
Covid-19 is declared a pandemic

# Bibliography

## On classics of feminism

Butler, Judith "Gender trouble" (Routledge, 1990).

De Beauvoir, Simone "Le Deuxième Sexe" (Paris: Gallimard 1949) [in EN "The Second Sex" (NY: Alfred Knopf, 1953)]

De Gouge, Olympe "The declaration of the rights of women : the original manifesto for justice, equality and freedom" (UK: Octopus publishing group 1791)

Friedan, Betty "The feminine mystique" (Norton, 1963)

Millet, Kate "Sexual Politics" (US: Double Day & Co., 1970)

Firestone, Shulamith "The dialectic of sex: the case for feminist revolution" (William Morrow and company, 1970)

Mill, John Stuart and Taylor Mill, Harriet, "The Subjection of Women" (UK: Longmans, Green, Reader and Dyer, 1869)

Wollstonecraft, Mary "A Vindication of the Rights of Women" (Routledge, 1792)

## On gender equality policy and the EU/European integration

Abels Gabriele, Krizan Andrea, Macrae Heather, van der Vleuten Anne "The Routledge Handbook of Gender and EU politics" (Routledge 2021)

Abels, Gabriele and MacRae, Heather "Gendering European Integration Theory, engaging new dialogues" (Barbara Budrich, 2016)

Abels Gabriele Mushaben Joyce "Gendering the EU, New approaches to old democratic deficits" (Palgrave Macmillan, 2012)

Hoskins, Catherine "Integrating gender, women law and politics in the European Union " (London: Verso, 1996)

Hubert Agnès "L'Europe et les femmes: identités en mouvement" (Apogée, 1998)

Jacquot, Sophie "Transformations in EU Gender Equality: From emergence to dismantling" (Palgrave Macmillan, July 2015)

Kantola, Johanna "Gender and the European Union" (Palgrave Macmillan 2010)

Kantola, Johanna and Lombardo, Emmanuella "Gender and the economic crisis in Europe" (Palgrave Macmillan, 2017)

Lombardo Emmanuela, Petra Meier, Mieke Verloo "The discursive politics of gender equality: stretching, bending and policy making" (Routledge 2009)

Rubery, Jill and  Maria, Karamessini (ed.) "Women and austerity, the economic crisis and the future for gender equality" (Abingdon: Routledge, 2014)

van der Vleuten, Anne "The price of gender equality" (Routledge 2007)

Walby, Silvia "The European Union and Gender Equality: Emergent Variety of Gender Regimes," *Social Politics* 11, no. 1, (2004)

## On gender mainstreaming

Hubert, Agnès and Stratigaki, Maria "Twenty Years of EU Gender Mainstreaming: Rebirth out of the Ashes?" *Femina Politika* 201

Stratigaki Maria "Gender Mainstreaming vs Positive Action: an Ongoing Conflict in EU Gender Equality Policy" *EJWS* (May 2005)

## On gender and covid-19

Rubery, Jill and Tavora, Isabel "The Covid-19 crisis and gender equality: risks and opportunities" in *Social policy in the European Union: state of play* (ETUI, 2020)

Kambouri, Nelly "Towards a gendered recovery in the EU: Women and Equality in the aftermath of the Covid19 pandemic" (Gender Five plus, 2020)

EIGE "The Covid-19 pandemic and intimate partner violence against women in the EU" (2020)

## On care work and jobs

Caracciolo di Torella, Eugenia and Masselot, Annick "Caring responsibilities in European law and policy: who cares?" (Abingdon: Routledge, 2020)

FEPS-FES Policy Study (2021). "Towards a fairer, care-focused Europe" by Barbara Helfferich. Available from: https://www.feps-europe.eu/attachments/events/policy%20study_care4care.pdf

FEPS-TASC Policy Study (2020). "Cherishing all Equally: Inequality and the Care Economy" by Robert Sweeney. Available from: https://www.feps-europe.eu/attachments/publications/report-care%20economy_tasc-feps.pdf

FEPS-TASC Policy Brief (2020). "Time to care! Work, life and inequality in the care economy". By Robert Sweeney & Laeticia Thissen. Available from: https://www.feps-europe.eu/attachments/publications/feps_tasc_policybrief_timetocare.pdf

FEPS-FES Policy Brief (2021). "Vital yet vulnerable: Europe's Intra-EU Migrant Caregivers" by Petra Ezzeddine. Available from: https://www.feps-europe.eu/resources/publications/815-com_publications.publications.html

FEPS-FES Policy Brief (2021). "Part-time work: risk or opportunity?" by Janna Besamusca and Mara Yerkes. Available from: https://www.feps-europe.eu/attachments/publications/211012_part_time_work_policy_brief_care4care.pdf

## On reproductive justice and anti-gender movements

Eszter Kováts (ed.) "Reproductive rights as a social justice issue in the EU" in *The future of the European Union: feminists perspectives from East-central Europe* (Friedrich Ebert Stiftung)

European Parliamentary Forum (2021). "Tip of the Iceberg: religious extremist – Funders against Human Rights for Sexuality & Reproductive Health in Europe." Available from: https://www.epfweb.org/node/837

FEPS-FES (2016). "Gender as symbolic glue: The Position and Role of Conservative and Far-Right Parties in the Anti-Gender Mobilisations in Europe". Available from: https://www.feps-europe.eu/resources/publications/309-gender-as-symbolic-glue.html

## On gender-based violence

FEPS-Fondation Jean Jaurès (2020). "Femicides: naming the phenomenon to better combat it." by Margot Giancinti. Available from: https://www.feps-europe.eu/resources/publications/763-femicides-naming-the-phenomenon-to-better-combat-it.html

FEPS-Fondation Jean Jaurès (2020). "Sexist and sexual violence in the workplace: lessons for public policies" by Sylvie Cromer and Adeline Raymond. Available from: https://www.feps-europe.eu/resources/publications/764-sexist-and-sexual-violence-in-the-workplace-lessons-for-public-policies.html

FEPS-Fondation Jean Jaurès (2020). "Progressive pathways to a Europe free from violence against women: Mapping the EU's institutional and policy maze" by Hannah Manzur. Available from: https://www.feps-europe.eu/resources/publications/768-com_publications.publications.html

FEPS-Fondation Jean Jaurès (2021). "Naming it, fighting it: a multi-level analysis of digital gender-based violence" by Chiara De Santis and Lilia Giugni. Available from: https://www.feps-europe.eu/resources/publications/785-com_publications.publications.html

FEPS-Fondation Jean Jaurès (2021). "Violence against lesbians, bi women and trans people: adapting the public response to the diversity of LGBT+ life experiences" by Flora Bolter. Available from: https://www.feps-europe.eu/resources/publications/791-violence-against-lesbians,-bi-women-and-trans-people-adapting-the-public-response-to-the-diversity-of-lgbti-life-experiences.html

FEPS-Fondation Jean Jaurès (2021). "Gender-based violence against women and girls with disabilities" by Pirkko Mahlamäki. Available from: https://www.feps-europe.eu/resources/publications/799-gender-based-violence-against-women-and-girls-with-disabilities.html

FEPS-Fondation Jean Jaurès Survey (2019). "Sexism and Sexual harassment at work". Available from: https://www.feps-europe.eu/

resources/publications/697-survey-european-observatory-on-sexism-and-sexual-harassment-at-work.html

FEPS-Fondation Jean Jaurès Survey (2018).” Women's Exposure to Gender-Based Violence and Harassment in the Street”. Available from: https://www.feps-europe.eu/resources/publications/636-com_publications.publications.html

FEPS (2019). “The #Metoo Social Media Effect and its Potentials for Change in Europe”. Minerva Publication. Available from: https://www.feps-europe.eu/resources/publications/698-the-metoo-social-media-effect-and-its-potentials-for-change-in-europe.html

## On EU gender equality law

Burri, S., Van Eijken, H. “Gender Equality Law in 33 European Countries: Update 2014” (European Commission 2015). Available from: http://www.equalitylaw.eu/downloads/2789-general-report-gender-2014.

Timmer, A., Senden L., “A comparative analysis of gender equality law in Europe 2017” (European Commission 2017). Available from: https://www.equalitylaw.eu/downloads/4553-a-comparative-analysis-of-gender-equalitylaw-in-europe-2017-pdf-847-kb

European Commission European network of legal experts in gender equality and non-discrimination “Gender equality law in Europe Justice and Consumers: How are EU rules transposed into national law in 2018?” Country reports available on the EELN website: http://www.equalitylaw.eu/country

## Annual gender equality monitoring references

European Commission (2021). “Annual Report on Gender Equality in the EU” Available from: https://ec.europa.eu/info/policies/justice-and-fundamental-rights/gender-equality/gender-equality-strategy_en

Joint Research Center Gender equality strategy monitoring portal https://composite-indicators.jrc.ec.europa.eu/ges-monitor

EIGE (2021). “Gender Equality Index 2021: Health”. (Vilnius: European Institute for Gender Equality). Available from: https://eige.europa.eu/publications/gender-equality-index-2021-health

European Commission (2021). "She Figures 2021 Handbook". Available from: https://op.europa.eu/en/publication-detail/-/publication/058103b5-4da0-11ec-91ac-01aa75ed71a1/language-en/format-PDF/source-245884703

World Economic Forum (2021). "Global Gender Gap Report". Available from: https://www.weforum.org/reports/global-gender-gap-report-2021

## On Sexual orientation and intersectionality

Fausto-Sterling, Anne. "Sexing the Body: Gender Politics and the Construction of Sexuality" (New York: Basic Books, 2000).

Crenshaw, Kimberlé. "On Intersectionality: Essential Writings" (Columbia Law School, 2017).

Davis, Angela. "Women, race and class" (1981)

Hook, Bell "Feminism is for everybody: passionate politics" (Cambridge MA: Southend Press, 2000)

Adiche, Chimamanda Ngozi "We should all be feminists" (USA: Rarewaves, 2015)

## On Multimedia

**Women's Europe: voices in times of covid** – Aware of the devastating impact on women the covid crisis is having and concerned with the fact that the policies designed to cope with the pandemic but also the post-covid agenda may be designed without sufficient input on the side of women or without their needs and priorities in mind, we, a group of 20 European academics, politicians, policy makers and civil society activists (both men and women) have produced four short videos under the title of Women's Europe: Voices in Times of covid. The videos provide a gender analysis of the covid crisis, warn about the risk of putting gender equality agendas under the carpet in reconstruction efforts and, more broadly speaking, articulate views about what could be a transformative recovery agenda and a new social contract. Available from: https://www.youtube.com/channel/UC-1VQmPv5dtfxfbHMxyR_rw/videos

**Eliane Vogel-Polsky "champion for women's rights in Europe"** – a 30-minute documentary. Eliane Vogel-Polsky was an exceptional woman. A brilliant Belgian lawyer and great European, she contributed to the cause of women in Europe. As a lawyer before the courts and tribunals, as a researcher and professor at the university, and as an expert for international institutions, she campaigned unceasingly for equal rights and opportunities, for parity and a social Europe. Through exceptional archives and rare testimonies, this film traces her struggles and successes and brings us back to important moments in the history of Europe and the women's struggle for equality.
https://vimeo.com/297136091

**Anne Laure Humbert "statistics that make the invisible visible"** https://www.youtube.com/watch?v=Mroak19i-6w&ab_channel=TEDxTalks

**"What we measure we treasure"** a theatrical engagement with gender equality at the LSE
https://www.facebook.com/events/377292582687282/

# Reviews

## MEP Robert Biedroń, Chair of FEMM Committee at the European Parliament

Agnès Hubert's new book "The European Union and Gender equality: Free, Thrive, Lead" is an interesting take on the parallels between the process of the European integration and the development of gender equality policies. The author takes us on a journey through the efforts and obstacles to keep women at the centre of European policymaking, as she assesses key milestones along the way, from equal pay to protection against domestic violence, from the first legislative measures to the impacts of the pandemic. Though-provoking and insightful, a must-read for all EU decision-makers.

## Zita Gurmai, President of PES Women and FEPS Vice President

Hubert's primer gives us a unique analysis of the paradoxical relationship between EU integration and gender equality, stretching back to the sixties and landing in our post-covid reality. With this comprehensive historical background and detailed state of play of feminism in the EU, Hubert brings her remarkable expertise to readers, and provides us with a heartening report of everything which has been achieved, with optimism for what is within reach, but also with concern for women's rights in a post-pandemic EU. An essential and valuable tool for anyone striving for a more gender-equal society, with clear guidelines on how to create a feminist Europe for all.

### Reka Safrany, President of the European Women's Lobby

Agnès Hubert with this FEPS Primer on Gender Equality is taking us on a journey about women's rights through the corridors of the EU's institutions and its Members States. It is a required reading for whoever wants to learn about the evolution, progress and hurdles in the fight for equality between women and men at the EU level. We are honored that the European Women's Lobby is seen as a key actor of what she calls the "Velvet Triangle" of feminists fighting for progress in Brussels and beyond. We share her conclusions that we need to end violence against women and girls through EU actions, ensure respect of women's Sexual and Reproductive Health and Rights, move to an economy of care and wellbeing, and ensure equal representation of women in all leadership spheres. This is what it will take to build a feminist Europe.

### Joyce Mushaben, Adjunct Professor - BMW Center for German and European Studies (CGES)

Feminist activists of the 1970s, 1980s and 1990s were too busy fighting for long overdue women's rights to reflect back then on the conceptual trails they were blazing, the networks they were building and the creative strategies they had to invent, all of which ultimately rendered gender equality a fundamental value across the European Union. Having participated directly in this transformational process, Agnès Hubert offers a detailed review of the key actors, institutions, inputs, outputs, victories and occasional set-backs that made it possible. The story she tells pays special homage to the women who worked so hard to fill the glass half-way, while providing tactical insights for younger EU citizens, eager to fill the other half. This "herstory" is well worth reading and remembering.

# About the Author

**Agnès Hubert** is an experienced policy maker and a recognised author on EU gender equality policy and social innovation in the EU. She is currently associate researcher with PRESAGE (Programme de Recherches et d'Enseignements des Savoirs sur le Genre) at Science Po/OFCE Paris, visiting professor at the College of Europe in Bruges, founding member and president of the first European feminist think tank Genderfiveplus.com and member of the Haut Conseil de l'Egalité, the advisory body to the French government on equality between women and men.

An economist by training, she was a journalist before joining the European Commission where she held senior advisory functions dealing with gender equality and social innovation, contributing to raising these issues at the highest levels in European institutions.

She has written books (L'Europe et les femmes, identités en mouvement, 1998; Democracy and information society in Europe, 1997), major policy documents on social innovation for the European Commission (Empowering people, driving change: Social innovation in the European Union, 2010; Social innovation a decade of changes, 2014) and a number of peer-reviewed academic articles and book chapters in her fields of expertise. She has also produced and co-directed the film Eliane Vogel Polsky, champion of the cause of women in Europe.

She has taught courses on gender and the European Union at the Fletcher School of Law & Diplomacy (Tufts University, Mass. USA), the Centro de Estudios Políticos y Constitucionales in Madrid, Science Po Paris, and in the Collège d'Europe (Bruges).

## Acknowledgements

I wish to thank my third wave feminist friend, Laeticia Thissen, officer in charge of Gender equality at FEPS for her meticulous reading of the first drafts, for adding useful comments and references and for the friendly discussions we had all along the writing and publishing of this primer. I also benefited greatly further along the line of the very pertinent remarks of Ania Skrzypek and Elena Gil and their enthousiastic support for this project.

# About the Illustrator

**Priscilla Beccari** is a multidisciplinary artist who expresses herself through video, sculpture, installation, photography, performance, drawing and also through music with Mono Siren, a work of art, photography, performance, drawing and also music with Mono Siren, an experimental electro disco funk duo. In 2017, she represented the Pavilion of the Republic of San Marino at the Venice Biennale.

https://priscillabeccari.com/

# The FEPS Primer Series

Following a decade of polycrisis that followed the great recession of 2009, progressive political thinking and practice in Europe needs a reconstruction. This FEPS Primer book series was launched to serve the creation of this new synthesis, connecting long established values of the European socialist and social democratic traditions with the lessons and innovations of the current experience.

Primers are booklets written with an educational purpose, to help new (typically young) audiences enter specific thematic fields, which can be diverse (in this case social science, politics, and policy). Accessible language is important, together with illustrations that highlight key elements of the content. The main text is always accompanied by a glossary as well as a section of recommended further reading.

The FEPS Primers are parts of a broader effort: the Foundation endeavours to raise progressive political education in Europe to a new level. Our volumes aim to provide useful analysis, instruction, and orientation for several years after publication. Some of them may well be considered 'must reads' for all those aspiring to play an active role in European politics at any level.

Our authors are not only recognised experts, but also active participants in political and policy debates, representing a diversity of European nations and career paths. However, they are connected by sharing the values and objectives of the progressive political family and concerns for the future of European societies, as well as sustainability and social cohesion as common goals.

The FEPS Primer series is edited by an Editorial Board. We keep in view the key current issues of the European Union, with a focus on critical discussion points that will influence the work of social movements as well as governance at various levels in the coming decade. We hope the selection of topics and the contributions of our distinguished authors will spark the interest of those participating in progressive political education, and also appeal to a wider readership.

Dr László Andor
FEPS Secretary General

## Image copyrights